"Drawing on three decades of experience in pastoring and in discipling students in the C. S. Lewis Institute Fellows Program, Thomas Tarrants guides readers through clear steps from biblical grounding to practical application. In conversation with Martin Luther, the Heidelberg Catechism, George Müller, Andrew Murray, C. S. Lewis, John Stott, J. I. Packer, and many others, he explores the fundamentals of discipleship, gently leading readers through core practices of the Christian faith. *Following Jesus Christ* offers a wide-ranging introduction to the Christian life from a wise and seasoned mentor."

Gwenfair Walters Adams, Professor of Church History and Spiritual Formation & Director of Spiritual Formation, Gordon-Conwell Theological Seminary

"Thomas Tarrants has authored a warm, accessible overview of what it means to be a disciple of Jesus. His presentation of key topics in the Christian life is practical, pastoral, and rooted in thoughtful engagement with Scripture. This is a fabulous resource to help you grow in your relationship with Christ or to equip you to help someone else who is looking to know more about what it means to follow Jesus."

Matthew D. Haste, Associate Professor of Biblical Spirituality and Biblical Counseling & Director of Professional Doctoral Studies, The Southern Baptist Theological Seminary

"Tom Tarrants has given us a book the American church needs. At a time when many professing Christians have settled for a tame, therapeutic spirituality that demands little and delivers less, Tarrants recalls us to what discipleship has always meant: following Jesus in the power of the Spirit through daily repentance and faith. Drawing on Scripture, the wisdom of church fathers, and decades of experience in spiritual formation through the C. S. Lewis Institute, Tarrants offers a guide that is theologically sound and practical. The questions at the end of each chapter make this an ideal resource for small groups and individual reflection."

Bryan Hollon, Dean, President, & Professor of Theology, Trinity Anglican Seminary

"Jesus' Great Commission was to make disciples (not merely converts) of all nations, and *Following Jesus Christ* lays out powerfully and comprehensively what authentic discipleship entails. For years, Tom Tarrants has devoted his life to that task, and here, with clarity and biblical faithfulness, he describes the key themes for being a faithful disciple and becoming a fruitful disciple. This book will serve pastors and lay leaders well in carrying out the Great Commission of our Lord. The key questions after each chapter enhance its practicality."

Dennis Hollinger, President Emeritus & Senior Distinguished Professor of Christian Ethics, Gordon-Conwell Theological Seminary

"This book provides just what the church needs—a trusted guide to help converts become true disciples, becoming more and more like their Master. Tom Tarrants is not only a student of this topic; he is also an experienced practitioner. He brings decades of reflection and practice to the task in creating this discipleship handbook."

Bill Kynes, Pastor (Retired), Cornerstone Evangelical Free Church, Annandale, VA, & Council and Staff Member, The Gospel Coalition

"What does it mean to follow Jesus into the abundant life of the kingdom of God? Tom Tarrants guides the way with wisdom, insight, and grace born of Bible study and personal experience. If you are ready to get serious about discipleship with Jesus, this book is an indispensable lifeline."

Philip Miller, Senior Pastor, The Moody Church, Chicago, IL

"I thank God for this timely book by Thomas Tarrants. As one who has been an intentional disciple-maker for over forty years and an author in the field of discipleship, I immediately recognized the value of this book as an essential companion and guide.

Tom initially zeroes in on the core qualities and characteristics of a disciple of Jesus and then very practically unfolds for us how those qualities are embedded in us by living in the fullness of the Holy Spirit. He covers each topic so comprehensively while bringing to the fore many pithy and supporting quotes from the giants of the faith who have gone before us. The best endorsement I give of this book is that I will give Tom's book to all I invite to join me on the journey of becoming a multiplying disciple of Jesus."

Greg Ogden, Executive Director of Global Discipleship Initiative

"Tom Tarrants speaks with wisdom acquired from a life of discipleship and reflection on the dynamics of the Christian life. His discussion of the Christian faith and its implications for life will challenge the reader with its depth and inspire with its practicality, while persistently presenting the person of Christ."

Scott Redd, Senior Pastor, Briarwood Presbyterian Church, Birmingham, AL

"The need for faithful followers of Jesus Christ has become urgent in North America and Europe. Tom Tarrants' inspiring study of authentic discipleship is a welcome solution to the common confusion that a disciple is a more advanced type of Christian rather than synonymous with true believers. If disciples are meant to follow Christ, they must grasp and grow more fully into the biblical teaching of the gospel, and this study provides insightful examination into those essentials.

These chapters are both engaging and practical and can nurture the lives of all Christians who desire to demonstrate the Good News of Jesus in our broken world. The church owes a huge gratitude to Tarrants for his passion and teaching on discipleship. I highly recommend it!"

Tom Schwanda, Associate Professor Emeritus of Christian Formation and Ministry, Wheaton College

"Having partnered with Thomas Tarrants in discipleship initiatives during my eight years of pastoral ministry in the Washington, D.C., area, I've witnessed firsthand the godly impact of his teaching. In this volume, Tarrants—former President of the C. S. Lewis Institute—offers a biblically grounded guide to what it truly means to follow Jesus. With pastoral wisdom and theological depth, he shows that authentic discipleship is not merely a profession of faith but a life of growing communion with Christ through the Holy Spirit. This book is both a challenge and an encouragement to every believer serious about becoming a faithful and fruitful disciple of Jesus."

D. Blair Smith, President, Reformed Theological Seminary Charlotte

"This book, *Following Jesus Christ*, is by a wise and godly man who has followed Jesus Christ for a very long time. The subtitle, *A Guide to Growing in Authentic Discipleship*, is a perfect description of the contents. Any believer—whether new in the faith or a seasoned disciple—can profit from this helpful and practical guide."

Donald S. Whitney, Professor of Biblical Spirituality & Director of the Center for Biblical Spirituality, Midwestern Baptist Theological Seminary

"Thomas Tarrants is a seasoned pastor, scholar, and preeminent practitioner of disciple-making. His newest book, *Following Jesus Christ*, is an excellent guide to growing in authentic discipleship to Jesus. Whether read individually or in a mutually supportive study group, this book is a full development of the Christian life by a wise, well-taught student and master of the Word of God. Tarrants speaks with authority, yet he does so with humility in helping believers of all ages grow in their discipleship to Jesus. This is a rich resource that draws upon faithful thinkers in church history.

Tom's book seeks to show believers at every stage of Christian maturity the way forward in following Jesus as an authentic disciple. And such it does! Highly recommended for all wanting a comprehensive overview of the core tenets of the life of following Jesus Christ."

Michael J. Wilkins, Distinguished Professor Emeritus of New Testament Language and Literature, Talbot School of Theology, Biola University

"I can think of no one better qualified to write a book on growing in authentic discipleship than Thomas Tarrants. His is a life truly transformed and shaped by the Lord Jesus. This book is Trinitarian, biblical, applicable, and accessible. A must-have for every church that wants to take discipleship seriously."

Jonathan Michael Youssef, Senior Pastor, The Church of The Apostles, Atlanta, GA

"*Following Jesus Christ: A Guide to Growing in Authentic Discipleship* exposed holes in the fabric of our Christian beliefs, showing where our actions are inconsistent with our theology and challenging us to think harder about the "why" of our spiritual practice. The women in our study group ranged widely in spiritual maturity and educational levels, but the book was accessible and stimulating to all. We read it aloud, and the discussion that followed was deep and inspiring."

Cynthia E., Bible Study Leader

"As one who has followed Christ for many years, I found *Following Jesus Christ: A Guide to Growing in Discipleship* a refreshing and profound guide to the lifelong journey of being a disciple of Jesus. The author not only engages our minds but also appeals to our hearts and our wills to wholeheartedly commit to following Christ. At the same time, he encourages us that it is God who calls and the Holy Spirit who divinely works to change us and build the kingdom of God."

Eleanor N., Church Missions Co-Chair

"*Following Jesus Christ: A Guide to Growing in Authentic Discipleship* left no stone unturned when it comes to life in Christ, and yet the book feels so light in my brain. There's nothing cumbersome or ponderous in the way it is written. In this book, the explanation of discipleship is truthful and thorough, yet gentle and accessible. Just as I believe the Holy Spirit would have it, I am both convicted and encouraged."

Aimee R., Wife and Mother

"*Following Jesus: A Guide to Growing in Authentic Discipleship* came at a time in my life when I was starved for spiritual mentorship and discipleship from godly men in the church. I was in my late twenties, attending a new church with my wife, when by the Lord's grace I found a group of about ten men of all different ages and life experiences who were committed to the learning and practice of biblical discipleship. It was through meeting with these men and discussing the book—chapter by chapter, week after week—that the Lord began to craft a vision for my life that was truly and solely lived for Him, through Him, and with Him. This book comprehensively, astutely, and meticulously teases out what the Holy Scriptures have to say about the Christian life and how we can draw near to God and live for his glory. I am so grateful to the Lord for a life changed!"

David S., Professional Musician

"*Following Jesus Christ: A Guide to Authentic Discipleship* presents gospel truths in ways that are both fresh and compelling—using current and historical examples to illustrate and enliven the text. And the proof is in the pudding: this material has been used in small group studies with dozens of men and women in our church and has 'landed' with them, giving them an accurate and inviting picture of what authentic discipleship looks like as followers of Christ seek daily to be more conformed in His image."

Jim T., Deacon and Elder

Following Jesus Christ

A Guide to Growing in Authentic Discipleship

Thomas A. Tarrants

Following Jesus Christ:
A Guide to Growing in Authentic Discipleship
Thomas A. Tarrants

Copyright © 2026 by Thomas A. Tarrants

Published by C. S. Lewis Institute Press

All rights reserved. This book or any portion thereof may not be reproduced or used in any manner whatsoever without the express written permission of the publisher except for the use of brief quotations in a book review.

Unless otherwise indicated, Scripture quotations are from the ESV® Bible (The Holy Bible, English Standard Version®), © 2001 by Crossway, a publishing ministry of Good News Publishers. ESV Text Edition: 2025. The ESV text may not be quoted in any publication made available to the public by a Creative Commons license. The ESV may not be translated in whole or in part into any other language. Used by permission. All rights reserved.

Scripture quotations marked "NIV" are from the Holy Bible, New International Version®, NIV®. Copyright ©1973, 1978, 1984, 2011 by Biblica, Inc.® Used by permission. All rights reserved worldwide.

Scripture quotations marked "NASB 2020" are from the New American Standard Bible®, Copyright © 1960, 1971, 1977, 1995, 2020 by The Lockman Foundation. Used by permission. All rights reserved.

Cover design: Christopher Tobias
Cover photo © Adobe Stock / Ma
Interior Design: Brian Zuckerman, The Perspectives Group

Library of Congress Control Number: 2026908378

ISBN (paperback): 978-1-7378543-6-4
ISBN (ebook): 978-1-7378543-7-1

First edition: March 2026

I dedicate this book to my family:
May you know, love, and serve Jesus Christ
ever more deeply all the days of your lives.

Contents

Prologue

Authentic Discipleship

At the age of thirteen, I made a profession of faith in Jesus Christ and was baptized. All was well with my soul now, and I would go to heaven when I died. Or so I thought. But the truth was that I was not born again and headed to heaven. I was still dead in sin—a Christian in name only, a false disciple, and my life began to show it. When Jesus saved me ten years later, I had been living a life of serious sin and was a total mess morally and spiritually, something which I deeply regret to this day. It took tragedy, pain, and suffering, all of my own making, to bring me to genuine faith in Christ. But when Jesus saved me fifty-five years ago, I became alive spiritually, a real Christian and authentic disciple, and my life began to change. It has been changing ever since.

During His ministry on earth, Jesus Christ invited people of all sorts and conditions to become His disciples and experience the abundant life that only He could give. He said, "Come to me, all who labor and are heavy laden, and I will give you rest. Take my yoke upon you, and learn from me, for I am gentle and lowly in heart and will give you rest for your souls. For my yoke is easy, and my burden is light" (Matt. 11:28–30). That is what Jesus did for me, and He still offers this life as a free, totally undeserved gift for needy people like you and me, a gift that is received by faith alone. Through it, God's grace abounds in our lives, giving us a new identity with meaning and purpose that were previously unknown, along with love, joy, peace, and much more.

In some believers, these graces are clearly present and testify to authentic discipleship. But in others the picture is less clear. Such graces seem partial or obscure, or they may be altogether lacking. Why is this?

A major reason (though not the only one) is a widespread misunderstanding about what it means to be a Christian and to be a disciple of Jesus. I'm not sure why, but this was not clear to me for several years after I was saved. However, it is clear in Scripture. Jesus commissioned His first disciples to "Go therefore and make disciples" (Matt. 28:19), and in the early church, those who came to faith in Jesus were referred to as "disciples" (the books of Acts records this 28 times). As the church spread into Gentile territory, Luke tells us the disciples were given a nickname: "In Antioch the disciples were first called Christians" (Acts 11:26).

As we will later see in more detail, in the New Testament, "disciple" and "Christian" are equivalent terms; thus, discipleship and the Christian life are actually one and the same—two words for a single thing. That single thing is a life of daily faith and repentance toward God and of discipleship with Jesus through the power of the Holy Spirit. The goal of discipleship is to become increasingly like Jesus (Matt. 10:24–25), "to walk in the same way in which he walked" (1 John 2:6). Or, as Paul puts it, "to be conformed to the image of his Son" (Rom. 8:29) and "to walk in a manner worthy of the Lord, fully pleasing to him: bearing fruit in every good work and increasing in the knowledge of God" (Col. 1:10).[1] Although such a life can be demanding at times, it produces joy and fruitfulness and glorifies God. Yet sometimes believers act as though being a Christian is just a matter of saying the right words, attending the right church (or the right number of services), volunteering for the right activities, giving enough money, or praying a certain prayer at some point in their lives—all while experiencing little if any lasting change and fruitfulness.

Being a true Christian—an authentic disciple of Jesus Christ—means living differently: maturing Christians shouldn't look the same as everyone else. They should not muddle along, satisfied with living mediocre Christian lives. Rather, they should heed the counsel of one

1 In theological terms, this is to be "progressively sanctified."

of Jesus' most notable disciples, Paul, who acknowledged that he had not reached perfection, and said, "One thing I do: forgetting what lies behind and straining forward to what lies ahead, I press on toward the goal for the prize of the upward call of God in Christ Jesus. Let those of us who are mature think this way" (Phil. 3:13–15). As we and our churches pursue authentic discipleship with Jesus, our lives will change dramatically, and we will become salt and light in the darkness of this fallen world (see Matt. 5:13–16), drawing others to Christ, spreading God's kingdom, and glorifying His name.

Such a life is a fruit of grace, not a burden of law. For following Jesus doesn't mean trying harder and harder to reach impossible goals or to "prove" our spirituality by checking certain boxes. During Jesus' life on earth, sinners in need found themselves drawn to Him, a man full of grace and truth (John 1:14, 17). He didn't load his followers with impossible, soul-crushing demands like the Pharisees did. He knows how broken and weak we fallen human beings are, and He promised rest for our souls. The grace-filled invitation we saw above is His call to everyone who has wearied of burdensome, legalistic, lifeless religion—to cast it off, take up the yoke of vibrant, life-giving discipleship to Him, learn from Him, and become like Him. And He accepts all who come to Him, no matter how flawed or broken they are.

Paradoxically, being a disciple of Jesus, while sometimes challenging, is easy, and His burden is light. How can that be? Because, by His Spirit, Jesus empowers His disciples to obey His commands and extends forgiveness when they fail. We need only consider how weak, sinful, and often clueless His original disciples were during their three years with Him and how patient, kind, and forgiving He was toward them. Jesus' persistent grace and gentle love brought transformation, fruitfulness, fulfillment, and joy to their lives, and it will do the same for us as we learn to follow Him and let Him disciple us.

That has certainly been true for me. In the early years of my conversion, I grew in knowledge of the truth, but I also struggled with living it—particularly with respect to certain sins that had troubled me in the past. I would describe myself as an authentic disciple, though a poor one. But Jesus was patient, merciful, and forgiving while helping me to overcome these sins, just as He was with His first disciples. And even now, all these years later, He is still patiently showing me areas that need to change in order for me to become more like Him.

This book seeks to show believers at every stage of Christian maturity the way forward in following Jesus as an authentic disciple. Many true believers today are hindered by lack of a coherent and comprehensive understanding of key transformational truths of the Christian life; their understanding has gaps that need to be filled in order to progress to a deeper faith. Others are like the people addressed in the book of Hebrews, who had made some progress but had stalled, and to whom the writer said, "You have become dull of hearing. For though by this time you ought to be teachers, you need someone to teach you again the basic principles of the oracles of God" (5:11–12). Still others are like the believers in Corinth, to whom Paul said, "But I, brothers, could not address you as spiritual people but as people of the flesh, as infants in Christ" (1 Cor. 3:1). I was each of those at one point or another in earlier years, but through His Word and Spirit, Jesus has brought me out of my blindness and into the light of His truth and freedom. This book can help in each of those situations, and it can also serve as a practical resource for believers who are more mature in the faith as they help younger believers to grow.

Does actively seeking to grow in Christlikeness really make a difference? It has made a difference for me. And during the past forty years, I have seen transformation and fruitfulness in the lives of hundreds if not thousands of ordinary men and women who have devoted themselves to the biblical truths shared here. It can be the same for you.

Each of the twenty chapters ahead focuses on a key transformational truth in the Christian life that will help you to become a more faithful and fruitful disciple of Jesus—an authentic disciple who glorifies God in thought, word, and deed. In Part 1, we will focus on what is necessary to become a true and sound disciple of Jesus. In Part 2, we will explore how we become an empowered disciple of Jesus.

In the companion volume to this book, *Abiding in Jesus Christ: A Guide to Maturing in Authentic Discipleship*, you will find additional teaching that builds on the foundations provided here. For details, see the book description in the back of this volume.

How to Use This Book

For Ordinary Believers Seeking to Grow in Authentic Discipleship

1. Read the book slowly and prayerfully. Do not rush through the chapters. Instead, take your time and ask God to show you how what you are reading applies to your life. An important step in that direction is to memorize and meditate on the Bible verse that appears at the start of each chapter. In addition, at the close of each chapter, reflect on the "Questions to Ponder"; they are intended to help you engage with and internalize what you have read.
2. Commit yourself to putting into practice what you discover to be God's will. If you do not do this, you may grow in knowledge, but you will not become more like Jesus.
3. Growing as a disciple of Jesus, as we see in the Gospels, is a process that occurs largely within groups. Although you can experience some measure of growth if you read this book by yourself, you will grow far more by doing so as part of a group.

   Today, learning as part of a group in a healthy church should be the norm. Either before or after you have read this book, pray for at least two or three other believers who want to become more like Jesus and who will work through the book with you. Meet with them weekly, if possible, for 60 to 90 minutes. Read the appropriate chapter before you meet. Choose one member of the group to be a facilitator, and use the "Questions to Ponder" at the end of each chapter to guide your discussion. Open and close your meeting with prayer. To build friendship and depth among group members, get together at other times for mutual encouragement, a meal, recreation, or joint ministry to others. As trust develops, share more about your life and your needs and challenges. Going through the book with a group will help you learn it at a deeper level.

4. The group of peers described above can be quite helpful for growth in discipleship. However, the impact can be substantially enriched through the involvement of a believer who is already mature in Christian experience and character and well-grounded in the Bible. Such a person can serve as a spiritual mentor and coach to younger, less mature believers in their growth as disciples of Jesus. This follows the pattern of Jesus as seen in the Gospels. Seek out such a believer in your church to mentor or facilitate your group, or to meet with you one-on-one if a group is not possible.
5. Let your pastor or elders know what you are planning and ask for any guidance or oversight they may be able to offer, including suggesting group members or mentors. If your group has questions that it cannot answer, check back with them to see if they can recommend trustworthy resources.
6. The free online version of this book features a PDF of each chapter that you can download and send to family, friends, and others, as well as curate to design your own curriculum for a study group if you wish. The online version also includes an annotated list of recommended books and resources to help you go deeper in the subject of each chapter. This list is updated as new resources become available.

For Pastors and Mentors Helping People Grow in Authentic Discipleship

1. This book is pastor- and church-oriented; it provides a range of potentially useful resources for preaching and teaching and is well suited for church-wide discipling programs. The chapters are grounded in the Bible and sound theology, quote highly respected Christian leaders past and present, refer to leading scholars where appropriate, illustrate with engaging stories, and are carefully footnoted.
2. The free online version provides additional recommended reading lists for each chapter as well as teaching outlines for classroom use. Special discipleship-related resources for pastors are also provided.
3. All chapters may be downloaded free of charge at the C. S. Lewis Institute website, www.CSLewisInstitute.org. For bulk or individual sales, the hard copy may be purchased online on amazon.com.
4. The entire book or selected chapters can be used as curriculum in adult education classes as well as church small groups.
5. Selected chapters can be recommended as follow-up reading for sermons where appropriate.

Part 1

Being a Faithful Disciple of Jesus

1

Who Is God?

The Lord, the Lord, a God merciful and gracious, slow to anger, and abounding in steadfast love and faithfulness.
Exodus 34:6

One might expect a book on discipleship to begin with Jesus—after all, it's *His* disciples that Christians claim to be. But rather than starting with Jesus and God's kingdom, we will begin at a more basic place. We will first ask: Who is God? This will give us a framework for understanding God's kingdom and the all-important ministry and mission of Jesus.

This is necessary because in much of the world today, a great inversion has occurred. In the West, for instance, the Enlightenment's revolt against God has given us a new normal, one described long ago by a Greek philosopher named Protagoras: "Man is the measure of all things."[1] Or, as a recent writer has put it, for some, "People are big, and God is small."[2] Postmodernism has only made matters worse. And sadly, this attitude is not unique to the contemporary West; people of all cultures and from all regions of the globe exalt themselves over God.

This skewed view of reality exerts a pervasive and powerful influence on our world. The church is not immune to this influence; many

1 Protagoras, fragment DK80 B1.

2 See Edward T. Welch, *When People Are Big and God Is Small* (Phillipsburg, NJ: P&R Publishing, 1997).

believers have unknowingly absorbed elements of it. Day in and day out, we rely much more on our own wit and wisdom than on God. As C. S. Lewis observed in *The Problem of Pain*, "We regard God as an airman regards his parachute; it's there for emergencies but he hopes he will never have to use it."[3]

The more we focus on ourselves, the less we attend to God. As a result, many no longer have even the most basic sense of who He is. Author George Orwell's observation about his day does not seem far from the truth about our own: "We have now sunk to a depth at which restatement of the obvious is the first duty of intelligent men."[4]

And even more so of intelligent believers.

The Root of the Problem

Not knowing the true God lies at the root of the problems that beset our personal lives, the church, and the culture—indeed, the whole world. Thus, the greatest need of every believer (and nonbeliever) today is to recover and maintain a right view of God. We receive this right view from the teaching of Scripture illuminated by God's Spirit.

Everything else flows from this. As the pastor and spiritual writer A. W. Tozer wisely said, "What comes into our minds when we think about God is the most important thing about us." This is so, says Tozer, because "we tend by a secret law of the soul to move toward our mental image of God. This is true not only of the individual Christian, but of the company of Christians that composes the Church."[5]

Distorted views of God influence today's church in significant and tragic ways. What Richard Niebuhr observed in the 1930s about "a God without wrath, who brings a man without sin, into a Kingdom

---

3 C. S. Lewis, *The Problem of Pain* (New York: HarperCollins, 2001), 94–95.

4 George Orwell, "The Taming of Power (review of Bertrand Russell's *Power: A New Social Analysis*)," *The Adelphi*, 15, no. 4 (1939), 206.

5 A. W. Tozer, *The Knowledge of the Holy* (New York: HarperOne, 1961), 1.

without judgment, through the ministrations of a Christ without a cross"[6] has returned.

One example that's popular in parts of the American church has been summarized as follows:

1. A God exists who created and orders the world and watches over human life on earth.
2. God wants people to be good, nice, and fair to each other, as taught in the Bible and by most world religions.
3. The central goal of life is to be happy and to feel good about oneself.
4. God does not need to be particularly involved in one's life except when [one needs God] to resolve a problem.
5. Good people go to heaven when they die.[7]

People who adhere to this worldview don't recognize the non-Christian ideas it contains; they simply think of themselves as Christians. But they have imported a very particular view of God into Christianity, and it isn't one that stands up to testing when we dive into God's Word.

Such a reductionist and human-centered view of God feels very comfortable and easy to live with. It makes no real demands, entails no cost, and allows one to live as one pleases with no concern about sin or accountability to God (and therefore no serious concern about forgiveness and reconciliation with God). This recently invented "god" is certainly not the God of the Bible, and adopting this viewpoint has the deadly effect of keeping people from the true God and the salvation He offers in Jesus Christ. To be sure, this new god has risen to some fame in the so-called "marketplace of religion." But the critical question is never what is fashionable. Rather, it is this: *What is true?* We must resist

6 Richard Niebuhr, *The Kingdom of God in America* (New York: Willet, Clark, and Co., 1937), 193.

7 Christian Smith (with Melissa Lundquist Denton), *Soul Searching: The Religious and Spiritual Lives of American Teenagers* (New York: Oxford University Press, 2009), 162–163. The technical name for this view is "moral therapeutic deism."

popular fashions, which regularly come and go, and anchor ourselves to the unchanging truths of God's Word, the Bible, which endures forever (Isa. 40:8; Matt. 24:35; 1 Pet. 1:24–25).

The Bible portrays God as the benevolent Creator and sovereign Ruler of the universe, a good, loving, and holy Being who created the heavens and earth and rules over them as King. He is all-knowing, all-wise, all-powerful, and eternal, and His character does not change. Clothed in majesty and splendor, He is worshipped by a vast company of angels—an army of powerful supernatural beings who number in the millions and carry out the Lord of Heaven's commands (Dan. 7:10, Rev. 5:11).

God created human beings in His own image to reflect His benevolent character and to be vice-regents—to share in governing—over His creation. But these first humans rebelled against Him, and their rebellion corrupted His kingdom (for the fuller story, see the first three chapters of the book of Genesis). As amazing as it may seem, God still loves His wayward creatures and offers them pardon and redemption if they will return to Him—unthinkable, except for the fact that God is gracious and deals with people on the basis of grace.

Through Jesus, His Son and Redeemer, God shows people kindness and favor that they do not deserve and could never earn. As more and more people enter God's kingdom, His creation moves toward the return of Christ and a glorious restoration in the new heavens and new earth (see Isa. 65:17; Rev. 21:1). Like a four-part novel, Scripture's account of humankind's creation, fall, redemption, and restoration tells the story of God's great work in this world and the world to come.

As we seek to better know this awe-inspiring God, we need humility, because He is infinite and we are finite; He is holy and we are unholy; and our sin hides Him from our sight. Yet, although we can never comprehend Him fully, we can indeed know Him personally and in ever-deeper ways, and that is what He desires.

To that end, we will look briefly in this chapter at two of God's most fundamental attributes: His holiness and His love. I hope this glimpse will inspire you to seek a deeper understanding of His other attributes. You can do that both by studying Scripture and by reading good books on these topics. And I encourage you to do so prayerfully, for getting to know God means more than just learning things *about* Him. It is more than simply giving assent to a set of rational propositions, no matter how biblically sound they may be. It means seeking a true relationship with Him, the One who loves you and gave His Son for you (Eph. 5:2; Gal. 2:20).

Before going further, we need to pause and ask: How it is that we can know God in the first place? The answer is simple: human beings cannot know God at all unless He chooses to reveal Himself. "If God is to be known by man," wrote biblical scholar R. T. France, "it will be on God's terms, and in God's chosen way. It is He who must take the initiative."[8] And when God takes the initiative, He does so in a personal way. France says it well: "The knowledge of God begins and ends in personal encounter with the living God. He does not send messages from outer space, but meets His people in a living, and sometimes disconcerting, relationship."[9] The knowledge God shares with us is not simply knowledge *about* Himself but knowledge *of* Himself.

Human beings today initially experience such a personal encounter with God when, through the gospel message found in His written Word, He opens our minds and hearts to His Son—Jesus, the Living Word. Jesus said it this way: "I am the way, and the truth, and the life. No one comes to the Father except through me" (John 14:6). Or, to say it in a slightly different way, we meet the Living Word through hearing God's written Word, inwardly illuminated by the Holy Spirit. This encounter opens the door to a life of communion with God—Father,

---

8 R. T. France, *The Living God* (Vancouver: Regent College Publishing, 2003), 42.

9 France, *The Living God*, 53.

Son, and Holy Spirit—which deepens as we walk with Him in faith and obedience.

God's written Word is the chief instrument through which the Spirit works in our lives. This written Word, sometimes called "Scripture" or the "Bible," was produced by men God chose, enabled, and inspired to accurately communicate what He desired to reveal about His nature, character, plans, purposes, and actions. In spite of differences in background, education, status, personality, and temperament, these men all said what God wanted them to say. When we step back for a moment and consider that God is the Creator of heaven and earth and all they contain, and that He raised Jesus from the grave, it is not difficult to believe that He could do whatever was necessary to produce people who would write what He wished to be written. Therefore, we can confidently affirm that what Scripture says, God says. And whatever God says should undoubtedly be the supreme rule of our lives.

Jesus and His apostles confirmed the divine origin and central importance of God's Word. Jesus regularly quoted the Scriptures and unequivocally held that they were the Word of God (Matt. 5:19) and could not be broken (John 10:35). He said that the words He spoke were given to Him by God (John 12:49), and He promised that after His departure the Holy Spirit would continue to teach His apostles and help them to remember all that He had taught them (John 14:24–26). Paul, for example, reminds Timothy that he came to know God through "the sacred writings, which are able to make you wise for salvation through faith in Jesus Christ. All Scripture is breathed out by God and profitable for teaching, for reproof, for correction, and for training in righteousness" (2 Tim. 3:15–16). And Peter tells us that "no prophecy of Scripture comes from someone's own interpretation. For no prophecy was ever produced by the will of man, but men spoke from God as they were carried along by the Holy Spirit" (2 Pet. 1:20–21). Peter also recognized the writings of Paul as Holy Scripture (2 Pet. 3:15–16). All these testimonies and more provide support for our confidence in the complete truthfulness and full trustworthiness of the Scriptures; it is the essential foundation for our lives. And this confidence is affirmed to us inwardly by the Holy Spirit.

Even though God's Word has been under relentless attack since the Garden of Eden, godly scholars continue to defend and demonstrate that it is completely trustworthy and deserving of full acceptance. Most important of all, as we will see ahead, is the fact that Jesus believed that Scripture is the Word of God. And as His followers we accept His verdict, for He cannot err. (For more, see some of the excellent resources that uphold the inspiration and authority of the Bible.[10])

God Is Holy

Two stories from the life of Moses give us a helpful starting point for understanding the holiness of God. Moses, who wrote the first five books of the Bible (that is, Genesis to Deuteronomy), was the greatest prophet and leader in ancient Israel. But why begin with Moses and the Old Testament? Because before Christ came, God revealed Himself most intimately to Moses, for "the Lord used to speak to Moses face to face, as a man speaks with his friend" (Exod. 33:11). God's dealings with Moses as recorded in Scripture still contain valuable lessons for us today (see Rom. 15:4).

Before looking at these stories in detail, it's helpful to pause and consider that apart from general conclusions from observing nature, our own unaided efforts will not result in the discovery of *anything* true about God. Everything we know of Him, we know because He chose to reveal Himself to us (see R. T. France's statement above).

10 For example, Walter C. Kaiser, *The Old Testament Documents: Are They Reliable & Relevant?* (Downers Grove, IL: IVP Academic, 2001); F. F. Bruce, *The New Testament Documents: Are They Reliable?* (Grand Rapids, MI: Eerdmans, 2003); Paul W. Barnett, *Is the New Testament Reliable? A Look at the Historical Evidence*, 2nd ed. (Downers Grove, IL: IVP Academic, 2003).

One of the most striking moments in the Old Testament is when God chooses to reveal Himself to Moses as he stands before a burning bush.

In the third chapter of Exodus, we read that one day, as Moses shepherded sheep in the desert, God changed his life. Moses was not seeking God, but God was seeking him. In an act of pure grace, God took the initiative and revealed Himself to Moses in an unexpected and extraordinary way. Moses saw a burning bush, unconsumed by flames, and approached it to investigate.

Out of the flames, God spoke: "Moses, Moses!"

"Here I am," Moses replied.

"Do not come near," God said. "Take your sandals off your feet, for the place on which you are standing is holy ground" (Exod. 3:4–5).

In this dramatic encounter, God immediately announced His holiness, lest Moses come too close. The Bible emphasizes God's holiness as one of His key attributes and one of its central themes. The terrified Moses hid his eyes. God then commissioned Moses to deliver the Israelites from bondage in Egypt. The Lord would graciously take the initiative to rescue a people who did not deserve His help (as the unfolding story starkly demonstrates). This encounter begins a long journey in which Moses comes to know this holy God personally and ever more deeply.

What Is God's Holiness?

"Holiness" is not a word that we often use outside the context of a church. What does it mean for God to be "holy"? In the Old Testament, the English word "holy" is a translation of the Hebrew word *qadosh*, which stresses separateness and also moral purity.

The holiness of God refers to His being "wholly other," set apart and separated from the created order which He has made. God's holiness also includes His absolute moral purity and perfection in every aspect of His being. When the seraphim declare "Holy, holy, holy is the Lord of hosts" (Isa. 6:3), they are emphasizing by their threefold repetition that God's holiness is the essence of His being. Because of God's holiness, even the ground becomes holy in His presence. This is why Moses had to remove his sandals before God (Exod. 3:5), a sign of respect and even worship. Places, physical objects, and people also become holy when they are devoted to God.

Moses' encounter with God's blazing holiness made a profound impact on him, one that would powerfully shape his life and produce a deep, lasting humility—so deep that we learn "the man Moses was very meek, more than all people who were on the face of the earth" (Num. 12:3). The impact of God's holiness becomes clear when we hear Moses exclaim, "Who is like you, O Lord, among the gods? Who is like you, majestic in holiness, awesome in glorious deeds, doing wonders?" (Exod. 15:11).

Knowing God More Deeply

Moses' encounter and growing relationship with God inspired in him (as it should in us) profound awe, reverence, and a deep desire to know God more intimately. No matter where you are with God, there is always more!

After Moses led the people of Israel out of Egypt, delivering them from lives of slavery and hard labor, God summoned him to Mount Sinai to receive the terms of God's covenant with the Israelites. Here Moses prayed, "Please show me your glory" (Exod. 33:18). God's response represents the high point in His self-revelation in the Old Testament. "I will make all my goodness pass before you and will proclaim before you my name … But," God said, "you cannot see my face, for man shall not see me and live." God therefore declared to Moses, "I will cover you with my hand until I have passed by. Then I will take away my hand, and you shall see my back, but my face shall not be seen" (vv. 19–23).

Because it pleased God to see Moses' desire to know Him more intimately, He granted Moses' prayer. Listen to how the Lord describes Himself:

> The LORD passed before [Moses] and proclaimed, "The LORD, the LORD, a God merciful and gracious, slow to anger, and abounding in steadfast love and faithfulness, keeping steadfast love for thousands, forgiving iniquity and transgression and sin, but who will by no means clear the guilty, visiting the iniquity of the fathers on the children and the children's children, to the third and the fourth generation." (Exod. 34:6–7)

This deeper revelation of God's attributes and disposition toward human beings shows that God's holiness and love are inextricably bound up with one another. We see this in words such as "merciful, gracious, slow to anger," "abounding in steadfast love and faithfulness," "forgiving … sin." Only after those words does He add that He "will by no means clear the guilty" (those who reject Him and continue in their rebellion and sin) but will visit "the iniquity of the fathers" on their children and grandchildren.

With these words to Moses, which were then written down for all God's people to hear, God shows that His inmost being is holy love. For that reason, these words became the classic description of God in the Old Testament, reappearing over the centuries in several important passages (for example, in Num. 14:18; Neh. 9:17, 31; Ps. 86:15; 103:8; 145:8; Jonah 4:2; Joel 2:13). This is also how Jesus and the writers of the New Testament saw God and why they called people to love Him in response (Mark 12:28–34; Rom. 13:8–10; Gal. 5:6, 13–14; 1 John 4:7–12). It has provided a bedrock for God's people over the centuries.

When we look more closely at how God described Himself to Moses, a beautiful picture emerges—one that can enrich our relationship with God. Hebrew scholar Douglas Stuart helps us discern the nuances of Exodus 34:6–7:

> The first attribute of Yahweh listed is that he is a "compassionate" [ESV: "merciful"] God, meaning that he genuinely cares about humans and holds toward them a tender attitude of concern and mercy. Second, he called himself "gracious," meaning that he does things for people they do not deserve and goes beyond what might be expected to grant truly kind favor toward people, favor of which they are not necessarily worthy.[11]

Grasping these two characteristics of God's character is essential for appreciating the next two:

> Third, he described himself as "slow to anger," meaning that his patience with people's less-than-satisfactory behavior and/or failures in any realm, including the moral, is very great. Fourth, he declared himself to be "abounding" (lit., great) in covenant "love."[12]

Twice in verse 6, God's "steadfast love" is highlighted. Stuart notes that the term used here in Hebrew, *hesed*, "connotes long-term, reliable loyalty of one member of a covenant relationship to another."[13]

What does this mean for you and me, and indeed for all of God's people throughout history? As Stuart puts it, "However fickle and unreliable humans may be in their relationship to God, he is nothing of the sort but can be counted on in every situation and at all times to be completely faithful to his promises for his people." And, finally, Stuart points out: "Next [God] described himself as '[abounding in] truth,' meaning that whatever he says is correct and reliable and may be trusted even to the extent of life and death issues, or indeed *eternal* life and death issues."[14] Keeping steadfast love for "thousands" could

11 Douglas K. Stuart, *Exodus, Volume 2*, The New American Commentary (Nashville, TN: B&H Publishing, 2006), 715.

12 Stuart, *Exodus, Volume 2*, 715–716.

13 Stuart, *Exodus, Volume 2*, 716.

14 Stuart, *Exodus, Volume 2*, 716. The word Stuart quotes as "truth" is translated "faithfulness" in the ESV.

mean for thousands of persons, but here it's more likely that it means thousands of generations. This statement assures us that God will not forsake His people as long as they do not abandon Him and give themselves over to evil that demands punishment.

God's self-description as "forgiving iniquity and transgression and sin" (v. 7) emphasizes that His forgiveness encompasses the full range of human sin. Unfortunately, however, the distorted views many people have of God prompt them to reject Him. One popular justification for this rejection focuses on God's wrath and judgment of sin. The idea of God expressing righteous indignation or sitting in righteous judgment offends the modern mind and causes some people to view God as an arbitrary, capricious, and vindictive tyrant. Our permissive, "nonjudgmental" culture finds it hard to grasp how God could be truly loving yet render judgment upon people for their sinful behavior "so long as they aren't hurting anyone else."

"Who does God think He is to judge me?" people ask. Or "How could a good God judge basically good people? Doesn't God say He wants me to forgive other people? So why can't He just forgive all of us for any kind of sin we commit?"

Ignorance of the true nature of sin is part of the problem here. So, a brief description of sin may provide important perspective, for, as Romans 3:23 tells us, all of us have sinned. Well-respected author and theologian J. I. Packer defines sin like this:

> Scripture diagnoses sin as a universal deformity of human nature, found at every point in every person. Both Testaments have names for it that display its ethical character as rebellion against God's rule, missing the mark God set us to aim at, transgressing God's law, disobeying God's directives, offending God's purity by defiling oneself, and incurring guilt before God the Judge.[15]

15 J. I. Packer, *Concise Theology: A Guide to Historic Christian Beliefs* (Wheaton, IL: Tyndale House Publishers, 1993), 82.

None of us can escape the fact of our sin. And sin is something that occurs in the context of our relationship with God. Packer goes on to say: "The root of sin is pride and enmity against God, the spirit seen in Adam's first transgression; and sinful acts always have behind them thoughts, motives, and desires that one way or another express the willful opposition of the fallen heart to God's claims on our lives."[16] So, the first appropriate response to those who challenge God's right to judge them is to point out that God is the Creator and righteous Judge of all the earth and that everyone must one day give an account of their life to Him.

But even more importantly, we must always see God's judgment against the backdrop of His holiness—His absolute moral purity and perfect justice, which requires punishment of unrepented sin. If God were to ignore moral evil, He would deny His very nature. God's wrath against sin is not an arbitrary, capricious expression of bad temper such as humans often display. Rather, it is the reaction of a *holy*, loving God against persistent and outrageous moral evil in His world. And it expresses His determination to ensure that justice is ultimately done, that the scales are ultimately balanced, either in this life or at the final judgment.

Because God is holy *love*, we also must see His judgment in the light of His love. This highlights one of the central issues in the drama of human existence: human freedom. God loves His creatures and desires that they love Him in return. But He does not compel such love; it must be freely given. To make that possible, God gave human beings the power of moral choice, and with that power came the possibility to choose not only good but evil.

When people choose to sin and violate God's laws, they offend Him. He responds first not with punishment, but with grace and mercy. He seeks to warn people and call them to repentance—to turn

---

16 Packer, *Concise Theology*, 82.

back to Him—as He did repeatedly with both Israel and Judah (2 Kings 17:6–23; 2 Chron. 36:15). He is patient and will use the gentlest means possible to bring people to repentance. However, if they ignore His repeated calls to repent and continue in deliberate, willful sin, God will let them have what they want—and with it, the consequences of their rebellion. C. S. Lewis puts it this way: "There are only two kinds of people in the end: those who say to God, 'Thy will be done,' and those to whom God says in the end, 'Thy will be done.' All that are in hell choose it."[17]

God's Holy Love

As we grapple with these issues, we must never let the reality of God's holy judgment obscure the reality of God's holy love. God is good and takes pleasure in blessing His creatures, not in punishing them. He is a God of grace, delighting to pour His undeserved kindness upon us when we deserve just the opposite.

Scripture assures us that "the Lord is good; his steadfast love [*hesed*] endures forever, and his faithfulness to all generations" (Ps. 100:5). He does good to all: "[Your Father] makes his sun rise on the evil and on the good, and sends rain on the just and on the unjust" (Matt. 5:45). God would rather show mercy than bring judgment: "Have I any pleasure in the death of the wicked, declares the Lord God, and not rather that he should turn from his way and live?" (Ezek. 18:23). But God *must* punish sin. From a human point of view, God's love and His justice seem to be irreconcilably in conflict. But both exist in God without conflict and, in fact, reveal His glorious character.

A vital aspect of God's glorious character that we must grasp is His fatherly love for His children (1 John 3:1). God's love and grace moved Him to take the initiative, at high cost to Himself, to rescue us when we were helplessly lost in sin, condemned, and could do nothing

---

17 C. S. Lewis, *The Great Divorce* (New York, NY: Touchstone Books, 1996), 72.

to save ourselves. No amount of our own obedience, good works, or sacrifice could erase our sins or make us right with God. But because the life of the sinless Son of God had infinite value, His death for us could atone for the sins of all who turn to Him seeking forgiveness and reconciliation with God.

In His holy and fatherly love, God sent Jesus, His only Son, to take on human flesh, live a sinless life, and willingly offer Himself as a sacrifice to pay the debt of our sin and bring us into His family as adopted sons and daughters (John 3:16; 10:7–18; Gal. 4:5; Eph. 1:5; 1 John 4:9–10). And so, God's justice and His love meet in the cross of Christ, where God punishes sin and visits that justice not upon us but upon His Son. Only through God's Son can we come to know God.

A supposedly true story about a Native American chief and a chicken thief has helped some people better grasp the atoning death of Jesus. During a long drought, an unknown member of a tribe began to steal chickens from others, putting the survival of the tribe at risk. The chief decreed that anyone caught stealing a chicken would be tied to a post and lashed twenty-five times. The thief was undeterred, and chickens continued to disappear. The chief then increased the punishment to fifty lashes, but still to no effect. Finally, the penalty was increased to one hundred lashes, a number no one could survive. Eventually, the thief was discovered—the chief's own mother.

The chief now faced an impossible dilemma. While he loved his mother deeply, he also had to enforce justice in the tribe. When the fateful day arrived, the chief's mother was led to the whipping post, where her arms were tied around it securely. A strong brave with a whip stood ready to carry out the chief's order. The eyes of all the tribe fixed on the chief as they waited for his signal to begin the lashing. But to the surprise of all, he removed his shirt, walked to the whipping post, placed his arms around his mother, and ordered the whipping to begin. He took upon himself the punishment his mother deserved, paying the full penalty she deserved. Then, he collapsed and died from the beating.[18]

This example gives us a picture of how God's justice and His love for sinners are satisfied through the death of Jesus on the cross. (It is an imperfect analogy, of course, because the chief might not have made the penalty so great had he known his mother was the offender. But God knew the full extent of our sin and imposed its full penalty on Jesus.)

The Amazing Love of Jesus

"Whoever has seen me," Jesus said, "has seen the Father" (John 14:9). Jesus perfectly reflected His Father's nature: "merciful and gracious, slow to anger, and abounding in steadfast love and faithfulness" (Exod. 34:6).

God's love and grace shine as a bright light in the darkness of this fallen world through the life, death, and resurrection of Jesus. He is the light of the world (John 8:12), full of grace and truth, the One who came into the world as God's Suffering Servant—"not to be served but to serve, and to give his life as a ransom for many" (Mark 10:45).

Day after day, Jesus went forth to seek and save the lost (Luke 19:10). And as He went, He was merciful and compassionate to all who sought His help, healing the sick, restoring sight to the blind, feeding the hungry, comforting the brokenhearted, delivering the demonized, teaching life-changing truth, and offering hope for the world to come. He became known as "the friend of sinners,"[19] reaching out in love to those rejected by proper society. Finally, for us and for our salvation, He took upon Himself the shame, humiliation, and excruciating pain of death on the cross to reconcile us to the Father and bring us into His family. Today, anyone who wants to know God personally can do so through Jesus, for He is "the way, and the truth, and the life." He

---

18 A slightly different version of this story is told in "The Indian Chief," *The Compass: A Tool for Disciplers*, Cru, https://www.cru.org/content/dam/cru/legacy/2012/01/theindianchief.pdf.

19 See Matt. 11:19; Luke 7:34.

clearly says that "no one comes to the Father except through me" (John 14:6) and "whoever comes to me I will never cast out" (John 6:37).

In all that Jesus said and did, we see the invisible God and His grace demonstrated concretely. With this overarching perspective in mind, we turn in the next chapter to the nature and character of Jesus Himself.

Questions to Ponder

1. Name some examples of how a person's view of God can affect his or her day-to-day experience. How do you typically think of God throughout the day?
2. What difference does your view of God make for your prayer life? When you pray, which do you tend to be more aware of—God's holiness or God's love?
3. Exodus 34:6–7 is a critical passage for understanding who God is because God defines Himself in this text. What did you learn about God from reflecting on Moses' encounter with Him?
4. How does the biblical view of love and holiness compare and contrast with the most common assumptions about love and holiness in your current cultural setting?
5. What are some views of God that you formerly had but you have now rejected or reshaped in alignment with biblical teaching?

2

Why Follow Jesus?

I am the way, and the truth, and the life.
No one comes to the Father except through me.
John 14:6

To better understand the spiritual crisis in the church and in many of our own lives, we must look to Jesus. He is the beating heart of what we call "Christianity," and we have strayed further from Him than we realize. The better we understand Jesus, His ministry, and His mission, the clearer our vision will become and the more obvious our life's direction will be.

Historians have sometimes described Jesus as the most significant person who ever lived. Commenting on how remarkable Jesus' influence has been in human history, the noted historian Philip Schaff wrote,

> Jesus of Nazareth, without money and arms, conquered more millions than Alexander, Caesar, Mohammed, and Napoleon; without science and learning, He shed more light on things human and divine than all philosophers and schools combined; without the eloquence of schools, He spoke words of life such as never were spoken before or since, and produced effects which lie beyond the reach of any orator or poet; without writing a single line, He has set more pens in motion, and furnished themes for more sermons, orations, discussions, learned

> volumes, works of art and sweet songs of praise, than the whole army of great men of ancient and modern times.[1]

Schaff summed it up well when he noted, "There never was in this world a life so unpretending, modest, and lowly in its outward form and condition, and yet producing such extraordinary effects upon all ages, nations, and classes of men."[2]

Schaff's words were written in retrospect, but what about the people of Jesus' own day? How do we make sense of the profound impact of Jesus of Nazareth on the men and women of His era? What drew them to Him? Why did they become His disciples despite the cost? How did following Jesus change their lives? What compelled them to urge others to become His disciples and set in motion what Schaff described above?

We might go on to inquire about Jesus' enduring influence. What has continued to attract people to Jesus over the centuries? Why should anyone in the modern world choose to become a disciple of Jesus? What does it even mean to be His disciple today? What does discipleship look like in *our* era?

The answers to these questions lie ahead and have profound implications. They open our eyes to the meaning and purpose of our lives. But to discover these answers and their transforming potential, we must start at the beginning.

Why People Felt Drawn to Jesus

Jesus did not launch His ministry in the normal way for Jews in His day, with rabbinical training and the endorsement of Israel's official religious establishment. He came in the power of the Holy Spirit, with a deep knowledge of the Scriptures, and spoke "as one who had authority" (Matt. 7:29). He taught in synagogues, preached good news, and

---

1 Philip Schaff, *The Person of Jesus Christ* (American Tract Society, 1913), 49.

2 Schaff, *Person of Jesus Christ*, 49.

promised rest to the weary. He forgave sins, healed the sick, gave sight to the blind, liberated those oppressed by demons, and raised the dead. He had a powerful and far-reaching impact.

People said of Him, "Never was anything like this seen in Israel" (Matt. 9:33), and "No one ever spoke like this man" (John 7:46), and "We never saw anything like this" (Mark 2:12). They "rejoiced" with His teaching (Luke 13:17) and heard Him "gladly" (Mark 12:37).

Some even recognized His true identity. Andrew told Simon, "We have found the Messiah" (John 1:41), while Philip told Nathanael, "We have found him of whom Moses in the Law and also the prophets wrote—Jesus of Nazareth, the son of Joseph" (John 1:45).

Waiting and Looking for the Messiah

By the time Jesus was born in Bethlehem, the prophets had been silent for more than four centuries and the faithful in ancient Israel were languishing under foreign domination, longing for God's promised Messiah. Many of God's people expected that the Messiah would be like King David, delivering the beleaguered nation from its enemies, establishing God's kingdom on earth, and ushering in a glorious era of peace and plenty.

Into this difficult political and religious climate, a new prophet appeared in Israel, tasked with announcing the impending arrival of the long-awaited Messiah. John the Baptist had a simple, direct, and electrifying message: "Repent, for the kingdom of heaven is at hand" (Matt. 3:2).

Multitudes came from far and wide to hear John preach, and he baptized those who accepted his message and confessed their sins. "I baptize you with water for repentance," he told them, "but he who is coming after me is mightier than I, whose sandals I am not worthy to carry. He will baptize you with the Holy Spirit and fire" (Matt. 3:11).

This soon-to-be-revealed Messiah, born of a virgin mother, lived in the quiet obscurity of the small mountain village of Nazareth until about the age of thirty. During these years, He worked as a tradesman while preparing for the public phase of His life's mission, which lasted only three years. An angel had revealed this mission even before His birth, instructing His adoptive father, Joseph, to "call his name Jesus, for he will save his people from their sins" (Matt. 1:21). By the act of naming Jesus, Joseph publicly accepted Mary's baby as his son, thereby bringing Jesus into the patrilineal family line of King David.

The name Jesus (*Yeshua* in Hebrew) means "Yahweh saves" ("Yahweh" is the Old Testament Hebrew name for "God," as recorded in Exodus 3:14). Contrary to the expectation of most Jews awaiting their Messiah, God considered deliverance from the oppression of sin infinitely more important than deliverance from Roman oppression. Jesus is God's solution to the rebellion at the heart of His creation, for Jesus comes as the rightful King who saves His people by atoning for their sin and rebellion and reconciling them to God.

The Gospel of Matthew tells us, "All this took place to fulfill what the Lord had spoken by the prophet: 'Behold, the virgin shall conceive and bear a son, and they shall call his name Immanuel' (which means, God with us)" (1:22–23). This unexpected and startling revelation—that Jesus the Messiah was God in human form—would prove very hard for most people to accept. And among some, it inflamed intense opposition.

When the fullness of time arrived, Jesus went to John the Baptist seeking baptism. He did so not because He had sinned or needed to repent, but to identify with fallen humanity and to "fulfill all righteousness" (Matt. 3:15). At His baptism, the Spirit of God visibly descended upon Jesus, and a voice from heaven said, "This is my beloved Son, with whom I am well pleased" (v. 17). In this dramatic moment, God announced Jesus the Messiah as His Son. This heavenly announcement confirmed to John and to his followers that Jesus really was the Messiah whom John had preached about and expected—but also that He was something *far* more (John 1:33).

At the same time, it confirmed the approaching end of John's brief but powerful and far-reaching ministry of preparing the way for the Messiah. While Jesus' mission would now begin and increase, John's would decrease and end (John 3:30). John's uncompromising proclamation of truth eventually brought him into conflict with Herod, the king of Judea, who imprisoned and then executed him.

John's arrest signaled that the time had arrived for Jesus to begin His public mission, and "from that time Jesus began to preach, saying, 'Repent, for the kingdom of heaven is at hand'" (Matt. 4:17). The long wait finally had ended! God's kingdom had drawn near in the person of Jesus: Messiah, Son of God, and King.

The Kingdom of God

Many scholars note that Jesus emphasized "the kingdom of God" as the main theme of His ministry. What is this kingdom? In his classic work *The Kingdom of God,* seminary professor John Bright observes that the concept "is ubiquitous in both Old Testament and New. It involves the whole notion of the rule of God over his people, and particularly the vindication of that rule and people in glory at the end of history."[3] He further says that "it lies at the very heart of the gospel message to affirm that the kingdom of God has in a real sense become present fact, here and now. … In the person and work of Jesus the Kingdom of God has intruded into the world."[4] And this unexpected intrusion isn't the endpoint; God's kingdom will one day come to its consummation at Jesus' second coming.

When we think about a kingdom on earth, we usually think of a geographic region and a group of people that are ruled by royalty. But

3 John Bright, *The Kingdom of God: The Biblical Concept and Its Meaning for the Church* (Nashville, TN: Abington, 1953), 18.

4 Bright, *The Kingdom of God,* 216.

when Jesus talks about establishing God's kingdom, he isn't talking about a bounded region. J. I. Packer elaborates:

> God's kingdom is not a place, but rather a relationship. It exists wherever people enthrone Jesus as Lord of their lives. When Jesus began preaching that "the kingdom of God is near," he meant that the long-promised enjoyment of God's salvation for which Israel had been waiting was now there for them to enter (Mark 1:15).[5]

This was a fundamental change that affected everything. But a question naturally arises—as Packer puts it, "How were they to enter it?" And, I might add, how are we to enter? Packer continues: "The Gospels answer that question very fully. Why, by becoming Jesus' disciples; by giving him their hearts' loyalty and letting him reshape their lives; by receiving forgiveness from him; by identifying with his concerns; by loving him without reserve and giving his claims precedence over all others."[6]

Doing these things is nothing less than inhabiting the kingdom of God on earth and fulfilling our purpose in life. We will explore this more fully in the next chapter.

What Is a Disciple of Jesus?

In the Gospels, we learn that Jesus spent a good deal of His three-year public ministry teaching and training His disciples. And after His resurrection, He charged them to "make disciples of all nations" (Matt. 28:19). But what exactly is a "disciple"?

In the Greco-Roman world of New Testament times, the word "disciple" (Greek *mathetes*) meant a learner and adherent of a master teacher. It was used to "designate a follower who was vitally commit-

5 J. I. Packer, *Growing in Christ* (Wheaton, IL: Crossway, 1994), 176.

6 Packer, *Growing in Christ*, 176.

ted to a teacher/leader and/or [a] movement."[7] In other words, it was something more than what we think of today as a "student," for disciples didn't just seek to learn intellectual truths; they adopted their teacher's way of life, often traveling with him and respecting his guidance. Philosophers commonly had such disciples, and many of these disciples aimed to mature, become teachers themselves, and gain their own followers. In the Gospels, we read about disciples of John the Baptist, disciples of Moses, disciples of the Pharisees, and disciples of Jesus.

When the Gospels use the word "disciple" to refer to Jesus' earliest followers, the term describes someone who has come to Jesus in repentant faith, is committed to Him, and is trying to learn and follow His teaching and become like Him (Matt. 10:24–25). We might call them students or pupils of Jesus, the righteous King, who is in the process of bringing God's kingdom to its fullness. Yet they are more than simply students trying to learn what Jesus knows; they are students who are *committed* to Jesus. This commitment begins in the hearts of His followers, and the more they become like Jesus, God's Son, the more the image of God is restored in their lives.

Although Jesus' first disciples did not yet have a full grasp of His true identity (or of their own), their understanding grew as their relationship with Him matured. By watching Him work, listening to His teaching, obeying His commands, and working with Him in various aspects of His ministry, they grew over the months and years. Their growth was slow and halting, but after the Lord's resurrection from the dead and their being filled with the Holy Spirit, certain things finally became clear to them, propelling them into rapid advance and greater spiritual maturity.

From that time on, the word "disciple" in relation to Jesus has meant "one who has come to Jesus for eternal life, has claimed Jesus

---

7 Michael J. Wilkins, *Discipleship in the Ancient World and Matthew's Gospel,* 2nd ed. (Grand Rapids, MI: Baker Books, 1995), 220–222.

as Savior and God, and has embarked upon the life of following Jesus. This is the common term for believers and is used in this sense at least 230 times in the Gospels."[8] Through such disciples God has been building His kingdom up to the present day.

But here's the big question for us: *How* did Jesus help His disciples grow and mature into fully formed disciples in God's kingdom? As we just saw, He used a process that unfolded over time. It began with a call to faith, personal commitment to Him, and joining His community, and it advanced through learning His teachings, obeying His commands, dying to oneself, suffering hardship, going on mission, following His example of humble, selfless love, and serving one another. All of these were essential for achieving Jesus' goal for these disciples: "for the disciple to be like his teacher, and the servant like his master" (Matt. 10:25). Their commitment and understanding would grow as they continued to walk with Jesus, through the ministry of the Holy Spirit, and to learn from Him alongside other disciples in the community.

Jesus' ultimate goal for His disciples, and how He plans to accomplish it, is described as follows by C. S. Lewis, who speaks here in the persona of Jesus:

> "Make no mistake," he says, "if you let me I will make you perfect. The moment you put yourself in my hands, that is what you are in for. Nothing less, or other, than that. You have free will, and if you choose, you can push me away. But if you do not push me away, understand that I am going to see this job through. Whatever suffering it may cost you in your earthly life … whatever it costs me, I will never rest, nor let you rest, until you are literally perfect—until my Father can say without reservation that he is well pleased with you, as he said he was

---

8 Michael J. Wilkins, *Following the Master* (Grand Rapids, MI: Zondervan, 1992), 42.

> well pleased with me. This I can do and will do. But I will not do anything less."[9]

That is what Jesus began to do with the first disciples and what He intends to do with everyone else who becomes His disciple.

What Do Today's Disciples Look Like?

Has the meaning of the word "disciple" or the true nature of discipleship to Jesus changed since the first century? No. The common understanding of the word, however, along with its meaning in practice, has become confused or distorted at various points in history. And *that* has caused problems.

Perhaps the most common confusion or error is the concept of "two tiers." This erroneous idea assumes the existence of two types of Christians: the "ordinary" Christian and the "highly committed" Christian—with only the latter being a "disciple." We will look at this idea in more detail just ahead.

The bitter fruit of this error is that professing Christians who remain uncommitted (or even unconverted) continue to live in ways that publicly undermine their profession of Christ and the credibility of the gospel. Their behavior sows seeds of unbelief among nonbelievers and produces much other bad fruit, creating widespread problems for the contemporary church.

On the other hand, despite this (and other corruptions and confusions that have plagued the church), God continues to raise up faithful, fruitful disciples of Jesus. Throughout the centuries, those disciples have brought glory to Him. And He continues to use faithful disciples to bring glory to Him today. In the next chapter we will learn more about how people become true disciples of Jesus and enter God's kingdom. Everyone who does so experiences in this life and the next the

9 C. S. Lewis, *Mere Christianity* (New York: Touchstone Books, 1996), 174.

blessings of those who faithfully follow the Son of God! Thus, may we daily pray with Richard of Chichester:

> Thanks be to thee, my Lord Jesus Christ,
> for all the benefits thou hast given me,
> for all the pains and insults thou hast borne for me.
> O most merciful Redeemer,
> Friend and Brother,
> may I know thee more clearly
> love thee more dearly,
> and follow thee more nearly, day by day.
> Amen.[10]

Questions to Ponder

1. Briefly explain how one becomes a disciple of Jesus, and what "disciple" means in the context of the New Testament and the church.
2. How would you describe the relationship between the kingdom of God and being a fully committed disciple of Jesus?
3. What qualities of Jesus impress you the most? As His disciple, which of these qualities do you find most challenging? Why?
4. How do you react to the idea that the Christian community has a major problem caused by the erroneous teaching that Jesus offers two levels of Christian commitment ("ordinary" and "highly committed")? Is this something you've heard or been taught in the past?
5. What would you say is your level of commitment to Jesus at this time? Where do you see evidence of being His disciple in your life, and in what areas do you hope to be strengthened or become more mature?

---

10 Prayer commonly attributed to Richard of Chichester (1197–1253).

3

Entering God's Kingdom

From that time Jesus began to preach, saying,
"Repent, for the kingdom of heaven is at hand."
Matthew 4:17

We have seen that Jesus continually focused His teaching on "the kingdom of God." We have also seen that "God's kingdom is not a place, but rather a relationship. It exists wherever people enthrone Jesus as Lord of their lives." The question before us now is how we enter this relationship with Jesus, enthrone Him as Lord of our lives, and become part of God's kingdom. Or, put differently, what must we do to be saved and receive eternal life?[1]

Many people today believe they have been saved, but their beliefs are misplaced and their lives give no evidence of salvation. Others believe they have been saved, and they may be, but cultural captivity, moral compromise, spiritual stagnation, and other maladies make it hard to see the fruit of salvation in their lives. However, some have a well-founded faith that shines through in their daily lives and bears abundant fruit because they have experienced true conversion through God's regenerating grace.

How can we have such a strong foundation that we feel confident of our salvation and bear the fruit of God's saving grace? This chapter seeks to show the way forward by returning us to God's Word.

1 To "be saved," "enter God's kingdom," and "receive eternal life" are synonymous in the Gospels, as are "the kingdom of God" and the "kingdom of heaven."

A New Era Has Arrived

When He was around thirty years old, Jesus launched His public ministry in Galilee, a fertile area in northern Israel dotted with about two hundred towns and villages and inhabited by perhaps as many as three hundred thousand people.[2] He established His base in Capernaum, a relatively prosperous fishing village on the northwestern shore of the Sea of Galilee.

Jesus' primary message was simple and clear: "Repent, for the kingdom of heaven is at hand" (Matt. 4:17). Or, as Mark 1:15 says, "The kingdom of God is at hand; repent and believe the gospel." With these words, Jesus proclaimed the arrival of a new era in history. He announced the advent of a new stage of God's kingdom—that sphere in human life where God's rule is recognized and received and where His restoring power is experienced—and urged men and women to become citizens of that kingdom. Embracing this offer of grace brought pardon for sins and a new spiritual life to those who received it with repentant faith.

From that time to this, sinful people have continued to enter God's kingdom as it moves toward its final consummation. But how does this happen? As Jesus would later tell the Jewish leader Nicodemus, there is an element of mystery in how the Holy Spirit brings people into God's kingdom: "The wind blows where it wishes, and you hear its sound, but you do not know where it comes from or where it goes. So it is with everyone who is born of the Spirit" (John 3:8). This "spiritual rebirth" involves the Spirit drawing people to believe and trust in Jesus as God's Son and Messiah and to follow Him in a life of faithful and fruitful discipleship (John 3:16; 8:31–32; 10:27; 15:8).

The story of Jesus' first followers, two pairs of brothers, describes the beginning of this life:

---

2 Michael J. Wilkins, *Matthew*, The NIV Application Commentary (Grand Rapids, MI: Zondervan, 2004), 180.

> While walking by the Sea of Galilee, [Jesus] saw two brothers, Simon (who is called Peter) and Andrew his brother, casting a net into the sea, for they were fishermen. And he said to them, "Follow me, and I will make you fishers of men." Immediately they left their nets and followed him. And going on from there he saw two other brothers, James the son of Zebedee and John his brother, in the boat with Zebedee their father, mending their nets, and he called them. Immediately they left the boat and their father and followed him. (Matt. 4:18–22)

This brief encounter provides a vivid example of God's grace at work as He calls people into His kingdom through a relationship with Jesus.

In the *foreground* of this report in Matthew 4, we see that, unlike the normal pattern of students choosing their rabbi, these men did not choose Jesus; *He* chose *them.* They had no special moral or intellectual qualities or unique abilities. They were just ordinary working-class men, business partners (Luke 5:10) engaged in the daily tasks of their vocation. Jesus took the initiative; He sought them out and called them to faith in Himself ("follow me") and service in God's kingdom ("I will make you fishers of men").

Jesus' authoritative summons required these men to make a firm and momentous decision. To answer His call, faith in Jesus and personal allegiance to Him had to become first and foremost in their lives, taking priority over all else. This meant a new way of thinking and living, a major turnabout—from lesser loves and loyalties to Jesus alone. Such a decision would require commitment and be costly. For them, it would mean leaving everything behind, including their hopes and dreams and plans as well as their livelihoods and closest family—all so that they might follow Jesus into an unknown future.[3] But with the call came the grace to trust and obey, and remarkably, they did so at once.

3 Along with being taught and formed as disciples, these four along with eight others would later be chosen to physically accompany Jesus in His travels in order to be trained for the additional unique role of apostles, His designated leaders of the church after His ascension (Luke 6:13).

In the *background*, we can also see God's grace at work in the mystery of His providence. The scene in Matthew 4 was not these brothers' first encounter with Jesus. The Spirit had been preparing them for this specific moment through a series of earlier events, as we see in John 1:35–2:11. Before meeting Jesus, Andrew and John[4] had been disciples of John the Baptist (John 1:35), from whom they heard the call to repent in preparation for the Messiah's impending arrival (they no doubt shared it with their brothers, Peter and James). They also had been present at Bethany when John pointed out Jesus and announced Him as the long-awaited Messiah, "the Lamb of God, who takes away the sin of the world" (John 1:29, 36). This revelation prompted them to immediately seek out Jesus for informal conversation.

They knew very little about Him other than what John had said, and their understanding of the Messiah was conflated with popular nationalistic expectations. Graciously, Jesus invited them to "come and ... see" (John 1:39), opening the door to a friendship and understanding of Him that would deepen over the next three years (Matt. 16:17; John 20:28). Immediately, Andrew found his brother, Peter, and introduced him to Jesus (John 1:41–42). Where James was at this point we aren't told, but we can be sure that he too was quickly introduced to Jesus.

We don't have an exact chronology of all that God was doing in these men's hearts at this exploratory "come and see" stage, but clearly the mysterious wind of the Spirit was blowing in their lives. We do know that a little later, as they were still getting acquainted with Jesus while in some informal sense following Him, they saw Him turn water into wine at Cana, and this increased their faith in Him (John 2:11). And we can reasonably assume that because Jesus had relocated from Nazareth to their town of Capernaum, they almost certainly would have heard His public teachings and frequent proclamation: "Repent, for the kingdom of heaven is at hand" (Matt. 4:17).

---

4 Widely assumed by scholars to be the unnamed disciple in John 1:37–40.

Did the nascent faith of these men become confirmed and established through these early encounters with Jesus? Only God knows. But what *is* clear is that Jesus' formal call to follow Him, as we saw above, was an action-forcing event that required them to respond to Him in a definite, concrete way that would crystallize what they had so far come to know and believe about Him into a decisive commitment.

Matthew's recounting of the event leaves no doubt. Soon after calling these four young fishermen, Jesus took the initiative again and called another young man, this one a despised tax collector. He too joined the group: "As Jesus passed on from there, he saw a man called Matthew sitting at the tax booth, and he said to him, 'Follow me.' And he rose and followed him" (Matt. 9:9). Like the others, Matthew immediately responded in faith, walking away from a lucrative career and leaving everything behind in order to follow Jesus into an uncertain future. These men would form the vanguard of the new community Jesus had come to establish—the church.

In each of these men, the drawing of the Holy Spirit and the call of Jesus combined to evoke the faith and repentance that He sought from everyone as He proclaimed God's kingdom throughout Galilee. Ever since then, His summons to "Follow Me" has called people to the same salvation, commitment, and costly service as the first disciples. For those today who are unconverted, the call is to faith, repentance, and wholehearted commitment to Jesus—to be His disciple. For those who have been converted but because of ignorance or bad teaching have not fully committed themselves to Jesus, the call is to repent and to give oneself completely to Jesus. In either case, this call is first and foremost to Jesus Himself, and then, as a supernatural outworking of that relationship, to His service. There is no repentance without change. And any "faith" that does not lead to discipleship is not saving faith.

Using a wider lens, we hear the same call in different words when Jesus invites the multitudes to trust Him, become His disciples, and enter the kingdom: "Come to me, all who labor and are heavy laden, and I will give you rest. Take my yoke upon you, and learn from me, for I am gentle and lowly in heart, and you will find rest for your souls. For my yoke is easy, and my burden is light" (Matt. 11:28–30). Note that these words, while comforting, cannot be interpreted as relieving followers of the need to repent or change.

The call of Jesus is not like the call of earthly rulers or teachers. In the words of Bible scholar Michael Wilkins, "Jesus' invitation is in stark contrast to the religious burden of Pharisaism. His yoke—a metaphor for discipleship to him—promises rest from the weariness and burden of religious regulation and human oppression, because it is none other than commitment to him. His disciples learn directly from him."[5] Jesus' call doesn't pile religious expectations on us; it urges us to put our trust in Him.

As we read in the Gospels, men and women of all sorts responded to Jesus' call. They came to Him in the obedience of faith and took up His yoke of discipleship through a decisive act of their will, a personal choice to follow Jesus. In response to the Spirit's drawing, they chose to repent, believe the Good News, and begin to internalize His teachings. They oriented their lives around Him by following His example and becoming increasingly like Him.

Unlike the first disciples, most of Jesus' later followers did not accompany Him in His travels. Although the call to discipleship was the same, the context in which they were to live it out was different; they remained in their homes, workplaces, and local communities as witnesses to Jesus—salt and light to those around them (see Matt. 5:13–16).

At the outset of His public ministry, Jesus enlarged His band of traveling disciples into a small community. In the culture of that time and place, it was normally expected that the disciple would choose the rabbi he wanted to learn from, but Jesus reversed that model and chose

5 Wilkins, *Matthew*, 424.

the disciples He wanted to follow Him—twelve in all. These men would have a dual role—disciples *and* apostles (Luke 6:12–16). Jesus taught and formed the twelve into disciples as they accompanied Him, and He also gave them training to later serve in the role of apostles. An apostle was someone who was "sent out" with a special mission, and their mission would be to lead the Jesus movement after He returned to heaven. Little did they know that their tiny community would serve as the forerunner to what later became the worldwide church!

After Jesus had suffered, died, been resurrected, and was preparing to return to heaven, He commissioned His original disciples to be apostles who would carry on His work of spreading God's kingdom by making disciples of others. He gave them this charge:

> All authority in heaven and on earth has been given to me. Go therefore and make disciples of all nations, baptizing them in the name of the Father and of the Son and of the Holy Spirit, teaching them to observe all that I have commanded you. And behold, I am with you always, to the end of the age (Matt. 28:18–20).

Even here, Jesus emphasizes the relationship: He will be *with them.* Jesus wanted not only His first disciples but those in every age and in every place around the globe to reproduce themselves. Everyone who becomes a disciple of Jesus is given the same mission to disciple others, thus forming an unbroken chain down through the ages. This is part of "all I have commanded you" and therefore is something every disciple is to learn and obey.

This was Jesus' plan for spreading God's kingdom: disciples making disciples. In the book of Acts, we see this happening when ordinary people who come to faith in Christ understand themselves to be His disciples—not merely converts—and take up His call. Like the original disciples, they were flawed, broken people who were learning to become more like Jesus. None were perfect. Some were outstanding disciples, others were mediocre, and still others were poor disciples. But they were all disciples, works in progress who bore witness to Jesus' life, message, and power.

Disciples, Not Merely Converts

"Disciples—not merely converts." Does it puzzle you to hear someone distinguish between "convert" and "disciple," or even between "Christian" and "disciple"? Few people today seem to realize that the entire early church understood themselves to be disciples of Jesus. They knew His commission to "make disciples." And they sought to make disciples of others, not only in Jerusalem but in Judea, Samaria, and throughout the world (see Acts 1:8).

These earliest believers consistently referred to themselves, and to those whom they won to Christ, as "disciples" (the term appears no fewer than twenty-eight times in the book of Acts). The early church was, in fact, a community of disciples on a divine mission, not individual converts on a path to self-discovery.

So, why didn't they call themselves "Christians"? Very simply, the word did not exist in that early period. It appeared only years later as a nickname given to Jesus' disciples by nonbelievers—probably as an insult. Luke tells us that "in Antioch the disciples were first called Christians" (Acts 11:26). Michael Wilkins explains:

> Although "Christian" is the most common name used today to designate followers of Jesus Christ, it occurs only three times in the NT: Acts 11:26; 26:28; 1 Pet 4:16. … The term is formed from Christ and indicates Christ's adherents, those who belong to, or are devoted to, Christ. … In the large metropolis of Antioch, with its many competing cults and mystery religions, those who spoke so much about *Christos* were soon called *Christianoi*, Christ's people. The term would

have then distinguished the disciples from unconverted Gentiles as well as from Judaism.[6]

As sometimes happens with labels assigned by an outside group, the name "Christian" eventually caught on among the public. Of its three uses in the New Testament, two of them come from the mouths of nonbelievers. The third comes from Peter, and he clearly uses the word of those who "share Christ's sufferings" and confess His name (1 Pet. 4:13–16).

As the gospel began to spread throughout the Greco-Roman world, where the word "disciple" was commonly used to describe followers of Pythagoras, Plato, Aristotle, and other philosophers, as well as in the Jewish world,[7] the apostle Paul and others developed a different vocabulary when talking to or about the church. They typically chose words such as "brother" or "sister," "saint," and "elect" to refer to the disciples of Jesus. By the early second century, Ignatius, the bishop of Antioch, was describing the believers in his city with the word "Christian." And in the middle of that century (AD 155), Polycarp went to his death proclaiming "I am a Christian." But because early believers saw the two words ("disciple" and "Christian") as essentially synonymous, no problem arose due to the switch in terms; it just clarified whom the disciple was following. Over time, however, the meaning of "Christian" evolved into something more like a cultural identity label, and so lost the crucial connection with its early focus on discipleship.

Sadly, in the American church, which is awash in cultural Christianity, the real meaning of the term "Christian" is often misunderstood. Too many in today's church remain unaware that a true Christian is, *by definition*, a disciple of Jesus. And because they do not know their identity as disciples, they do not realize that Jesus' teachings on discipleship apply to them. They see Jesus as their Savior, but little more.

6 Michael J. Wilkins, "Christian," in *Anchor Yale Bible Dictionary, Volume 1: A–C*, ed. David Noel Freedman (New Haven, CT: Yale University Press, 1992).

7 See Michael J. Wilkins, *Discipleship in the Ancient World and Matthew's Gospel*, 2nd ed. (Grand Rapids, MI: Baker Books, 1995), 95–116.

They often see discipleship as an optional, higher level of commitment to Jesus (for those few who might have interest in it).

The problem with this two-tiered concept is that Jesus never offered such an option. He sought only one kind of follower: a disciple.

Repentance, Faith, Conversion

So, how does one become a disciple of Jesus and enter God's kingdom? Or, to ask the question in a more common form, "How does one become a true Christian?"

It begins when God calls a person through His Word and Spirit. We have already seen God doing this in Jesus' calling of the first disciples, and we see Him doing the same with others throughout the New Testament.

The human action in response to God's call is typically referred to as "conversion." The Greek word is *epistrepho* and essentially means "to turn, turn back, or turn around." It is the outward manifestation of repentance, a Spirit-wrought inward change of heart and mind. "When men are called in the [New Testament] to conversion, it means a fundamentally new turning of the human will to God, a return home from blindness and error to the Saviour of all (Acts 26:18; 1 Pet. 2:25)."[8] Thus, conversion is "the act of turning *from* one's sin in repentance and turning *to* Christ in Faith."[9]

We become true Christians, then, through repentance toward God and faith in Jesus (Mark 1:15; Acts 2:38; 20:21). Note that true conversion involves *both* repentance and faith. Paul, the great apostle of grace, taught that Jew and Gentile alike should "repent and turn to God, performing deeds in keeping with their repentance" (Acts 26:20). These two elements, repentance and faith, are really just different aspects of the same process. Like the two sides of a coin, they are inseparable.

---

8 F. Laubach, "Conversion, Penitence, Repentance, Proselyte," in *New International Dictionary of New Testament Theology*, ed. Lothar Coenen, Erich Beyreuther, and Hans Bietenhard (Grand Rapids, MI: Zondervan, 1986), 355.

9 Millard Erickson, *Christian Theology*, 3rd ed. (Grand Rapids, MI: Baker Academic, 2013), 864.

In discipling others, I and other pastors have found that defects in one or both of these areas lie at the root of many of the problems we experience in seeking to live the Christian life. Ignorance, misunderstanding, or bad teaching often opens the door to these troubles. To ensure that we understand both terms and their implications clearly, let's take a closer look at each.

Repentance

Again and again in the Bible, we find the call to repent—that is, to wake up to our sin, confess it, and turn away from it and toward God. The Old Testament Hebrew word for this is *shub,* primarily meaning to turn from one's sin to God. The New Testament Greek equivalent is the verb *metanoeo,* usually referring to a change of mind that produces a change of life. This is the kind of repentance that John the Baptist taught, just like the Old Testament prophets before him and Jesus and the apostles after him. It could be described as making a U-turn in life, a 180-degree shift in the direction of one's life. Such a radical change of mind and heart involves both recognizing and feeling genuine sorrow for our sin against God; we then move in a new direction of life characterized by obedience to God. Scripture calls this shift "bearing fruit."

John made this clear when he told those who accepted his message to "bear fruits in keeping with repentance" (Luke 3:8). The crowds, seeking further instruction, asked him, "What then shall we do?" John answered, "Whoever has two tunics is to share with him who has none, and whoever has food is to do likewise." When the tax collectors who came to be baptized asked him, "Teacher, what shall we do?" John told them, "Collect no more than you are authorized to do" And to the soldiers who asked the same, he said, "Do not extort money from anyone by threats or by false accusation, and be content with your wages" (vv. 10–14).

In each instance, John gave a concrete example of what it means to turn in our hearts from sinful, self-seeking behavior to righteous, others-centered behavior. Such acts are the fruit of repentance, which, as we have seen, is "a godly sorrow for one's sin, along with a resolution to turn from it."[10]

Jesus, Peter, and Paul each called people to this kind of repentance, not as a good work to do before they could exercise faith but as a necessary condition and accompaniment of saving faith. For salvation is a matter of being delivered from sin and its consequences and control in our lives. It is important to remember that repentance is not a matter of getting our lives cleaned up before we can exercise saving faith. Rather, it is the fruit of conviction of sin, and it points us to our need for a Savior who saves us through faith.

Faith

Jesus, like John, launched His ministry with a call to repentance—but with a major difference. The kingdom of God had now drawn near and was actively present in the person and works of Jesus, the King. Thus, Jesus expanded John's call to include faith in Himself and in the good news He proclaimed: "Now after John was arrested, Jesus came into Galilee, proclaiming the gospel of God, and saying, 'The time is fulfilled, and the kingdom of God is at hand; repent and believe in the gospel'" (Mark 1:14–15).

What was the nature of the faith Jesus called for? Far from mere credence or mental assent to a set of rational propositions, Jesus championed the same faith God has always required of His people: "the assurance of things hoped for, the conviction of things not seen" (Heb. 11:1). This involves a confident trust that the invisible God of the Bible exists, that He is who He says He is, and that He will do what He promises to do, even when human eyes cannot yet see it. True faith counts God's Word as trustworthy and acts accordingly regardless of appearances, circumstances, or feelings. This kind of faith pleases God

10 Erickson, *Christian Theology*, 868.

(Heb. 11:6) and is illustrated in the lives of Noah, Abraham, Sarah, Moses and many others mentioned in Hebrews 11.

Did the faith Jesus called for have any specific focus? Yes: it centered on Jesus Himself. *He* was the object of true faith. Jesus called people to a confident assurance that He was not merely a great religious teacher or prophet but that He was God's Son. He also called them to believe His message, that He "came to seek and to save the lost" (Luke 19:10) and "to give his life as a ransom for many" (Mark 10:45) so that "everyone who looks on the Son and believes in him should have eternal life" (John 6:40).

Jesus calls us today to believe and trust that He did what He said He would do. At the cross, He willingly took upon Himself the penalty for our sins, paying a debt we could never pay. By doing so, He satisfied God's wrath against our sin, reconciled us to Him, and gave us eternal life. Faith in Christ includes believing that God vindicated Jesus as Savior and Lord by raising Him bodily from the dead, even though we have not yet seen Him in His resurrected body. These are the most basic elements of faith required for salvation.

Going a little deeper, saving faith has three aspects that intricately intertwine at the deepest level of the human person, what the Bible calls the heart. Each one is essential, though they may differ in strength.

The *intellectual* aspect (knowledge) involves understanding and accepting as true that the God of the Bible exists, that one is a sinner, and that God offers forgiveness and salvation to those who believe the gospel and put their faith in Jesus Christ. True conversion does not depend on a deep or broad knowledge of the Bible. The amount of knowledge one must have, in fact—the gospel message—is quite small. But we must believe the key truths already noted.

The *emotional* aspect (assent) involves what has been called "an absorbing interest" in Jesus Christ as the greatest need of one's life. We desire Him and feel a compelling sense of needing Christ and His salvation. However, we do not need an "emotional experience" to be saved; some people have that, others do not.

The *volitional* aspect (trust), building on the intellectual aspect, involves personal trust in Jesus Christ and His atoning death on the cross to save us from sin and give us eternal life. This trust roots itself in the heart, the core of who we are, and involves embracing Him as our Savior and Lord. The will takes a prominent and essential role in this act of self-giving.

What Does Faith Do?

What does saving faith do? How does it act? The Reformer Martin Luther (1483–1546), a great teacher of the faith, taught that true faith

> is a divine work in us which changes us and makes us to be born anew of God. … Because of it, without compulsion, a person is ready to do good to everyone, to serve everyone, to suffer everything out of love and praise to God who has shown him this grace.[11]

Even when certain Scripture texts don't mention both faith and repentance, we should keep in mind that the two always go together in true conversion.

Jesus sometimes calls people to "repent and believe," other times to "repent," still other times to "believe"; but whenever He uses only one term, He implies the other, like two sides of one coin. As noted above, repenting of sin and trusting in Christ by faith requires us to turn from the direction we were traveling in life and to proceed in the opposite direction.

---

11 Martin Luther, *Commentary on Romans*, trans. J. Theodore Mueller (Grand Rapids, MI: Zondervan, 1954), xvii.

The Early Church's Main Message

The apostles and members of the early church issued a clarion call to believe the good news about Jesus, repent and be baptized, receive the gift of the Holy Spirit (Acts 2:38), and follow Jesus as they went forth to fulfill Jesus' Great Commission to make disciples of all nations. They focused their message on presenting the key facts Peter cited in his Acts 2 sermon, especially verse 38:

- Jesus was the Son of God and Messiah[12]
- Jesus died on a Roman cross to satisfy God's wrath against our sins
- God raised Jesus physically from the dead
- God now offers salvation to all those who repent and turn to Jesus in faith.

They followed this message with an urgent appeal to believe the good news, repent, be baptized, and receive the Holy Spirit. These four elements were at the heart of true conversion then and still are today. The late pastor John Stott wrote, "Repentance and faith are in fact the constituent elements of conversion, when viewed from the standpoint of man's experience ... [R]epentance plus faith equals conversion, and no man dare say he is converted who has not repented as well as believed."[13] All those who truly repent and believe are disciples of Jesus.

I had to learn about repentance the hard way. At the age of thirteen, I became worried about going to hell and made a profession of faith in Jesus. But I lacked repentance of sin, and my "faith" was little more than mental assent to the facts about Jesus. Although I was duly baptized, became a member of the church, and was considered a Christian by others, my life did not change. In fact, it gradually became worse—much worse. I was a nominal Christian—that is, a Christian in name only.

---

12 The Messiah is the "anointed one," God's promised Redeemer.

13 John Stott, "Must Christ Be Lord to Be Saviour?" *Eternity Magazine*, September 1959, 15.

By God's grace, ten years later, through a series of tragic circumstances, I came to see my sins and my need for forgiveness. I was brought to repentance for my sins and to faith in Jesus as Lord and Savior. I became a real Christian—a disciple of Jesus. At that point, my life changed dramatically, and it has continued to change over the fifty-five-plus years since then.

Because so much confusion exists about the nature of repentance, we should recognize that the Bible speaks of two types of repentance: godly and worldly. Godly repentance does not mean simply feeling remorse or regret about past sins. Nor does it merely involve a resolution to reform or turn over a new leaf. Rather, it roots itself in the recognition of our sin nature (our inborn propensity to sin) and our specific personal sins against a holy God to whom we are accountable, along with a determination to forsake them. Professor J. I. Packer's expanded description is helpful:

> The New Testament word for repentance means changing one's mind so that one's views, values and ways are changed and one's whole life is lived differently. This change is radical, both inwardly and outwardly: mind and judgment, will and affections, behavior and life-style, motives and purposes, are all involved. Repenting means starting to live a new life.[14]

This is what was missing when I made my first profession of faith. In true repentance, the Holy Spirit awakens us to our sins and shows us our need for God's forgiveness through Christ.

Godly repentance has three aspects.[15] The *intellectual* aspect involves a change in our thinking and awakens us to the seriousness of our sins against God and our corruption and guilt before Him. The *emotional* aspect prompts a godly sorrow for our sin and its utter offen-

---

14 J. I. Packer, *Concise Theology: A Guide to Historic Christian Beliefs* (Wheaton, IL: Tyndale House Publishers, 1993), 162.

15 Louis Berkhof, *Systematic Theology* (Grand Rapids, MI: Eerdmans, 1941), 486–487.

siveness to God. The *volitional* aspect (the aspect of the will) involves an inner change of purpose and direction in life. Like a cable of three strands, the intellect, emotions, and will all intertwine in genuine repentance, though some aspects may be stronger than others in any given instance.

Worldly repentance looks very different. Worldly repentance lacks godly grief and merely involves regretting the consequences of sin (whether loss of reputation or resources or some other highly valued good in life). It focuses on this world, on the negative effects of sin *for me*, and not on my offenses against God (2 Cor. 7:9–10). It is self-centered.

The distinction between godly and worldly repentance raises the uncomfortable question of whether simply believing the facts about Jesus without godly repentance, personal trust, and wholehearted commitment to Jesus is true saving faith. Theologian John Murray is helpful on this point: "The life of true faith cannot be that of cold metallic assent. It must have the passion and warmth of love and communion because communion with God is the crown and apex of true religion. 'Truly our fellowship is with the Father and with His Son Jesus Christ' (1 John 1:3)."[16]

The Heidelberg Catechism's answer to the question "What is true faith?" beautifully expresses this truth:

> [It] is not only a certain knowledge, whereby I hold for truth all that God has revealed to us in His Word; but also a hearty trust, which the Holy Ghost works in me by the Gospel, that not only to others, but to me also, forgiveness of sins, everlasting righteousness and salvation, are freely given by God, merely of grace, for the sake of Christ's merits.[17]

---

16 John Murray, *Redemption Accomplished and Applied* (Grand Rapids, MI: Eerdmans, 1955), 170.

17 The Heidelberg Catechism (1563), Q21.

In other words, saving faith starts with mental assent to the truth of God but doesn't stop there. It moves on to active trust in the God of truth and in His Son, Jesus Christ.

New Testament Examples

The New Testament gives us several examples of the place of true conversion in following Jesus and entering God's kingdom. Paul describes how the members of the church in Thessalonica "turned to God from idols to serve the living and true God, and to wait for his Son from heaven" (1 Thess. 1:9–10). We also read many stories of individual conversions, and no two are quite the same. This should not surprise us, for as Jesus said, "The wind blows where it wishes, and you hear its sound, but you do not know where it comes from or where it goes. So it is with everyone who is born of the Spirit" (John 3:8).

The sudden, dramatic conversion of Paul is the most stunning in the Bible (Acts 9:1–19). The conversion of the Ethiopian governmental official who was reading the Bible as he traveled home from Jerusalem (Acts 8:26–39) also provides an exciting and stark example of God's sovereign, converting grace. By contrast, the quiet, gradual conversion of Timothy came about as he learned the Holy Scriptures at the knees of his mother and grandmother (2 Tim. 1:5; 3:14–15). Lydia, a businesswoman whose heart God opened in a very gentle way as she listened to Paul's preaching, is yet another example of true conversion (Acts 16:11–15).

The variety of these examples illustrates that no one standard pattern exists. Each one differs in outward circumstances, but some inner commonalities remain. They all display a supernatural work of God that produced the same inner change: being raised from spiritual death to spiritual life, followed by a life of wholehearted devotion to God; commitment to Jesus as Lord; increasing conformity to His likeness through the Holy Spirit; and love for others. Many factors come into play regarding how quickly these changes occur in individual lives, but these same elements are key in the life of every true believer.

By Grace Alone

While on one level true conversion involves human actions, on a deeper level these acts are divinely enabled gifts of God's grace. They are the fruit of a mysterious work in which He draws us to faith in Jesus (John 6:44). Only as the Holy Spirit opens our hearts and minds and draws us to Jesus can we respond.

As the renowned theologian Augustine (354–430) wrote in his *Confessions*, "I call upon you, my God, my mercy. You made me and, when I forgot you, you did not forget me. … Before I called to you, you were there before me."[18] Augustine could say this not only from firsthand experience but also because he knew well the teaching of Paul, who wrote, "[God] chose us in [Christ] before the foundation of the world" (Eph. 1:4) and "By grace you have been saved through faith. And this is not your own doing; it is the gift of God, not a result of works, so that no one may boast" (2:8–9). Only through God's free grace—His completely unwarranted kindness to us—are we saved.

God does not save us because of any good works we have done or ever will do, nor because He knew in advance that we would respond to the gospel when someone offered it to us. As Anglican archbishop William Temple said so well, "All is of God; the only thing of my very own which I can contribute to my own redemption is the sin from which I need to be redeemed."[19] God saves us entirely because of His own love and mercy, overflowing in grace toward us. His salvation is not something we deserve but is His gift to us. As C. S. Lewis said,

---

18 Augustine, *Confessions*, trans. Henry Chadwick (Oxford: Oxford University Press, 1991), XIII.i.1.

19 William Temple, *Nature, Man, and God* (London: Macmillan, 1949), 401.

"God loves us: not because we are lovable but because He is love, not because he needs to receive but because he delights to give."[20]

Those who are truly converted, saved by God's grace, do not remain the same as they were before. How could they? The Holy Spirit has come to dwell in them. The Spirit awakens them to God, imparts a desire to better know God, convicts of sin, prompts confession, and gives them the power to obey and publicly confess Jesus Christ. God's grace produces spiritual growth, from the inside out. Depending on a variety of factors, that growth may come quickly or slowly, but it *will* produce works of love in our lives as the fruit and evidence of our salvation. Martin Luther puts it well:

> Although I am an unworthy and condemned man, my God has given me in Christ all the riches of righteousness and salvation without any merit on my part, out of pure, free mercy, so that from now on I need nothing except faith which believes this is true. Why should I not therefore freely, joyfully, with all my heart, and with an eager will do all things which I know are pleasing and acceptable to such a Father who has overwhelmed me with his inestimable riches? I will therefore give myself as a Christ to my neighbor, just as Christ offered himself to me; I will do nothing in this life except what I see is necessary, profitable, and salutary to my neighbor, since through faith I have an abundance of all good things in Christ.[21]

---

20 C. S. Lewis, *The Collected Letters of C. S. Lewis, Volume III: Narnia, Cambridge, and Joy 1950–1963*, ed. Walter Hooper (New York: HarperCollins, 2007), 119.

21 Martin Luther, *Three Treatises*, 2nd ed. (Minneapolis, MN: Fortress Press, 1970), 304.

Questions to Ponder

1. How would you explain to someone in your own words what Jesus taught about how a person can enter the kingdom of God?
2. What problems might result from a failure to understand the relationship of repentance to faith?
3. What are the three aspects of saving faith? Why must we understand all three aspects as we personally embrace the gospel and when we share the good news with others?
4. What is the difference between "believing that" and "believing in," and why are both essential to saving faith?
5. What does the concept of grace tell us about God's motivation for His saving actions in Christ? Where do you see God's grace operating in your life, either in your conversion, or, if you don't remember your conversion, in your daily life?

4

Living in God's Kingdom

But seek first the kingdom of God and his righteousness.
Matthew 6:33

As we have seen, Jesus made the kingdom of God (or kingdom of heaven) the central theme of His ministry and the centerpiece of His plan for the world. If we wish to fully embrace Jesus' work, along with the life and mission to which He calls us as His disciples—to fulfill His purposes for our lives—we will gain much from learning more about His kingdom and kingship.

Old Testament and New

Although the exact phrase "kingdom of God" does not appear in the Old Testament, God is often depicted there as king over His creation and over His people, Israel. Many Bible passages describe God as king:

> Yours, O Lord, is the greatness and the power and the glory and the victory and the majesty, for all that is in the heavens and in the earth is yours. Yours is the kingdom, O Lord, and you are exalted as head above all. (1 Chron. 29:11)
>
> The Lord is king forever and ever. (Ps. 10:16)
> For God is the King of all the earth; sing praises with a psalm! (Ps. 47:7)
>
> The Lord has established his throne in the heavens,
> and his kingdom rules over all. (Ps. 103:19)

> Your kingdom is an everlasting kingdom,
> and your dominion endures throughout all generations.
> (Ps. 145:13)

Then, in the New Testament—especially in the Gospels—the phrase "kingdom of God" moves to the forefront. This phrase points to God's kingship over His creation, yet it also has a special focus on God's reign in the lives of His people in this world *and* in the glorious world to come.

God's people experience His kingdom today through Jesus, the appointed King who comes to rule and reign in their lives through the Holy Spirit (Eph. 5:18–6:20; Gal. 5:22–23). They experience this reign most fully in the church, the body of Christ (Col. 1:24), which is a colony of heaven. God's reign reveals itself as the church operates under the lordship of Christ, with members wholeheartedly committed to Jesus and the Father and rejecting conformity to the values and behaviors of the fallen world. When the church is truly being the church, it is not simply a religious institution but a countercultural society, a society in which the values of the kingdom are displayed in the lives of God's people: a foretaste of heaven on earth.

Jesus the King

The coming-to-earth of Jesus, the Son of God and promised Messiah, marked a new stage in the spread of God's reign. The true King of Israel had come to dwell for a time among His people. Yet Jesus came without the regal trappings and fanfare of popular expectations. Rather, He was born in a stable to poor parents. And, as we noted earlier, He lived and worked in obscurity as a humble tradesman in a small village while preparing for His mission.

When Jesus' preparation was complete, He began to proclaim that "the kingdom of God is at hand" (Mark 1:15) and to urge men and women to enter it while they could. Jesus Himself was the door into that kingdom (John 10:9). Anyone who recognized Him as the Messiah, the true King of Israel and the Son of God, and trusted Him in repentant faith could enter God's kingdom.

No one expected this new stage of God's kingdom to begin in such an insignificant and seemingly weak way. "The kingdom of God has arrived in minute [i.e., small, hidden] form. … while the mature, fruit-bearing tree of the kingdom of God has not yet come."[1] God's kingdom was present in the person of Jesus, the King, and in the hearts of all who had entered, but absent as a visible political regime. Jesus, when "asked by the Pharisees when the kingdom of God would come," explained it like this:

> The kingdom of God is not coming in ways that can be observed, nor will they say, "Look, here it is!" or "There!" for behold, the kingdom of God is in the midst of you. (Luke 17:20–21)

Jesus also likened the kingdom to a tiny mustard seed that would grow into a huge tree over time as more and more people entered—human beings of every kind from every place on earth (Matt. 13:31–32). It would reach full fruition when He returned in power and great glory to raise the dead, judge all people, abolish evil, and establish God's eternal reign in the new heavens and new earth. On that day it will truly be shouted, "The kingdom of the world has become the kingdom of our Lord and of his Christ, and he shall reign forever and ever" (Rev. 11:15)!

The Highest Priority in Life

Jesus frequently insisted that the highest priority in life, worth any sacrifice, is entering God's kingdom. Listen to His teaching:

> The kingdom of heaven is like treasure hidden in a field, which a man found and covered up. Then in his joy he goes and sells all that he has and buys that field. Again, the kingdom

1 George Eldon Ladd, *The Presence of the Future: The Eschatology of Biblical Realism* (Grand Rapids, MI: Eerdmans, 1974), 218.

> of heaven is like a merchant in search of fine pearls, who, on finding one pearl of great value, went and sold all that he had and bought it. (Matt. 13:44–46)

Although the kingdom began spreading in the world as soon as Jesus began His earthly ministry, it would not immediately come in all its fullness, as He revealed in Luke 19:11–27. Since Pentecost, when God's Spirit was poured out on the church (Acts 2), God's kingdom has continued to advance as more and more people come under the reign of Jesus in His church. At a time known only to God, it will reach its glorious consummation. Until then, we live in a tension often called the "already/not yet" period. The rightful King has already landed! His people rally to His side as He marches forward! But the final victory is not yet here: it lies ahead.

Theologian Oscar Cullmann likened this period to the phase of World War II in between the Allied invasion of Normandy in the summer of 1944 and the final victory over the Nazis in the autumn of 1945.[2] By securing the French beachhead, the Allies assured their ultimate victory. But many more months of fierce enemy resistance would result in heavy casualties before the war finally ended. While victory was certain, it had not yet been experienced.

Our spiritual situation today parallels that wartime reality. Through His atoning death on the cross, Jesus has already won the ultimate victory. His kingdom is advancing. But the fierce cosmic warfare between God and His angels and the devil and his angels (who were cast out of heaven when they joined his rebellion, see Revelation 12:9 and Ephesians 6:12) will continue to rage until Jesus returns to bring final victory.

Jesus described this victory of God's kingdom over the kingdom of this world in terms of a final judgment on the devil and his minions.

---

2 Oscar Cullmann, *Christ and Time: The Primitive Christian Conception of Time and History*, rev. ed., trans. Floyd V. Filson (London: SCM, 1962), 3, 39, 84.

That victory also will result in the eternal judgment of all those who had refused to accept God's pardon and enter His kingdom (Matt. 25:31–46).

What Does It Look Like?

As we await His return, what does life in Jesus' kingdom look like in the here and now? What does it mean to grow and mature as a disciple of Jesus and to be part of His advancing kingdom?

Jesus gave us some crucial foundational teachings to guide us, teachings essential to directing and shaping our growth and service. We find these teachings presented most fully in the Gospel of Matthew, which seems to have been designed as a handbook for discipleship.

The Gospel of Matthew deeply shaped the post-apostolic church: "It was to Matthew's Gospel that the Christians of the first two centuries automatically turned for the essential data about Jesus."[3] During this formative period in church history, Matthew was considered "the Gospel par excellence"[4]; it has been described as "the Gospel in the form of a catechetical manual" and "a first textbook for congregational teachers."[5] And it still has much to teach us today.

The core of Jesus' teaching about kingdom life is contained in the Sermon on the Mount (Matthew 5–7), the first and longest of the five teaching blocks in Matthew. The other sections also have important kingdom teaching, but the Sermon on the Mount is the foundation and starting place for learning about life in a kingdom that upends the values and behaviors of the fallen world. As Michael Wilkins has written, "The kind of kingdom life elucidated in the [Sermon on the Mount] is the foundation for each Christian's personal discipleship to Jesus … . From the biblical point of view, all Christians are disciples, so

---

3 R. T. France, *Matthew: Evangelist and Teacher* (Downers Grove, IL: InterVarsity Press, 1989), 14.

4 France, *Matthew*, 17.

5 France, *Matthew*, 18.

the teaching of the [Sermon] is not for a few more-committed believers. This is the heart of Jesus' teaching for all Christians."[6]

In my decades of discipling, spiritual direction, and pastoral counseling, it has amazed me how few believers have awareness of these basic truths. In some cases, they have received no instruction about them at all; in others, they feel overwhelmed simply by reading them and cannot imagine how in their weakness they could possibly live such a life. Yet others cannot imagine how such truths could be applied in today's world. If you haven't done so lately, I encourage you to read Matthew 5–7 again now. This sermon gives us remarkable insight into who Jesus is and what following Him looks like.

Jesus addressed the Sermon on the Mount primarily to His disciples, though others listened in. His frequent reference to "your Father" in speaking to His disciples confirms that by this point they were children of God and already in the kingdom. Therefore, Jesus' teaching here is not a rigorous program by which one earns admission to the kingdom, nor a set of impossibly high ethical standards that expose our sins and force us in desperation to turn to Christ with repentant faith. Neither do His statements present a set of guidelines intended for a future life in the millennium. Rather, in this sermon Jesus teaches about life in God's kingdom *here and now*—about how God's children are to conduct themselves in this present world. Or, to put it differently, Jesus presents to us the family code of conduct—a code that doesn't merely address our external behavior but actually changes us from within. He can give us this code (and the power to live it) because He is God's Son and we share in His sonship.

As J. I. Packer points out, three all-embracing principles frame Jesus' description of kingdom life in this sermon: *imitating* the Father (Matt. 5:43–45, 48), *glorifying* the Father (v. 16), and *pleasing* the Father

---

6 Michael J. Wilkins, *Matthew*, The NIV Application Commentary (Grand Rapids, MI: Zondervan, 2004), 199.

(6:17–18).[7] In the context of these principles, Jesus gives a variety of important instructions about the life of grace to which He calls us as sons and daughters of God—a life that is countercultural in relation to the fallen world around us (and also, in many cases, to the culturally Christian world). Jesus does not give a detailed, comprehensive set of laws, but rather provides guidance on key life issues from which we can make inferences, draw conclusions, and learn to make applications to other issues. We could also describe this sermon as a collection of basic principles of discipleship essential for every believer to know and live by.

To be sure, the way of life Jesus calls us to adopt is challenging! Some have considered it impossible—and it *is* impossible in merely human strength. But it is *possible* through God's grace and the empowering of the Holy Spirit, which Jesus pours out on all His followers.

A key point to bear in mind in reading and studying the Sermon on the Mount is that Jesus consistently emphasizes that our God is a loving Father. In fact, Jesus refers to God as "Father" seventeen times in the three chapters that comprise the sermon. The most notable of these we find in His pattern-prayer for us, which He begins with, "Our Father in heaven," an affirmation of our sonship and the joyful reality that our God is not distant and impersonal.

Jesus weaves into His teaching some of the important ways we are to imitate, please, and glorify the Father. He addresses a range of essential matters in an understandable, down-to-earth way that anyone can readily grasp, easily memorize, and regularly meditate upon to transform the heart and guide daily life. "The emphasis in the [Sermon on the Mount] will be on inside-out transformation," Wilkins writes. "Jesus will continually go to inner motivation, not external performance. The inner life will naturally transform the outer life. The heart

7 J. I. Packer, *Knowing God* (Downers Grove, IL: InterVarsity Press, 1973), 211.

that treasures the kingdom of heaven above all else will be the starting point for transformation of the entire life."[8]

A Quick Overview

The Sermon on the Mount begins with the Beatitudes, which describe the blessed life to which God calls all His children (Matt. 5:2–12). It then gives much-needed comfort and encouragement, speaking of disciples as salt and light in this world's darkness (vv. 13–16), people whose lives are to glorify God.

Then we see Jesus' supreme devotion and total commitment to God's Word and to fulfilling it in His life. Likewise, He proclaims the blessedness of disciples who love God's Word and reject the legalistic externalism of the Pharisees, instead living in true righteousness, rooted in grace and producing works of love (vv. 17–20). Jesus follows this by addressing common problems such as anger, lust, divorce, making oaths, revenge, and loving one's enemies (vv. 21–48).

Drawing a stark contrast to the attention-seeking Pharisees, Jesus next describes the proper approach to private devotional practices such as giving to the poor, prayer, and fasting, which are intended to nurture the soul's intimacy with the Father. These practices please the Father, Jesus tells us, and He rewards them when they are done with right motivation, in agreement with His will, and in secrecy (6:1–18).

Jesus goes on to teach that disciples must forsake the idolatrous pursuit of money and possessions, a great snare to the soul. Instead, they should make their love for the Father supreme, seeking first His kingdom and righteousness, trusting Him to provide for their needs and free them from anxiety (6:19–34).

Jesus condemns judgmental self-righteousness and encourages self-examination as an antidote (7:1–6). He then returns to prayer, instructing us to keep on asking, seeking, and knocking (7:7–11).

---

8 Wilkins, *Matthew*, 199.

Jesus thus emphasizes the importance of persevering in prayer, essential for life in the kingdom.

The summit and heart of the Sermon focuses on loving our neighbor and treating him as we would want him to treat us (7:12).

Jesus begins to conclude His sermon by calling all His listeners to reject the popular and much-traveled road of easy religion. Rather, they must enter God's kingdom by the narrow gate and hard way that leads to eternal life. He warns that as we travel the road to eternal life, we will encounter false prophets and false believers, and then He gives us instructions about how to recognize them (7:13–23).

Jesus completes His sermon by highlighting the profound importance of hearing and obeying His words:

> Everyone then who hears these words of mine and does them will be like a wise man who built his house on the rock. And the rain fell, and the floods came, and the winds blew and beat on that house, but it did not fall, because it had been founded on the rock. And everyone who hears these words of mine and does not do them will be like a foolish man who built his house on the sand. And the rain fell, and the floods came, and the winds blew and beat against that house, and it fell, and great was the fall of it. (Matt. 7:24–27)

Obedience to Jesus' words—that is, to God's words stripped clean of the Pharisees' distortions—will ground His disciples in truth and wisdom that will sustain them in the challenges they will inevitably encounter on the road that leads to eternal life. Disobedience to His Word is folly and leads to eternal ruin.

Start Where They Did

If we want to follow Jesus, we need to begin where the first disciples did. We must begin as truly converted disciples and learners, committed to Jesus and seeking to understand and to put into practice Jesus' teaching about life in God's kingdom. Gratitude to the Father, who has touched our hearts with His grace and love, prompts such a response, which the Holy Spirit empowers.

Questions to Ponder

1. How does Jesus' announcement that "the kingdom of God is at hand" (Mark 1:15) relate to the depictions of God as King in the Old Testament?
2. To what does Jesus compare the kingdom of God? What do those comparisons teach us?
3. Taking the Sermon on the Mount in Matthew 5–7 as a whole, what stands out to you about Jesus' teaching? Which sections do you find particularly challenging or compelling?
4. Throughout His sermon, Jesus contrasts the Pharisees' religiosity with the true nature of Christian discipleship. How would you describe this contrast in your own words?
5. What is the significance of Jesus' referring to God as "Father" or "our Father" in the Sermon on the Mount? What does this indicate about God and about those who are in His kingdom?

5

Obeying Jesus

If you love me, you will keep my commandments.

John 14:15

Jesus explained to his disciples that those who love Him will keep His commandments; they will obey Him. For some people, Jesus' emphasis on obedience feels unsettling. It may strike them as rigid or harsh. Or it may arouse fears of legalism or suggest a desire to control, both of which have a long, sordid history.

Perhaps for all of us, obedience to anyone other than ourselves challenges our inherent drive toward autonomy and the independent, individualistic bent that is especially prevalent in American culture. Many of us do not want anyone telling us what to do, not even God.

Our reservations about obedience may dissipate when we realize that Jesus stresses obedience not to oppress and afflict us, but to bless us. We have only to think of a father insisting to his little daughter that she not ride her bicycle on the driveway, which slopes down to the busy street in front of the family home. Obedience to Jesus does us good and gives God glory (see Deut. 10:13; 1 Cor. 7:35).

Disobedience to God's words is what plunged His pristine world into the sin, suffering, sorrow, and death that each of us lives with today. Obeying His words—starting with the gospel call to repent and believe—can reconcile our relationship with Him and set us on the path of deliverance from these evils.

Obedience Flows Out of Gratitude

We'll discuss more specifics about obedience to God in this chapter and the next. But first, let's consider something more basic: our motivation to obey.

It helps to remind ourselves often that we are not meant to obey God or do good works to gain His favor. Rather, we are to obey Him from hearts of grateful love. We are to seek to please our Father in heaven, the same God who loves us, has redeemed us, watches over us, and daily seeks our good. Obedience is a loving response to the One who loves us, not a forced effort on our part to earn His love.

Our Father delights to bless and reward our obedience. At great cost to Himself, He gave up His beloved Son on the cross to pay the penalty for our sins. He now offers us a complete pardon and a new life empowered by His Spirit. The greatest of His blessings, of course, is to know Him personally. Our obedience plays a key part in how this happens. As John Calvin said, "All true knowledge of God is born of obedience."[1]

Knowing God begins when we obey the command of Jesus to "repent and believe in the gospel" (Mark 1:15). It deepens as we obey Jesus' call to follow Him as a disciple. In doing so, we experience what C. S. Lewis found as he sought to follow Jesus: "Obedience is the key to all doors; feelings come (or don't come) as God pleases."[2] Every act of obedience has its own reward.

The importance of obeying Jesus becomes clearer when we remember that He did not come into this world simply to rescue us from hell and eternal damnation (as important as that is). Our rescue was the first step in a much more glorious plan, which includes leading us out of the sinful ways of this present evil age and into the fullness of life and righteousness in God's kingdom.

---

1 John Calvin, *Institutes of the Christian Religion*, ed. John T. McNeill, trans. Ford Lewis Battles, vol. 1 (Philadelphia: The Westminster Press, 1960), I.6.2.

2 C. S. Lewis, *Letters of C. S. Lewis*, ed. W. H. Lewis (New York: Harcourt, Brace, & World, 1966), 225.

We will explore this more fully ahead, but a few words here will be helpful preparation. Imagine that each of us is lost in a dense jungle infested with deadly snakes and predators. A skilled and experienced guide has set out to rescue us. First, he must come to where we are, for we certainly can't go to him. Once he finds us, he must liberate us from the vines and underbrush that entangle us. Then he must lead us on the long, difficult, and perilous journey back to safety. We can survive the journey only by following his expert guidance and protection. Obedience to his instructions means life or death. Our state in this fallen world looks much like this.

Jesus' call to obey really is a life-or-death matter. He does not give arbitrary or capricious commands, but loving directives filled with life-giving grace. They flow out of His love for us and His desire to see us transformed and prepared for the world to come. And He wants us to glorify God along the way.

Jesus' work in us does not come easy, for it involves helping us, through His Spirit, to fight a lifelong battle with the world, the flesh, and the devil (see the companion volume to this book, *Abiding in Jesus Christ: A Guide to Maturing in Authentic Discipleship*). The enemy within all of us—the Trojan horse of our fleshly desires—makes this battle difficult.

Jesus described some of the deeds of the flesh when He said, "What comes out of a person is what defiles him. For from within, out of the heart of man, come evil thoughts, sexual immorality, theft, murder, adultery, coveting, wickedness, deceit, sensuality, envy, slander, pride, foolishness. All these evil things come from within, and they defile a person" (Mark 7:20–23). Some of these sins of the old, fleshly nature can dominate our lives before the new birth.

But thanks be to God, once the Holy Spirit brings us into union with Christ through faith in His death and resurrection, thus giving us newness of life, sin can no longer dominate and enslave us as it once did. The Spirit breaks the bondage of our will to sin and its ability to control us. We then become *able* to live in obedience to God.

Such a life does not come automatically, however. Like a low-level infection held in check by medication, sin still resides in us (albeit in a weakened state) and can sometimes flare up. This explains why certain sins, often ones from our past, can rise and tempt us. But because the Holy Spirit now indwells and empowers us, we can oppose and overcome sin by choosing to resist it and obey God (Gal. 5:16–18, 25). If we do not choose to resist, we will go down in defeat.

Each time we feel tempted, we face this choice again. The flesh beckons us to give in; but if we do so, we betray our Redeemer and interrupt our fellowship with Him. We turn away from the safe and secure path that He is offering us through the Spirit. Capitulating has other consequences as well, for disobedience brings darkness to the soul, and the more we disobey, the greater the darkness becomes. This includes the strengthening of the sinful desire to which we have just yielded ourselves—making it harder to resist the next time. Whatever we feed grows stronger. A toehold can grow into a foothold and then into a stronghold. Like a rip current that can sweep us far from shore, we cannot know in advance how far our disobedience may take us from God or what the consequences will be.

A young man from a Christian family in a church I pastored had allowed pornography to gain a foothold in his life. He talked about it each time we met, but he would never take the radical steps necessary to deal with the roots of the problem. The foothold became a stronghold, and he began visiting prostitutes. The computer security department where he worked eventually discovered a trail of his visits to porn sites on his office computer, leading to dismissal from a good job with much potential for advancement. Yet he continued with his addiction to pornography, which led him to even darker places.

By contrast, we can choose to resist and reject the temptations that entice us. We do so by praying for God's help, repenting of and forsaking whatever idol produces our addiction, yielding to the indwelling Holy Spirit, obeying the word of Christ, and rejecting whatever tempts us. In especially difficult temptations we may need the prayers, counsel, and accountability of others, including pastors and Christian counselors. Some instances may even require fasting (see *Abiding in Jesus Christ: A Guide to Maturing in Authentic Discipleship*). Our active resistance to sin glorifies the Lord, deepens our fellowship with Him, and brings blessings in its wake. These blessings include strengthening our self-control against that sin, making it easier to resist the next time. Whatever we starve gets weaker.

That was the experience of another man I once mentored. He wanted to get married, and a friend in a large church offered to introduce him to a "strong Christian woman." As their first date came to an end, she wanted to go to bed with him. He refused and broke off the relationship. Another friend introduced him to a woman who was described as a mature Christian. The same thing happened, and he broke off that relationship too. The third woman he was introduced to was different; she wanted to wait until after the second date. The appalling disregard for God's moral standards in each instance is all too common today in the church. But my friend was a praying man who knew God's Word and was committed to obeying Him. He knew where the red lines were and would not cross them. With each temptation, his determination to resist became stronger. (Sadly, many single godly Christian women find the same problem with men in our churches.)

This battle with sin is far more serious than many of us realize. As C. S. Lewis observed, "Every time you make a choice you are turning the central part of you, the part of you that chooses, into something a little different from what it was before. And taking your life as a whole, with all your innumerable choices, all your life long you are slowly turning this central thing either into a heavenly creature or a hellish creature."[3] Our daily choices make us into something better or worse. We make our choices, and then our choices make us.

How to Make Godly Choices

How can we consistently choose to obey God? How can we regularly make godly decisions? Some people think they can overcome sin simply by making up their mind to stop sinning. They correctly reason that God's ordinary way of working with us is to present His truth, instructions, and commands to our minds in order to be understood and then obeyed. But that misses the hugely important fact that the process of choosing is ultimately rooted in the heart, not the mind alone. Biblically speaking, the heart is the core, the center, of a person and encompasses mind, will, emotions, and desires, all of which interact with each other. The human psyche is complex, and it is not easily compartmentalized. But, as Augustine observed long ago, human beings are ultimately driven by what they think is desirable and love. What are the implications of this understanding?

Drawing on his study of the Protestant Reformer Thomas Cranmer, theologian Ashley Null gives penetrating insight into Cranmer's view of how the heart works: "What the heart desires, the will chooses and the mind justifies. The mind doesn't direct the will. The mind is actually captive to what the will wants, and the will itself, in turn, is captive to what the heart wants."[4] Null (via Cranmer) expresses an important truth here that points us in the right direction.

The key to making godly choices lies in the desires of the heart—and this is a good news/bad news scenario. The bad news is that the

---

3 C. S. Lewis, *Mere Christianity* (New York: Touchstone Books, 1996), 87.

4 Ashley Null, interview by the Anglican Church League, September 2001, https://acl.asn.au/resources/dr-ashley-null-on-thomas-cranmer/. For in-depth discussion, see Ashley Null, *Thomas Cranmer's Doctrine of Repentance: Renewing the Power to Love* (Oxford: Oxford University Press, 2000), 100–101.

temptation to love the world and the things in the world—"the desires of the flesh and the desires of the eyes and pride of life" (1 John 2:16)—always lies before us. Our hearts can easily become ensnared with sinful desires, moving our will to choose sin while our minds rationalize and defend the choice. We then tell ourselves that we love God while at the same time indulging in sins that displease God, draw us away from Him, and weaken our souls.

But the good news? Through God's grace, the desires of our heart really *can* change. He can give us new, holy desires and affections that are far better than the ones that once bound us. If we pray and ask with sincerity, He will change our hearts so that we regularly desire to do His will; as David said, "I delight to do your will, O my God" (Ps. 40:8). Such a desire is the fruit of a new affection for God. The only new affection strong enough to displace the sinful desires and idols that ensnare the human heart is the love of God and of Jesus, His Son.

How does this new affection get control of our heart? We cannot generate love for God in our own strength. God must take the initiative. He does this at the most basic level when He draws us to trust Jesus as our Savior and Lord and then justifies us by that faith, uniting us with Christ, forgiving our sins, adopting us into His family, giving us peace, and pouring His love into our hearts through the Holy Spirit (see Rom. 5:1–2, 5). In Ephesians Paul explains, "But God, being rich in mercy, because of the great love with which he loved us, even when we were dead in our trespasses, made us alive together with Christ—by grace you have been saved … . For by grace you have been saved through faith. And this is not your own doing; it is the gift of God, not a result of works, so that no one may boast" (2:4–5, 8–9).

God's grace brings deep changes in us. His mercy and the undeserved gift of His grace and love awaken in us a grateful love for Him and for Jesus who died for us. As John says, "We love because he first loved us" (1 John 4:19). We could call this love a new affection, one more powerful than anything of the flesh or the world. It produces in us a desire to please God by obeying Him, for "this is the love of God, that we keep his commandments. And his commandments are not burdensome" (1 John 5:3). This love grows stronger the more we meditate on God's great love for us, expressed in the many good things He does for us and most of all in the giving of His only Son to pay the debt of our sins.

"That's great," you may say, "but what if I *do* find obeying God's commandments burdensome?" When this happens, the most frequent cause is trying to obey only as a matter of duty to God as the Creator, Lawgiver, and Judge to whom we owe submission and obedience. While no doubt it certainly *is* our duty to submit to God and obey Him, simply "doing our duty" doesn't go far enough. If we stop there, we risk falling into what older theologians called "legal obedience." That is, we obey merely as a legal obligation to satisfy God and be considered righteous in His sight. Legal obedience usually comes out of "servile fear and dread" of God and the punishment He may visit on us if we disobey.

Such a works-based righteousness—one that tries to appease God and maintain His favor through rule-keeping, trying harder, and striving in our own strength—puts an impossibly heavy burden on the human soul. What's more, it tends to produce either pride (if we believe we've successfully managed our behavior) or despair (if we do not).

How can we break free of this miserable state? The key is discovering (or rediscovering) God's completely undeserved mercy and love for us. This grace becomes real to us when we come to know in our heart by faith and remind ourselves often that our Creator and Judge is also our Father in heaven, who:

- has chosen us to be His child
- loves us with an everlasting love

- has demonstrated His love by giving His Son to atone for our sins
- has drawn us to faith in Him
- has given us His Holy Spirit
- has adopted us into His family
- forgives our sins when we repent and return to Him
- always seeks our good
- and will never leave or forsake us.

All of this makes our hearts sing and reorients them to obey God, not because we must but because we want to. We delight to obey and please such a gracious Father who loves us and has done so much for us. As we repeatedly remind ourselves of these precious truths and meditate on them, preferably audibly, they become embedded more and more deeply in our hearts, reinforce our grasp of God's grace, and shape our lives.

The Danger of Drifting

Why do those who know these things sometimes lose sight of them and find themselves drifting into reliance on their obedience and good works for God's approval? What goes wrong in these cases?

Even the strongest believers never reach perfection in this life. Each of us is always a work in progress, and none of us grasps the depths of our own sin or the full riches of God's grace, nor do we experience the fullness of His love all at once. This comes by degrees, over time, as we seek to know Him better and love Him more.

As our lives unfold, we experience seasons, sometimes long ones, when grace looks as bright and clear as the noonday sun. But times and circumstances can come when our grasp of grace grows dim, as when dark clouds obscure our view of the sun. In such times, we can imperceptibly drift into thinking that God's love and acceptance depend on our works, on how well we live the Christian life. We can become performance-oriented in our relationship with God.

What can we do in such a situation? We must regularly preach the gospel to ourselves, as Christian author Jerry Bridges often advised,[5] and never forget that God saves us by His grace through faith, not by our works (Eph. 2:8–9). Our works do not gain our salvation; rather, they are the fruit and the evidence of it. We need to remind ourselves again and again that nothing we do can make God love us any more or any less. He loves us, not because we are lovable, but because He *is* love. He has chosen us and accepts us as righteous, not because of our works, but because of the works of Another, His Son Jesus, who paid for our sins on the cross. Keeping these truths fresh in our minds and hearts will help protect us from drifting into legalism.

Does such an emphasis on grace mean our works have no relevance? Not at all, because the faith that saves is a faith that obeys and abounds in good works. We are not saved *by* good works but *for* good works, as Paul, the great apostle of grace, made clear (Eph. 2:10; Titus 2:7, 14; 3:8, 14). The more deeply we grasp the riches of God's grace—how much He loves us and how much He has done for us and continues to do for us—the more our love, gratitude, and affection will grow, and with these, our desire to please and obey Him.

How Grateful Love Works

Let me share with you a story I heard from a dear friend, Jack Moore, a Southern Baptist pastor. It helped me better grasp how such a grateful love works, and I think it may help you too. A cemetery worker noticed a young woman who every year brought flowers to the grave of a man who had been buried there many years earlier. On one of her visits, he said to her, "You must have loved him very much."

"Actually," she replied, "I never knew him. But I owe everything to him. When I was a little girl, our house caught fire, and the flames spread quickly. I was trapped in my upstairs bedroom, and my parents could

---

5 See, for example, Jerry Bridges, *Respectable Sins: Confronting the Sins We Tolerate* (Colorado Springs, CO: NavPress, 2007).

not get to me. They had to run for their lives. But a fireman ran into our blazing house, reached my bedroom, and handed me out the window to another fireman on a ladder. As he tried to get out of the house, he got trapped and died in the flames. He gave his life for me, and I owe him everything. Though I never knew him, I have always loved him and been filled with gratitude to him for what he did for me."

This young woman's response was a natural one: the fireman had sacrificed himself to save her, and she was enduringly grateful. Our situation as Christians is the same, but with two notable differences. First, unlike the young woman who never knew the man who gave his life to rescue her, we can know the Man who gave His life to rescue us. His death for us should evoke a deep gratitude as we live in ongoing relationship with Him. Gratitude to God for sending His Son to rescue us lies at the heart of the Christian life. What's more, Jesus didn't just save us from physical death as the fireman did for the little girl, but from spiritual death. The gift He offered us is so much greater.

Thus, we do not obey God to earn His favor; rather, we obey Him in response to His favor—out of love—a sincere, grateful love that seeks in all things to please our heavenly Father. This kind of obedience demonstrates that our love for God is genuine.

Just as love for the Father moves us to gratefully obey His commandments, so does love for Jesus move us to gratefully obey Him. Jesus says, "If you love me, you will keep my commandments. And I will ask the Father, and he will give you another Helper, to be with you forever … . You know him, for he dwells with you and will be in you" (John 14:15–17). This indwelling Helper, the Holy Spirit, strengthens and empowers us to understand and obey the words of Jesus.

And to the one who loves and obeys Jesus through the power of the Spirit, Jesus says, "I will love him and manifest myself to him" (John 14:21). He also says, "My Father will love him, and we will come to him and make our home with him" (v. 23). John Stott summarized these stunning promises like this: "The test of love is obedience and the reward of love is the self-manifestation of Christ."[6]

This promise of deeper intimacy with the Father and the Son, through the Spirit, takes us into the very heart of the Christian life: a life of love and of grace-filled obedience free from looking to the law for life. In that life, we gratefully and joyfully do the will of the Father and the Son from the heart and seek to please God in all things.

What's Next?

Where do we go from here? Each day, let us give ourselves to God afresh, body and soul, and seek to abide in Jesus and walk as He walked, asking the Holy Spirit to fill, lead, and empower us to do the will of God from the heart. Our aim? To obey Him in all things, great and small, including when the very next temptation or trial presents itself, and the next, and the next.

Whatever the reasons for our uneasiness about obedience, the fact remains that we express our love for Christ through our obedience to Christ. And we express our love for God through obedience to God. Those who want to live in God's kingdom must decide before putting their hand to the plow whether they are willing to follow Jesus, which means obeying His words (see Luke 9:62). Jesus' words are God's words.

Scripture is clear that merely hearing God's words is not enough. In both the Old and New Testaments, true hearing always produces obedience. The supreme test of faith in God and love for God is not feeling, but obedience. James summed up this truth in one crisp sentence: "But be doers of the word, not hearers only, deceiving yourselves" (James 1:22). To those who obey God's words not simply from duty but from a grateful heart, Jesus promises a firm foundation that will sustain them in all the temptations, trials, and challenges they will encounter as they follow Him on the road to life. "Obey God and

---

6 John R. W. Stott, *Christ the Liberator* (Downers Grove, IL: InterVarsity Press, 1971), 39.

leave all the consequences to him," says preacher and author Charles Stanley.[7] Memorize that phrase, meditate on it, and rely on the Spirit to help you apply it every day.

All who have come to a living faith in Jesus Christ and follow Him enjoy this marvelous heritage. This also explains why Jesus stresses the importance of obedience to Him and His words. Such obedience liberates and gloriously transforms.

Do you want to be a faithful disciple and enjoy the fullness of God's abundant life? If so, then in gratitude embrace the obedience of love and daily seek to walk by the Holy Spirit, through whom all these blessings come (see Gal. 5:16–26).

Questions to Ponder

1. How do you respond to hearing that Jesus calls His disciples to obey him?
2. Why does obedience to Jesus seem so unnatural to us as human beings?
3. Explain the relationship between love, gratitude, and obedience.
4. What do you typically do when you face temptation? What does God encourage us to do?
5. List some positive outcomes of living a life of obedience. What "fruit" comes from a life of disobedience?
6. If you feel resistance to the call to obey Jesus, ask Him to change the desires of your heart and help you delight to please Him in all things.

---

7 Charles F. Stanley, *30 Life Principles* (Nashville: HarperChristian Resources, 2022), 7.

6

Committing to Jesus

And calling the crowd to him with his disciples, he said to them,
"If anyone would come after me, let him deny himself
and take up his cross and follow me.
Mark 8:34

The obedience to Jesus that we have just considered, rooted in grace and love, concretely expresses our commitment to Jesus. And wholehearted commitment to Jesus is essential for growing as His disciple.

The world saw a clear illustration of the cost of commitment to Christ in 2015, when the Islamic State terrorist group lined up twenty-one Christians on the shores of the Mediterranean Sea in Libya. Twenty of them were Egyptian Copts, and one was an African from Chad. Their captors gave them an ultimatum: reject Jesus Christ or be beheaded.

None of the Egyptian Copts turned away from their faith, and all were killed. It was widely reported that the African worker from Chad was not previously known to be Christian. But he told his captors, "Their God is my God," confessing his faith in Christ and therefore dying as a martyr. Anba Angaelos, the Archbishop of London for the Coptic Orthodox Church, later spoke these words of faith and encouragement as he looked back on the deaths of these men and on persecution of Christians more broadly:

> Egyptian Christians have long experienced persecution. The interesting thing is that we live it with a sense of resilience, but we have never fallen into a state of victimhood or triumphalism. We realize that it is the cross of Christ . . . It is not the end of the road because there is a resurrection that comes after the cross and the empty tomb. And so it is in that hope that we continue to live. And it is in that hope that we continue to carry the cross, knowing that it will be removed from us.[1]

When put to the ultimate test, these men stood firm in the faith: they gave their lives for Jesus Christ.

What would you have done?

The Cost of Following Jesus

Jesus neither minimized nor ignored the cost of following Him; instead, He honestly and clearly declared it. He had no interest in attracting multitudes of halfhearted people. The Son of God sought fully committed disciples, for unconditional commitment to Him was essential to live the life to which He was calling them. Jesus made this clear on several occasions, not just to His disciples but also to the crowds that followed Him. C. S. Lewis vividly described this commitment as follows:

> Christ says, "Give me all. I don't want so much of your time and so much of your money and so much of your work. I want you. I have not come to torment your natural self but to kill it. No half-measures are any good. I don't want to cut off a branch here and a branch there, I want to have the whole tree down … . Hand over the whole natural self, all the desires you think innocent as well as the ones you think wicked—the whole out-

1 Morgan Lee, "Five Years Ago, ISIS Executed 21 Christians on a Beach in Libya," podcast, Quick to Listen, ep. 200, *Christianity Today*, February 19, 2020.

> fit. I will give you a new self instead. In fact, I will give you myself; my own will shall become yours.'"[2]

Is this depiction by Lewis right? Early in Jesus' ministry, a scribe declared, "Teacher, I will follow you wherever you go." Jesus commented on the cost: "Foxes have holes, and birds of the air have nests, but the Son of Man has nowhere to lay his head." When another disciple asked for a reprieve, saying, "Lord, let me first go and bury my father," Jesus replied, "Follow me, and leave the dead to bury their own dead" (Matt. 8:19–22). No easy road here.

We again see Jesus' candid teaching about the cost of discipleship in Luke 14, where He addresses a large group of interested listeners:

> Now great crowds accompanied him, and he turned and said to them, "If anyone comes to me and does not hate his own father and mother and wife and children and brothers and sisters, yes, even his own life, he cannot be my disciple. Whoever does not bear his own cross and come after me cannot be my disciple. For which of you, desiring to build a tower, does not first sit down and count the cost, whether he has enough to complete it? Otherwise, when he has laid a foundation and is not able to finish, all who see it begin to mock him, saying, 'This man began to build and was not able to finish.'" (vv. 25–30)

Jesus further compares the would-be disciple to a king directing an army of thousands:

> Or what king, going out to encounter another king in war, will not sit down first and deliberate whether he is able with ten thousand to meet him who comes against him with twenty thousand? And if not, while the other is yet a great way off, he sends a delegation and asks for terms of peace. So therefore,

2 C. S. Lewis, *Mere Christianity* (New York: Touchstone Books, 1996), 169.

any one of you who does not renounce all that he has cannot be my disciple. (vv. 31–33)

What did Jesus mean by these shocking words? Did He expect His disciples to literally hate their families? Must they give up everything they have? These are crucial questions for us today if we would follow Him.

A moment's thought helps us realize that Jesus did not mean people had to literally hate their families in order to follow Him. Jesus consistently taught wholehearted love for God, sacrificial love for neighbor, and love even for enemies. In the passage from Luke above, He used hyperbole to emphasize in a startling way that love for and devotion to Him must take precedence over all earthly relationships, obligations, and concerns. Love for Jesus fuels the costly discipleship He seeks, for a commitment undergirded by love is far stronger than one based on duty alone. Faithful preacher Charles Spurgeon says it well: "I feel that, if I could live a thousand lives, I would like to live them all for Christ, and even then, I would feel that they were all too little a return for His great love to me."[3]

While Jesus' challenging words may sound harsh to our modern ears, Jesus spoke them in love, truth, and utter realism. He refused to minimize the cost of following Him for the sake of gaining larger crowds. Nor did He encourage anyone to follow Him before that person was ready. He wanted *everyone* to count the cost of putting Him first and so to prepare for the separation, rejection, persecution, suffering, and possible death that such a commitment might bring.

In another instance, Jesus said, "If anyone would come after me, let him deny himself and take up his cross and follow me. For whoever would save his life will lose it, and whoever loses his life for my sake will find it. For what will it profit a man if he gains the whole world and forfeits his soul?" (Mark 8:34–36)). Here is the same theme again. And

---

3 Charles Spurgeon, "Love's Lamentation," Sermon 2782 in *The Metropolitan Tabernacle Pulpit*, vol. 48 (London: Passmore & Alabaster, 1856), 280.

these words are recounted in multiple Gospels,[4] which signals their importance. Let's look more closely now at the three conditions that Jesus spelled out as essential for *anyone* desiring to follow Him.

Deny Self

Jesus first says, "Let him deny himself." The Lord doesn't have in mind here simply denying ourselves some pleasure or enjoyment, but rather forsaking *our self* to live instead for Him. Or to put it differently, to exchange our self-centeredness for Christ-centeredness. This means denying every form of sin and self-seeking we are aware of that stands in the way of trusting Jesus and faithfully obeying His words. It means saying "no" to something lower so we might say "yes" to something higher and infinitely more important: Christ and His will.

Unfortunately, our era has trivialized this important phrase, as Professor F. F. Bruce, one of the leading New Testament scholars of the twentieth century, explains:

> Here too is a phrase that has become unconscionably weakened in pious phraseology. Denying oneself is not a matter of giving up something, whether for Lent or for the whole of life: it is a decisive saying "No" to oneself, to one's hopes and plans and ambitions, to one's likes and dislikes, to one's nearest and dearest, for the sake of Christ. It was so for the first disciples, and it is so for many disciples today.[5]

Doing this requires coming to a definite point in our lives when, with firm intention and commitment, we say a decisive "no" to our fallen self so we might say "yes" to Jesus and follow Him—normally when

---

4 See Matt. 16:24–26; Mark 8:34–38; Luke 9:23–25.

5 F. F. Bruce, *The Hard Sayings of Jesus* (Downers Grove, IL: InterVarsity Press, 1983), 152.

we first repent and believe the gospel.[6] We start there and then continue to reaffirm this commitment daily and grow into it. If we don't do this, our fleshly tendencies of self-seeking and self-preservation will frustrate our efforts to follow Him and so lead to compromise and failure as disciples.

Dietrich Bonhoeffer, a German pastor who was martyred by the Nazis, expressed this succinctly when he said, "When Christ calls a man, he bids him come and die." Only as we die to ourselves and to the world can we truly embrace the life of grace and faithfully follow Jesus.

John Stott, one of the most influential pastor/scholars of the twentieth century, elaborates on denying self:

> What we are (our self or personal identity) is partly the result of the Creation (the image of God), and partly the result of the fall (the image defaced). The self we are to deny, disown, and crucify is our fallen self, everything within us that is incompatible with Jesus Christ (hence Christ's command, "let him deny himself and follow me"). The self we are to affirm and value is our created self, everything within us that is compatible with Jesus Christ (hence his statement that if we lose ourselves by self-denial we shall find ourselves). True self-denial (the denial of our false, fallen self) is not the road to self-destruction, but the road to self-discovery.[7]

---

6 Flawed and inadequate preaching of the gospel message is not uncommon today and causes spiritual confusion about this issue. But God is gracious and can use even a weak message to save people; He then leads them to a fuller understanding the call to discipleship and full commitment to Jesus. Their problem is not lack of willingness to follow (as with nominal Christians) but lack of understanding about the call. And when that light is given, they will respond. Are such people disciples? If they have come to repentance and trusted Jesus and they want to follow Him, they are His disciples, though not yet adequately instructed in the life of discipleship.

7 John Stott, "Am I Supposed to Love Myself or Hate Myself?" *Christianity Today*, April 20, 1984.

Take Up His Cross

What is this "cross" disciples must take up? Does Jesus refer to some disagreeable circumstance we must endure in life? F. F. Bruce again explains,

> The sight of a man being taken to the place of public crucifixion was not unfamiliar in the Roman world of that day. Such a man was commonly made to carry the crossbeam, the *patibulum*, of his cross as he went to his death. That is the picture which Jesus' words would conjure up in the minds of his hearers. If they were not prepared for that outcome to their discipleship, let them change their minds while there was time—but let them first weigh the options in the balances of the kingdom of God: "for whoever would save his life will lose it; and whoever loses his life for my sake and the gospel's will save it."[8]

Jesus would die on just such a cross, and those who would follow Him must prepare themselves for the same fate should faithfulness to Him require it. Many did pay that price during the first three centuries of the church. And many continue to pay it today in parts of the non-Western world. The Christians who died in Libya are but one example.

This demand strikes some as extreme. But the legendary C. T. Studd put it in perspective when he said, "If Jesus Christ be God and died for me, then no sacrifice can be too great for me to make for him."[9] Jesus asks of His disciples exactly this attitude of heart. Taking up the cross of Jesus doesn't mean simply walking through a hard time in life, but rather walking daily in Jesus' footsteps, the very One who carried His cross for us. Whether that means dying the death of a martyr or living a long life in active service to our Lord, the call is the same: take up your cross.

---

8 Bruce, *Hard Sayings of Jesus*, 150 (Bruce is paraphrasing Matthew 16:25).

9 Widely attributed to C. T. Studd and expresses his sentiments but not confirmed in any of his known writings.

Follow Me

Finally, says Jesus, "Follow me." This means following Jesus' teaching and example, which is possible only if we first deny self and take up our cross.[10]

Which of Jesus' *teachings* should we follow? All of them. As we do, we keep in mind that the call to wholehearted devotion to Christ, love for God, and love for our neighbor—even when that neighbor is an enemy—lies at the heart of His teaching.

What part of Jesus' *example* are we to follow? As the long-awaited Suffering Servant (see Isaiah 53), Jesus came in wholehearted devotion to the Father, to fulfill the Father's will. He came "not to be served but to serve, and to give his life as a ransom for many" (Mark 10:45). Everything He did expressed servanthood that was grounded in sacrificial love, and His self-giving service culminated on the cross with the greatest act of love in human history.

While we cannot give our lives to redeem the souls of others, we can live in humble servanthood as Jesus did (John 13:14–17). We can love God and our neighbor as He did. We can love fellow disciples as He loves us (John 15:12). We can lay down our lives for our friends (John 15:13). We can show compassion for those who don't yet know Him and share the gospel with them. And we can follow His steps in suffering (1 Pet. 2:21). As the apostle John said, "Whoever keeps his word, in him truly the love of God is perfected. By this we may know that we are in him: whoever says he abides in him *ought to walk in the same way in which he walked*" (1 John 2:5–6; my emphasis). We will not do these things perfectly, but as we seek to faithfully follow Jesus in the power of the Holy Spirit, we will grow stronger and more consistent over time.

---

10 In the Greek New Testament, the words translated "deny self" and "take up" are aorist imperative verbs indicating a decisive action, while "follow" is present tense, indicating continuous action.

What is at stake here in the conditions of discipleship Jesus lays before those who would follow Him? He leaves no doubt when He goes on to say, "For whoever would save his life will lose it, but whoever loses his life for my sake and the gospel's will save it." If we choose to live for self and the best we can gain in earthly life, we will lose eternal life. But if we deny self, take up the cross and follow Jesus, even at the cost of our earthly lives, we will gain eternal life.

Count the cost, says Jesus: "For what does it profit a man to gain the whole world and forfeit his soul? For what can a man give in return for his soul?" (Mark 8:36–37). Compare the value of gaining all that you desire in this earthly life with the loss of eternal life. That is exactly the issue, because "whoever is ashamed of me and of my words in this adulterous and sinful generation, of him will the Son of Man also be ashamed [that is, will disown] when he comes in the glory of his Father with the holy angels" (v. 38).

Hard, yet Easy

These three conditions of discipleship may sound hard, but by embracing them, we paradoxically discover the reality of Jesus' promise that "my yoke is easy, and my burden is light" (Matt. 11:30). We find that they provide the path of grace in God's kingdom—a path that leads us into freedom, righteousness, peace, and joy. They free us from the prison of self-centeredness and guide us in loving obedience. They give peace of heart and deliver us from the fear of death, and they enable us to walk in joyful fellowship with Jesus, who strengthens and empowers us through His indwelling Spirit.

It can help to think about the commitment Jesus asks of us as something like the mutual devotion of husband and wife in marriage, an idea I first heard from Pastor Bill Kynes.[11] Not knowing what the future may hold, husband and wife pledge themselves exclusively to

11 Dr. William Kynes, former Senior Pastor of Cornerstone Evangelical Free Church, Annandale, VA, is now retired and serves as a council member for the Gospel Coalition.

one another and commit "to have and to hold from this day forward, for better, for worse, for richer, for poorer, in sickness and in health, to love and to cherish, till death us do part."[12] Similarly, not knowing what the future may hold, we commit ourselves to Christ, who loved us, gave Himself up for us, and remains committed to us. Just as we enter marriage realizing that, sooner or later, challenges will come (and therefore we vow in advance to remain faithful no matter the cost), so we commit to follow Jesus and remain faithful to Him throughout our lives, no matter the cost.

Does this sound daunting? It may, but Jesus assures us that we can do it through the Holy Spirit's empowerment. It also helps to remember that countless believers through the ages already *have* done it.

While some conclude the price of following Jesus is too high, the cost of not following Him is infinitely higher. Throughout the centuries, those who have faithfully followed Jesus have declared it worth every sacrifice and more. The American missionary to Ecuador Jim Elliot, who died as a martyr, spoke for all followers of Jesus when he said, "He is no fool who gives up what he cannot keep to gain what he cannot lose."[13]

Truly, as we follow Jesus, we gain something far more valuable than anything we may give up. In this world, God gives us a new life, a new identity, a new family, a new purpose, and a new power for living. We begin to live out what Paul calls the "fruit of the Spirit": "love, joy, peace, patience, kindness, goodness, faithfulness, gentleness, [and] self-control" … like we see in the life of Jesus (Gal. 5:22–23). And in the world to come, God will completely deliver us from all sin and give us a place in His presence, life with His people, citizenship in a

---

12 *Book of Common Prayer* (Oxford: Oxford University Press, 1928), The Form of Solemnization of Matrimony, 302.

13 Elisabeth Elliot, *The Journals of Jim Elliot* (Old Tappan, NJ: Fleming Revell, 1978), 174 (journal entry dated October 28, 1949).

kingdom of love, and satisfactions and enjoyments beyond anything we can imagine.

Keep Eternity in View

Charles Thomas (C. T.) Studd, whom I quoted above, was the son of a wealthy English merchant. He met Christ while a student at Eton. He went on to Cambridge, where he became a nationally celebrated cricket player and joined with five other Cambridge students and one from the Royal Military Academy to form, in 1855, the famous Cambridge Seven. Each of the Cambridge Seven made a wholehearted commitment to Christ, left behind a life of wealth and privilege, and devoted himself to foreign missions with Hudson Taylor in China. Studd's legendary ministry made a powerful impact over the years—first in China, then in India, and finally in Africa.[14]

Studd wrote a powerful poem to express the commitment he made to Christ and used it to urge all other believers to live with similar devotion. The famous refrain of the poem declares,

> Only one life, 'twill soon be past,
> Only what's done for Christ will last.

A similar thought is expressed at more length by Puritan pastor Richard Alleine and was adapted by John Wesley and later called the Wesley Covenant Prayer:

> I am no longer my own, but yours. Put me to what you will, rank me with whom you will; put me to doing, put me to suffering; let me be employed for you, or laid aside for you, exalted for you, or brought low for you; let me be full, let me be empty, let me have all things, let me have nothing: I freely and wholeheartedly yield all things to your pleasure and disposal. And now, glorious and blessed God, Father, Son and Holy

14 See Norman Grubb, *C. T. Studd, Cricketer & Pioneer* (Fort Washington, PA: Christian Literature Crusade, 1972).

> Spirit, you are mine and I am yours. So be it. And the covenant now made on earth, let it be ratified in heaven. Amen.[15]

Does wholehearted commitment to Christ seem like too high a price to pay? If we view it only through the lens of this world, it probably does. But if we believe in a world to come that makes this one look like mere shadows and ghosts—the glorious, brilliant age of Christ to come—then it's no sacrifice at all. Instead, we begin to see things as the apostle Paul did:

> Whatever gain I had, I counted as loss for the sake of Christ. Indeed, I count everything as loss because of the surpassing worth of knowing Christ Jesus my Lord. For his sake I have suffered the loss of all things and count them as rubbish, in order that I may gain Christ and be found in him, not having a righteousness of my own that comes from the law, but that which comes through faith in Christ, the righteousness from God that depends on faith—that I may know him and the power of his resurrection, and may share his sufferings, becoming like him in his death, that by any means possible I may attain the resurrection from the dead. (Phil. 3:7–11)

That's a life worth living! And it lasts forever.

Where are you? Did you understand and accept the call to discipleship when you first came to Jesus? Or did the call become clear later? If you have not made a wholehearted commitment to Jesus, take time to count the cost now and decide how you will respond to His call to you. If you *have* fully committed yourself to Jesus, prayerfully examine yourself to see if you are still walking in it daily.

15 J. I. Packer, *Growing in Christ* (Wheaton, IL: Crossway, 1994), 181.

Questions to Ponder

1. What does Jesus mean when He calls us to "take up [our] cross and follow him" (Matt. 16:24)?
2. Name some practical implications of saying "no" to yourself and "yes" to Jesus.
3. List some characteristics of a person seeking to live a life of "humble servanthood."
4. How does having an eternal perspective help us make sense of Jesus' call to be wholeheartedly committed to Him?
5. What fears do you have about wholehearted commitment to Jesus? Lay them before Him and ask Him to deliver you from them.

7

Praying Kingdom Prayers

Pray then like this.
Matthew 6:9

After reading the Sermon on the Mount in full, with its call to obedience, followed by the call to wholehearted commitment, many people feel overwhelmed. "How can I possibly live such a life?" they ask. "I know how weak I am. How could I possibly obey the words of Jesus?"

Here's the answer: God gives us everything we need to live in His kingdom: "His divine power has granted to us all things that pertain to life and godliness" (2 Pet. 1:3). The next five chapters explore some of the vital means of growth in godliness.

One of the most important of those resources we receive from God is prayer. God answers prayer! Throughout the Bible, God encourages His people to pray. Jesus does the same. And Jesus leads by example: the Gospels show us that He was constantly in prayer. Even as the Son of God, led and empowered by the Holy Spirit, Jesus knew the necessity of prayer for daily communion with His Father in heaven. As He grew up, He was taught to pray as one of the three pillars of Jewish piety (alongside almsgiving and fasting). Through prayer, Jesus daily received the wisdom, guidance, and strength He needed to do the Father's will.

If Jesus prayed, then how much more should you and I! Yet most believers have never tapped into the full power of prayer.

Six Essential Aspects of Prayer

Because Jesus knew the vital place of prayer in our relationship with God, He taught us how to pray. We commonly call the centerpiece of this instruction "the Lord's Prayer," but that term misleads a bit. Perhaps we should call it instead "the Disciples' Prayer," because Jesus gave it to His disciples as an essential resource to shape their prayer lives.

This prayer has held such a prominent place in many church liturgies for so long that, unfortunately, congregants often pray it by rote in less than thirty seconds with little, if any, reflection. But if we learn to pray this remarkable prayer in all its depth and richness, it can revolutionize our prayer lives. Rather than praying "empty phrases" (Matt. 6:7), we can enter into communion with our Father, who "knows what you need before you ask him" (v. 8). Let's briefly explore this well-known prayer and some of its practical applications.

We find this prayer in both Matthew 6:9–13 and Luke 11:1–4 (with minor differences of wording; the versions may have been given on separate occasions). Here let's focus on the fuller version in Matthew, where the prayer forms an important part of Jesus' basic teaching about discipleship.

By more fully appreciating each of the six petitions that comprise this prayer, we can strengthen the foundations of our prayer life. This pattern isn't the only way to pray, of course, as we can clearly see from the prayers of Jesus, Paul, the psalmists, and others in the Bible. But it is the cornerstone, which explains why believers from earliest times have deeply valued it. Church fathers such as Tertullian (c. 155–220), Origen (185–254), and Cyprian (c. 210–258) each wrote whole books on it,[1] as many others have done since.

1 See Alistair Stewart-Sykes, trans. and intro., *On the Lord's Prayer: Tertullian, Cyprian, and Origen* (Crestwood, NY: St. Vladimir's Seminary Press, 2004).

Pitfalls to Avoid

At the outset, we should note a couple of cautions Jesus gives us about our prayer lives.

The first concerns hypocrisy: praying to be seen and noticed by others. This was a huge problem among the Pharisees in Jesus' day (as it is in our own). When praying in the presence of others, we must guard against the temptation to think of those with whom we pray as an audience before whom we can display our "spirituality." So, Jesus says, "When you pray, go into your room and shut the door and pray to your Father who is in secret" (6:5). Such private prayer (which may include the Lord's/Disciples' Prayer) eliminates a human audience and allows greater honesty and intimacy with the Father. On the other hand, public prayer, and especially repeating the Lord's/Disciples' Prayer, which is communal (as indicated by plural pronouns such as "our," "us," "we"), requires us to be alert to the motives of our heart and avoid trying to impress others.

Jesus' second caution is our tendency to pray in a mechanical or an ostentatious fashion, which characterized the pagans, who "heap up empty phrases" because "they think that they will be heard for their many words" (6:7). This isn't necessarily a rejection of long prayers or even repeated prayers: there are some things we pray for every day, such as bread. Jesus cautions us not against praying for daily necessities, but against a kind of mechanical repetition, day in and day out, that degenerates into mere pious performance. How easy we find it to pray in rote fashion, as though our requests were items on a checklist! Jesus urges us to avoid these common snares.

Jesus also reminds us that we do not pray to inform God of something He does not already know. Jesus said, "Your Father knows what you need before you ask him" (6:8). God knows, and He cares.

This raises a puzzling question: If God is a loving Father and is all-powerful, all-knowing, and fully aware of what we need, then why doesn't He just give it to us without requiring us to pray for it? John Calvin answered that God-ordained prayer is "not so much for His own sake as for ours."[2] C. S. Lewis took it a step further by quoting the Christian mathematician and philosopher Blaise Pascal: "God instituted prayer in order to lend His creatures the dignity of causality."[3] God has designed His creation in such a way that our prayers, when offered in agreement with His will and in faith, can make a real difference in human affairs—enabling us to join Him in His work in the world. Other possibilities for why God requires us to pray include drawing us closer to Him; helping us remain dependent on Him as the source of all our blessings and provider of our needs; building up our faith as we see Him answer specific requests; and increasing our love and gratitude toward Him for His goodness to us. Very likely, all of these apply at one time or another. Whatever the case, we know that God asks us to pray, to make requests of Him, and to expect Him to answer.

Many people seem unaware that if we fail to pray, we can actually miss out on things God would otherwise be happy to give us. As James said, "You do not have, because you do not ask" (James 4:2). Many Christian leaders have echoed this point over the centuries. We might turn again to John Calvin, who said, "To us nothing is promised to be expected from the Lord, which we are not also bidden to ask of Him in prayers … and He is inactive, as if forgetting us, when He sees us idle and mute."[4] And John Wesley said, "God will do nothing except in answer to prayer"[5]—an overstatement, perhaps, but not too far from what Calvin said.

---

2 John Calvin, *Institutes of the Christian Religion*, ed. John T. McNeill, trans. Ford Lewis Battles, vol. 2 (Philadelphia: The Westminster Press, 1960), III.20.2–3.

3 C. S. Lewis, *God in the Dock* (Grand Rapids, MI: Eerdmans, 1970), 106.

4 Calvin, *Institutes*, III.20.2–3.

5 John Wesley, *A Plain Account of Christian Perfection* (Grand Rapids, MI: Christian Classics Ethereal Library, n.d.), 60 (section 25). Paraphrased.

A Pattern for Prayer

Notice that Jesus said, "Pray then *like* this" rather than "pray *this*." The word "like" alerts us that the Disciples' Prayer is a *pattern* to guide our praying. Its six petitions combine to give us a model for how to pray.

The fact that the Greek word for "pray" appears here as a present imperative verb (a tense that indicates a command for continuous action) communicates that we are called to use this prayer regularly. We might loosely translate the phrase as "Habitually pray like this." Doing so can lead us into many adventures, for as we discover the breadth and depth of this pattern-prayer, we can discern many subcategories under each petition.

About four centuries ago, poet and theologian Jeremy Taylor observed, "The Lord's Prayer is short and mysterious, and like the treasuries of the Spirit, full of wisdom and latent senses: it is not improper to draw forth those excellencies which are intended and signified by every petition, that by so excellent an authority we may know what it is lawful to beg of God."[6]

When we pray, then, let us meditate on each petition and pray for any concerns the Spirit brings to mind—an important consideration, because sometimes "we do not know what to pray for as we ought" (Rom. 8:26). We need the Spirit to prompt and guide us in naming specific requests, alongside His regular ministry of praying *for* us.

Finally, we should note that the prayer in Matthew 6 divides quite naturally into two sections. God, His glory, and His kingdom come first (vv. 9–10), while we and our needs come second (vv. 11–13). This order reflects the priorities that should guide us—not only in our prayers, but in all of life. Faithful and effective disciples are God-centered, kingdom-focused people who entrust their lives to God.

---

6 Jeremy Taylor, *The Great Exemplar*, vol. 2 (New York: R. Carter & Brothers, 1859), 302.

Petition 1: Our Father in Heaven...

The Fatherhood of God is the crucial starting point in prayer. J. I. Packer rightly says that we can sum up the whole of New Testament religion if we describe it as knowing God "as one's holy Father."[7] Packer suggests that if we want to judge how well a person understands Christianity, we should consider how much the individual values "the thought of being God's child, and having God as his Father. If this is not the thought that prompts and controls his worship and prayers," Packer says:

> it means that he does not understand Christianity very well at all. … "Father" is the Christian name for God. Our understanding of Christianity cannot be better than our grasp of adoption.[8]

Our Father

Before praying the words "Our Father," whether privately in our room or publicly in church or a small group, we do well to reflect on God as *our* Father. We pray as part of God's family, not as isolated individuals or orphans. He is our Father, and we are His dearly loved children. This helps to clarify our relationship to God and its implications for how we pray. As C. S. Lewis wisely observed, "The prayer preceding all prayers is, 'May it be the real I who speaks. May it be the real Thou that I speak to.'"[9]

What we believe about "the real Thou" is an all-important question, because our image of God shapes all our perceptions, feelings, and attitudes toward Him. As we prepare to pray, therefore, we must remind ourselves that our God is a holy, loving Father. He tenderly cares for us, always seeks our good, and delights to hear from us. He is good, loving, merciful, gracious, wise, powerful, and pure (Exod. 34:6;

---

7 J. I. Packer, *Knowing God* (Downers Grove, IL: InterVarsity Press, 1973), 201.

8 Packer, *Knowing God*, 201.

9 C. S. Lewis, "Letter 15," in *Letters to Malcolm: Chiefly on Prayer* (London: Geoffrey Bles, 1964), 109.

Jer. 32:17; Hab. 1:13a). Nothing is too difficult for Him (Jer. 32:27; Isa. 40:21–31; Matt. 19:26) as He shepherds His sheep throughout their lives (Psalm 23).

If we often ponder how God in grace and love took the initiative to provide atonement for our sins and reconcile us to Himself; how He gave us new life and adopted us into His family (Rom. 8:15); how we are now His beloved children (Eph. 5:1; 1 John 3:1); how He truly delights in us (Ps. 147.11; Zeph. 3:17); and how intimacy with Him is our spiritual birthright (Ps. 149:4; Eph. 1:3–14)—our hearts will soar and our love for Him will grow. Pondering these realities gives us firm footing to approach Him with confidence, assured that He looks upon us with a smile, not a frown, and delights to hear our prayers through the merits, mediation, and intercession of Jesus His Son, our Great High Priest (Prov. 15:8: Matt. 7:11).

All of this prepares us to "enter his gates with thanksgiving and his courts with praise" (Ps. 100:4). These preparations can help orient our hearts and lift them up to God. Then, as preacher and teacher Andrew Murray advises, "Just place yourself before him, and look up into his face; think of his love, his wonderful, tender, pitying love."[10]

Pondering the Father's love for us at the outset of prayer helps to give us assurance that God will hear and answer us. If we think of Him as anything less than a loving Father, our ability to believe and trust Him will shrink, weakening our prayer life. As Murray also said, "The knowledge of the Fatherhood of God, the revelation of His infinite Fatherliness in our hearts; the faith in the infinite love that gives us His Son and Spirit to make us children, is indeed the secret of prayer in spirit and truth."[11] And it should move our hearts to pray, "Help me love you with all my heart and be a good son (or daughter). May I please you today and bring you glory!"

---

10 Andrew Murray, *With Christ in the School of Prayer* (Old Tappan, NJ: Fleming H. Revell Company, 1981), 24.

11 Murray, *With Christ*, 21.

Sadly, many believers struggle to have a right view of God, sometimes because they had problems with their earthly father. The image we have of our earthly father—normally, the first male authority figure in our lives—can significantly influence the image we have of our heavenly Father, the ultimate authority figure. If we had a loving, patient, kind, compassionate, and reliable earthly father who cared for and took an interest in us, we gain a helpful analogy, a lens through which it becomes easier to see those qualities in our heavenly Father. On the other hand, if our father was cold, distant, harsh, judgmental, authoritarian, critical, unreliable, self-centered, too busy for us, or absent, we will likely suffer emotionally from a negative father-image and will unconsciously transfer this image onto God. This error will keep us from seeing Him as He really is and thereby hinder our trust in and intimacy with Him. I have seen this problem quite often in the process of helping believers to grow as disciples of Jesus. It also was a problem in my own life for many years, although now, by God's grace, it seems largely resolved.

On the other hand, some people have an innate sense that their negative ideas about God do not represent His reality. This recognition draws them to seek the truth about His fatherly love. The best place to turn for our image of God is to Scripture. Our life experiences will certainly shape our ideals concerning what a father is and does. But God has provided us a rich image of His Fatherhood in the pages of His Word. Psalm 103 is a good example, among many others.

Whether we must peel away a negative image of fatherhood or can build upon a positive one, thankfully, God transforms our view by the renewal of our minds through truth (Rom. 12:2). The Spirit uses our prayerful meditation on the Scriptures to show us the true character of the Father and of Jesus and to produce this important change in us. A wise, mature pastor or a godly Christian counselor or friend may also help us to work through questions or challenges in this area. Of course, attending a loving church that faithfully preaches and teaches the Bible and bears witness to God the Father's love is essential.

... in Heaven

The phrase "in heaven" further orients us as we call to mind God's transcendence and sovereignty. It reminds us to approach Him with humility and reverence. Although God is exalted far above all earthly and human realities, He is also somehow present with us and cares for us in our weakness and frailty: "For thus says the One who is high and lifted up, who inhabits eternity, whose name is Holy: 'I dwell in the high and holy place, and also with him who is of a contrite and lowly spirit, to revive the spirit of the lowly, and to revive the heart of the contrite'" (Isa. 57:15). God resists the proud and knows them from afar, but He welcomes and delights in those with a contrite and humble heart (Ps. 138:6; Prov. 3:34; James 4:6).

... Hallowed Be Your Name.

In biblical thought, there is often a close connection between a person's name and his or her character. God's name is essentially the same as His person. Thus, when we pray for His name to be "hallowed," or set apart as holy, we are asking that He display His holiness and glory more fully in the world and that He be honored, revered, and held in awe.

One significant way God answers this request is through the lives of His people. As men and women love God, seek to faithfully follow Jesus, and live holy lives, they bring glory to Him. They bring light to the world's darkness. We therefore pray that our lives will hallow His name.

God also loves to get glory through His church in both its global and its local expressions. There are some wonderful congregations that make God's character a visible reality. But in places where sinful beliefs and behaviors shape the church more than do those of God's kingdom, we often see God's name defamed, scorned, and trivialized, thereby reinforcing unbelief. We therefore need to pray earnestly for God to revive and reform His church, both wherever we live and around the world. We should work toward that end in the ways He makes plain to us. As we pray, the Holy Spirit will teach us how we may glorify Him.

Petition 2: Your Kingdom Come

When we ask for God's kingdom to come, we look ahead to that great, glorious day of consummation when, after defeating the devil and all who oppose His rule, God will reign supreme as King in the lives of His people and over His entire creation. But as we have seen, that day comes in stages.

A new stage in the advance of God's kingdom began with the arrival of Jesus, the Messiah, God's own Son. His advent signaled that the present evil age had begun to pass away and the age to come had commenced. Through faith and trust in Jesus, lost people began to enter God's kingdom, come under His reign, and make more and more disciples throughout the world. These disciples gathered into communities (local churches) as public and visible colonies of God's kingdom.

Today, we are rapidly moving toward the final stage in redemption history, the glorious day of consummation when Jesus will return and unite with His bride, the church. At a time known to God alone, He will send Jesus back to earth in power and great glory with His holy angels—to defeat the devil and his minions, raise the dead, preside at the final judgment, and bring this present evil age to an end (Rev. 19:11–20:6). Then Jesus shall turn over the kingdom to the Father and shall reign forever as King over His people in the new heavens and new earth (1 Cor. 15:24–28; Rev. 11:15; 21:1–4). It should thrill our hearts to frequently reflect on this reality while we are "waiting for our blessed hope, the appearing of the glory of our great God and Savior Jesus Christ" (Titus 2:13). So praying "Your kingdom come" involves far more than many of us commonly suppose!

God's rule and reign in our personal lives becomes living and active when we give ourselves wholeheartedly to Him and His purposes through Jesus. Our cry becomes, "May Your kingdom, Your rule and reign, come *in me*!" This cry may include similar petitions for our family, friends, and neighbors.

We also pray for the triumph of God's kingdom through the powerful preaching of the gospel—the good news about Jesus—throughout the world, such as via the ministries of pastors, missionaries, and Christian workers. We pray for believers to share the gospel with unbelievers and to abound in God-honoring works of love and compassion for the poor, the needy, and those who suffer. We pray for the defeat of the devil and of all his schemes against God's people and kingdom, including heresies, false teaching, doctrinal error, divisions, false religions, and hostile philosophies. We ask for all this and more when we pray, "Your kingdom come." The Spirit will guide us in the particulars.

Petition 3: Your Will Be Done, on Earth as It Is in Heaven

This petition sums up the previous two, asking that the life of heaven, where our Father's name is honored and revered and His will is done, will come in all its fullness to the earth. And it asks that, until then, His will shall increasingly be done in our lives on earth. As C. S. Lewis said, "Thy will be done—by me—now."[12] That means complete submission to God expressed in wholehearted love for God, sacrificial servant love for others, and moral purity.

12 C. S. Lewis, *Letters to Malcolm*, 25–26.

Petition 4: Give Us This Day Our Daily Bread

With this request, the focus shifts from God's glory to our essential needs as His children. Because God loves and cares for us, He wants to provide what is needed to sustain our lives and encourages us to ask for it.

Over the many years that Israel wandered in the wilderness (for the full story, read Exodus through Deuteronomy), God showed His love and faithfulness by supernaturally providing food day by day (except on the day before the sabbath, when He provided a double portion [Exod. 16:22]). This is the historical background of our request for daily bread, which speaks of what we need to sustain our life each day—food, clothing, shelter, and more.

Nonessentials and luxuries are not in view here, though our gracious and generous God sometimes gives us far more than the bare essentials. In kingdom life today, Jesus assures His disciples that as they trust the Father, who knows all their needs, and seek first His kingdom and His righteousness, He will provide for them (Matt. 6:31–33). This promise applies as much to us now as it did to His disciples in the first century. Believers throughout history have testified to how God has daily supplied their bread, sometimes in extraordinary ways.

God can still provide for His people in miraculous ways if He chooses, so we should be open to the possibility. However, this is not His usual way of providing for His children. Rather, in most cases, He gives us honest work that enables us to buy our daily bread. This petition, then, is an acknowledgement that everything we have ultimately comes from God. It is by His hand that we are fed.

Petition 5: Forgive Us Our Debts

When Jesus says "forgive our debts," He means our spiritual liabilities or sins (see Matt. 6:14–15). Our sins offend God and disrupt our fellowship with Him. We must deal properly with them to restore our fellowship with Him. We should therefore confess our specific sins as soon as we become aware of them, and certainly no later than by the end of the day. A prayerful review of our day is a valuable practice and can help us remember anything we need to confess (as well as any blessings for which to thank God).

Unconfessed sin can hinder God's answers to our prayers (Ps. 66:16–19; Isa. 59:1–2). Earlier generations sometimes called prompt confession "keeping a short account with God." Our confession must be completely honest and forthright, with no rationalizing or blame-shifting and with a firm intention of forsaking the sin. Because of our natural tendency to deceive ourselves, we will sometimes need to ask God to search our hearts and shine His light on our offenses, both known and unknown. Psalm 139:23–24 helps us pray in this way.

Our offenses may include sins of commission (the wrong things we do) as well as sins of omission (the good things we leave undone). It is also important to ask God to help us hate sin, love righteousness, and walk in holiness. To this end, the great missionary William Carey and his Serampore brotherhood[13] called prayer essential for a healthy spiritual life, saying that "Prayer—secret, fervent, believing prayer—lies at the root of all personal godliness."[14]

We do not (and cannot) *earn* the Father's forgiveness of our sins; rather, His forgiveness is a gift that flows from His abounding grace. He delights to grant it whenever we seek it with repentant hearts. Such repentance produces the fruit of joy and heartfelt gratitude.

---

13 Eponymously named for Carey's mission location in Serampore, West Bengal, India.

14 William Carey, *Carey's Serampore Form of Agreement*, Article 10. Paraphrased from George Smith, *The Life of William Carey, Shoemaker & Missionary* (London: John Murray, 1885), 450.

... As We Also Have Forgiven Our Debtors

In principle, all believers agree on the importance of forgiveness. But as C. S. Lewis observed, "Everyone thinks forgiveness is a lovely idea until he has something to forgive."[15] God's people continually need forgiveness for their own sins, and failure to extend it to others has wrecked many lives, relationships, ministries, and churches. Yet how often do believers minimize and ignore it, thus dimming the light of Christ in their lives by their refusal to forgive?

God's grace, which He has so lavishly poured out upon us, changes our hearts and obligates us to graciously forgive those who sin against us. In fact, God conditions His forgiveness of our sins on our forgiving others. But don't think *quid pro quo* here. Instead, it's more like this: as we have received so much undeserved forgiveness from God, how could we presume to refuse to forgive our neighbor's offenses against us? Regardless of how grievous those sins may seem, we *must* forgive.

True forgiveness is not a feeling; it is a choice, an act of our will to pardon one who has sinned against us, to cancel the moral debt they owe us and forsake anger, resentment, bitterness and the desire for revenge. As we do so, feelings will follow—if not immediately, then eventually. Quoting Lewis again, "To be a Christian means to forgive the inexcusable because God has forgiven the inexcusable in you." May it be hard and take time? Yes. May we sometimes need to reaffirm it again and again? Yes. But however difficult it may be, we must forgive.

Jesus emphasized this because He knew that others will offend us, sin against us, and injure us many times and in many ways over the course of our lives. We will need to forgive *repeatedly*. If we want to live in communion with God, we cannot withhold forgiveness, carry grudges, or bear animosity against those who have hurt or offended us. Refusal to forgive from the heart is not an option for any follower of Jesus (as He makes clear in Matthew 6:14–15 and states even more strongly in

---

15 C. S. Lewis, *Mere Christianity* (New York: Touchstone Books, 1996), 104.

18:32–35). If we refuse, Jesus says, God will withhold forgiveness of our sins until such time as we do forgive (Matt. 6:14–15; Mark 11:25). In his classic work *The Weight of Glory*, C. S. Lewis explains:

> We believe that God forgives us our sins; but also that He will not do so unless we forgive other people their sins against us. There is no doubt about the second part of this statement. It is in the Lord's Prayer, it was emphatically stated by our Lord. If you don't forgive you will not be forgiven. No exceptions to it. He doesn't say that we are to forgive other people's sins, provided they are not too frightful, or provided there are extenuating circumstances, or anything of that sort. We are to forgive them all, however spiteful, however mean, however often they are repeated. If we don't, we shall be forgiven none of our own.[16]

Noted preacher Charles Spurgeon said, "Unless you have forgiven others, you read your own death warrant when you repeat the Lord's prayer."[17] Persistent refusal to forgive raises questions about whether we have received God's grace in the first place. If you are struggling to forgive, Martin Luther's advice is helpful: "Anyone who feels unable to forgive, let him ask for grace so that he can forgive."[18] (For more on Jesus' teaching on forgiveness, see Chapter 9.)

Petition 6: Lead Us Not into Temptation

The word "temptation" in Matthew 6:13 is a translation of the Greek *peirasmos*, which can mean temptation, test, or trial, depending on the context. Some scholars have suggested that it is probably better

16 C. S. Lewis, "On Forgiveness," in *The Weight of Glory and Other Addresses* (New York: HarperCollins, 2001), 178.

17 Charles Spurgeon, "Forgiveness Made Easy," Sermon 1448 in *The Metropolitan Tabernacle Pulpit*, vol. 24 (London: Passmore & Alabaster, 1856), 694.

18 Martin Luther, *A Simple Way to Pray* (Louisville, KY: Westminster John Knox Press, 2000), 27.

to translate it in this passage as "test."[19] Since the Bible tells us that God is morally pure, hates sin, and "tempts no one" (James 1:13), this petition cannot be a request that He refrain from tempting us to sin. Is it, then, a request to be spared from testing or trial? No, because the Bible also tells us to "count it all joy" when we face trials that test our faith (see James 1:2–3). God uses trials to reveal our character or commitment and to help us grow in faith, virtue, and a deeper knowledge of Himself.

So then, how should we understand this petition? We stand on solid ground when we understand this request as asking God to spare us from tests or trials *greater than we can bear*. As Professor Donald Hagner puts it, "The disciple thus prays not to be led into such a situation, i.e., not to be led into a testing in which his or her faith will not be able to survive."[20]

What one can endure, another cannot—and only God knows each person's limits.

. . . But Deliver Us from Evil

When we pray for God to "deliver us from evil," do we mean from the corruption of this present evil world? Or from the evil one, the devil, the chief architect of evil in the world, who tempts people with the aim of corrupting and destroying them? The Greek word here for "evil," *poneros*, can be either neuter ("it") or masculine ("he") in its grammatical form and therefore can be translated either "evil" (ESV) or "the evil one" (NIV). Perhaps Jesus intended both. "The difference between Satan and evil is small in the present petition: to pray to be free from one is to pray to be free from the other."[21]

---

19 C. L. Blomberg, "Trial," in *The International Standard Bible Encyclopedia of the Bible, Revised*, ed. Geoffrey W. Bromiley (Grand Rapids, MI: Eerdmans, 1988), 904.

20 Donald A. Hagner, *Matthew 1–13*, vol. 33a, Word Biblical Commentary (Dallas: Word, Inc., 1993), 151.

21 Hagner, *Matthew 1–13*, 151.

Thus, we do well to pray for freedom and deliverance from any specific influences of the world, the flesh, or the devil. This unholy trinity will oppose us as long as we live on earth, but we do not have to fall down in defeat. As we will see in more detail later, the Holy Spirit will enable and empower us to overcome evil. We are also assured that when temptation comes, God will not allow it to go beyond what we can resist but will provide a way of escape so we can endure it (1 Cor. 10:13). For more on this topic, see the companion volume to this book, *Abiding in Jesus Christ: A Guide to Maturity in Authentic Discipleship.*

It Stands the Test of Time

The Disciples' Prayer has stood the test of time, and its treasures have blessed countless believers. When we explore its depth, breadth, and riches, and devote ourselves to making it our own, we enter into deeper communion with God and develop greater spiritual strength for the life of discipleship.

Questions to Ponder

1. Why is faith-filled prayer so essential to life in the kingdom of God?
2. Name two potential problems related to prayer that Jesus warned against in the context of what we are calling "the Disciples' Prayer" (see Matt. 6:5–7). Why do you suppose these two problems seem so prevalent?
3. How do you respond to the thought of God as your Father? Is that a comforting idea or a troubling one? Why, and how can gaining a more accurate view of God's character help you?
4. Since, as Jesus taught, we do not pray to inform God about various situations, then why do we pray?
5. Make a list of the six petitions of the Disciples' Prayer and briefly describe the focus of each petition. Which one stirs your mind and imagination most? Why?
6. Many of Christ's disciples have used Jesus' model prayer in Matthew 6 as a framework for developing a prayer life that focuses on the priorities of the kingdom of God. Describe your own experience with using the Disciples' Prayer as a guide for your practice of prayer.

8

Persevering in Kingdom Prayer

Ask, and it will be given to you; seek, and you will find;
knock, and it will be opened to you.
Matthew 7:7

Jesus teaches us not only to pray but to persevere in prayer.

We can find many examples of persevering in prayer in the Bible, in church history, and in the present day. I know of one woman who prayed for more than thirty years for the salvation of her husband—and in a time of great need, the man finally reached out to Jesus and asked Him to become his Lord and Savior. Stories such as this one point us to the fact that Jesus calls believers to follow His command to persevere in prayer.

Jesus made earnest prayer and communion with the Father a vital part of His own life and ministry. They are just as vital for everyone who wants to be a faithful and fruitful disciple of Jesus.

God Wants to Answer Our Prayers

Jesus encourages us to pray by assuring us that our Father in heaven loves us and wants to answer our prayers (Matt. 7:11; John 16:23–24; see also 1 John 5:14–15). He wants us to discover, as Martin Luther and many others have, that "prayer is not a matter of overcoming God's reluctance but laying hold of his willingness."[1] Knowing that He will both hear and answer us gives us a powerful incentive to pray.

Discovering how lavish and breathtaking God's promises are gives us another incentive. Once we grasp how much God wants to bless us through prayer, we will begin to pray with stronger faith and see answers that both amaze us and glorify Him.

As we have seen, the Disciples' Prayer is the centerpiece of Jesus' teaching on prayer, providing the foundation and framework for our prayer lives. But having a pattern for prayers is one thing; believing that God will answer our prayers is another.

Many of us have found ourselves in seasons in which we recite a list of routine requests only to realize that our prayers have become stale—we go through the motions but expect little to come of it. Such tepid praying disillusions and demotivates us and can damage our faith.

For a vital and effective prayer life, we need confidence that God loves us, listens to us, and will answer our prayers. Prayer then becomes a delight instead of a duty. As we see His answers, our trust in Him grows stronger. We come to know Him better and love Him more, and we increase in our zeal to serve Him and spread His kingdom.

Jesus' second major teaching on prayer in the Sermon on the Mount can help us in this area. Here is what He says:

> Ask, and it will be given to you; seek, and you will find; knock, and it will be opened to you. For everyone who asks receives, and the one who seeks finds, and to the one who knocks it will be opened. Or which one of you, if his son asks him for bread, will give him a stone? Or if he asks for a fish, will give him a serpent? If you then, who are evil, know how to give good gifts to your children, how much more will your Father who is in heaven give good things to those who ask him! (Matt. 7:7–11)

---

1 This quotation is commonly attributed to Martin Luther but is not found in modern editions of his works and has sometimes been attributed to others.

With these striking words, set in the warm glow of family life, Jesus teaches us that our Father in heaven delights much more in granting good requests to His children than a loving earthly father enjoys giving good things to his sons or daughters. Receiving God's answers makes a powerful impact on us and provides one reason why Jesus so strongly urges us to pray.

In these verses, Jesus simply and clearly insists that persistent, believing prayer will be answered. He exhorts believers to ask, seek, and knock in prayer to their Father in heaven. The verbs are imperatives, which means they are commands to be obeyed, not suggestions to be considered. They also appear in the present tense in Greek (likely indicating continuous action, as we saw above), meaning we should *regularly* ask, seek, and knock at God's door with our requests. Some Bible translations therefore render these words as "keep on asking, keep on seeking, keep on knocking" (see, for instance, the New Living Translation).

Moreover, John Stott has suggested that these three verbs may represent an "ascending scale of urgency."[2] Whether Jesus intended this increasing urgency or not, it certainly reflects the experience of many believers. Jesus goes on to assure us that God will answer everyone who prays in this way for something within His will (John 14:13–14; 15:7). Therefore, we should pray with expectation that He will answer.

A remarkable example of urgent, persevering prayer dates from 1800 and is still bearing fruit today. Ann Hamilton, a godly Scottish woman, prayed faithfully and earnestly for her family's salvation. "On her deathbed she was troubled in spirit," wrote her biographer,

> but then suddenly her face became radiant and she said, "I've got the promise." The promise she referred to was Isaiah 59:21: "'And as for me, this is my covenant with them,' says the Lord: 'My Spirit that is upon you, and my words that I have put

---

2 John Stott, *Christian Counter-Culture: The Message of the Sermon on the Mount* (Downers Grove, IL: InterVarsity Press, 1978), 184.

> in your mouth, shall not depart out of your mouth, or out of the mouth of your offspring, or out of the mouth of your children's offspring,' says the Lord, 'from this time forth and forevermore.'"[3]

Generation after generation, Hamilton's descendants have known Christ, and many of them have served in vocational ministry. My pastor is one of them; he once told me that in his branch of the Hamilton family line, there were twenty-one men and women who were currently committed followers of Christ. Fifteen of them are in full-time ministry as pastors, missionaries, or parachurch workers in various orthodox Christian denominations.

God's love for us is the basis for such a strong command and lavish promise. As a gracious and good Father, by nature He gives good things to His children. They are not rewards for good works we have done. They are more like a divine hug, saying, "I love you. You can trust me." The more we experience this, the better we come to know and love Him and the deeper our trust and intimacy grow. The more instances of such answered prayer that we can look back on, the more our hearts will feel lifted and strengthened for present and future challenges.

What Good Things Will God Give Us?

How can we experience more of the Father's answers to our prayers? It will help to understand what Jesus means when He says our heavenly Father will give us "good things." Does He mean good things in the form of meeting all our wants and desires? Or good things according to *His* definition of good and *His* knowledge of what is best for us at any given time?

Surely the latter—which cautions us against the worldly, self-seeking directions our prayers can sometimes take. As James 4:3

---

3 Susan Hunt, *Heirs of the Covenant* (Wheaton, IL: Crossway Books, 1998), 126.

says, "You ask and do not receive, because you ask wrongly, to spend it on your passions."

We saw earlier, for example, that Jesus taught us to pray for our daily bread (necessities). A few verses later, He promised, "Seek first the kingdom of God and his righteousness, and all these things will be added to you" (Matt. 6:33). In the context of the Sermon on the Mount, what are "these things"?

Jesus has just discussed our anxieties about what we eat, drink, and wear (6:31)—in other words, our basic needs. If we meet the condition of seeking first God's kingdom and righteousness, we can confidently expect that God will answer our prayers for basic necessities. Does this mean that He has no interest in providing *any* of our wants and desires?

It depends.

Because God is gracious, He gives us things that we do not deserve and have no right to expect. In instances where our wants and desires align with His will and purpose—things that will do us good and bring Him glory—we can expect Him to grant them. When they do not, He will do what any good earthly father would do and say "no." Often He gives us something better than we asked for, something that we *would* have asked for had we known the best thing for us.

Luke's version of this prayer helps us at this point; he tells us which is the best of the good gifts God can give. It is the Holy Spirit (Luke 11:13). Prayer for the Spirit's fullness in our lives should be our highest priority each day.

In practical terms, then, one key to seeing more of our prayers granted is simply to pray for alignment with God's will, that He will bring our desires and requests into agreement with His will. Our aim is to pray God-centered prayers, ones that seek God's purposes and glory rather than our own.

Learning to pray God-centered prayers has had a major effect on my prayer life and on the prayer lives of many people I have known over the years. The more often we pray according to God's will, the more often we see God's answers. A number of times, Jesus gives us strong invitations and extravagant promises to encourage us to pray this way: "Whatever you ask in my name," He said, "this I will do, that the Father may be glorified in the Son. If you ask me anything in my name, I will do it" (John 14:13–14). At first glance, this looks like a promise for anything and everything we may want, *carte blanche*, and prosperity-gospel preachers misapply it this way. But when we remember that, in the Bible, a person's name represents his or her character, it becomes clear that Jesus means "anything" that is in agreement with who He is and all that He stands for—things He would endorse. Such prayer glorifies God.

Jesus reaffirms this understanding a few verses later when He says, "If you abide in me, and my words abide in you, ask whatever you wish, and it will be done for you" (John 15:7). If we enjoy unhindered fellowship with Jesus, and His words shape our thinking and requests, our prayers will conform to His will—and He will grant them.

The apostle John reinforces this idea when he tells his congregation, "This is the confidence that we have toward him, that if we ask anything according to his will he hears us. And if we know that he hears us in whatever we ask, we know that we have the requests that we have asked of him" (1 John 5:14–15). This gentle but direct reminder tells us that our prayer does not persuade God to do *our* will. Rather, we are to align our prayer with *His* will. Then He will answer.

Jesus modeled this approach as He prayed about His impending arrest and crucifixion, saying "not as I will, but as you will" (Matt. 26:39). When we learn to subordinate our will to God's will as a basic part of our Christian life, we put ourselves in position to see our prayers answered. God simply will not grant prayers that do not agree with His will, no matter how much we pray or how many people we recruit to join us in prayer. The sooner we recognize this, the faster we will mature in prayer … and the more often our prayers will receive an affirmative answer!

Putting This into Practice

How do we put this into practice? If we want to pray according to God's will—that is, to ask Him to do what He already wants to do—we need to understand His will regarding the matters that concern us. We come to such an understanding through reading, studying, and meditating on God's Word, the Bible, in dependence on the Holy Spirit, who helps us to see the Lord's intention and how it applies to our issue.

A special focus on the teachings of Jesus also will help us better grasp how to "pray in His name," which does *not* mean simply tacking the phrase on the end of our prayer. We must learn to pray for things consistent with His character and will—things He Himself approves of and endorses as He intercedes for us at the throne of grace.

As we discover God's promises in Scripture, understand them in context, and meet any conditions that He may require, we can ask Him with confidence to fulfill them in our lives and in the situations that concern us.

In some cases, we may know God's will in general, but not its application to a specific situation. For example, how do we pray for a sick person or for someone who doesn't yet know Christ? Here we need a special sensitivity to the Holy Spirit's guidance, for God clearly does not heal every sick person or save every lost person, nor did Jesus so do in His earthly ministry. Scripture contains many wonderful, exciting, extravagant promises, and we should aim to familiarize ourselves with them and ask the Spirit to show us how and when to pray them in specific situations.

More generally, what good things might God be pleased to give us? Both the Disciples' Prayer and its companion passage here in Matthew 7:7–11 give us a sound starting place since they give us specific categories for focusing our prayer. When we pray each of these petitions, we pray

God's will. And if we enlarge our focus to include the entire Sermon on the Mount, with all its challenging teachings about how God wants us to live, we will find much more to pray about. We will discover still more when we expand our sights to the full scope of Scripture.

What about Delayed Answers to Prayer?

Persevering in faith gives us another key to answered prayer. We are to continue to believe God for the answer even when we see no sign of it on the horizon, for God's timing is not necessarily our timing. Thus, we are to "be constant in prayer," says Paul (Rom. 12:12), and "continue steadfastly in prayer" (Col. 4:2). As Charles Spurgeon once said, "Faith is the foundation stone; prayer comes next. Prayer without faith would be an empty mockery; it would win nothing of God."[4] Faith is not merely optimism, wishing, or hoping, but a confident assurance that God is who He says He is—and that He will therefore do what He promises at the time He knows is best.

As Scripture says, faith is "being sure of what we hope for and certain of what we do not see … and without faith it is impossible to please him, because anyone who comes to him must believe that he exists and that he rewards those who earnestly seek him" (Heb. 11:1, 6 NIV 1984). God wants us to continue to grow stronger in faith, hope, and love. Like a muscle, faith grows stronger the more we exercise it.

This helps to explain why Jesus commands us to keep on asking, keep on seeking, keep on knocking *in faith*. Those of us in the Western world find this hard to do because secularization has created a climate in which it is difficult for us to believe in anything we cannot see or measure (or at least build a rational probability for). We want to see *before* we believe.

God, however, tells us to believe and *then* we will see. He instructs us to walk by faith, not by sight (2 Cor. 5:7). Perhaps many of us

4 Charles Spurgeon, "The Necessity of Increased Faith," *The New Park Street Pulpit, Volume 1* (1855), 550.

should pray for ourselves like a desperate father did as he sought help from Jesus: "I believe; help my unbelief" (Mark 9:24).

Many of us also struggle with impatience. So much about our culture conditions us to want instant gratification. The microwave, instant coffee, immediate credit approval, online orders that arrive the same day (or even the same hour), and so on are but a few examples. Conditioned to expect immediate action, we may pray about something once or twice and then give up if no answer quickly arrives. But God doesn't operate on our timetable, nor does He necessarily do things as we expect. "My thoughts are not your thoughts," He tells us, "neither are your ways my ways … . For as the heavens are higher than the earth, so are my ways higher than your ways and my thoughts than your thoughts" (Isa. 55:8–9). God knows the right time to answer our prayer, and He never answers late. He calls us to trust Him even if we don't see answers when we want them. In those situations, we must "wait on God" in active faith, a hard thing for most of us.

And yet, as we wait on God, He uses our waiting to teach us patience and increase our faith. As Isaiah said, "From of old no one has heard or perceived by the ear, no eye has seen a God besides you, who acts for those who wait for him" (Isa. 64:4). In Scripture, this refrain echoes again and again: "Wait on the Lord!"

Abraham, the "man of faith" (Gal. 3:9), gives us an example of the kind of perseverance in faith that Jesus calls us to exercise and grow in. God promised Abraham a son, but Isaac didn't show up until twenty-five years later. Abraham did not have an easy walk of faith. He made mistakes along the way (e.g., fathering Ishmael in a vain attempt to fulfill God's promise on his own). But as Abraham persevered in faith, he grew stronger and eventually received the promise *in God's appointed time*: "No unbelief made him waver concerning the promise of God, but he grew strong in his faith as he gave glory to God, fully convinced that God was able to do what he had promised" (Rom. 4:20–21).

Abraham's example of continuing to trust God during the "wait of faith" provides us with a valuable lesson today. The wait of faith—the time between when we pray and when God answers—can purify our motivation and deepen our trust as we continue to rely on God despite no sign of an answer.

Why does God sometimes take such a long time to answer certain prayers? The psalmists frequently asked this question (Ps. 13:1–2; 69:3; 89:46), and many believers through the centuries have echoed it. I ask it too. For more than forty years I have been praying for the salvation of one person, and nearly that long for another. But I am confident that God will answer, even if it happens after I die.

In many instances, we cannot discern why certain prayers are answered more quickly than others. We can say only that God has good reasons, whether we can fathom them or not. Our prayers for the salvation of unbelievers may be answered quickly, but usually it takes a long time. God does not violate a person's freedom to choose, and as He draws people to Christ, He may orchestrate their life circumstances over a period of years to draw them to the point of willingly choosing Him. An oft-quoted story from the life of George Müller illustrates the importance of persevering in prayer for as long as it takes to get the answer. In 1844, George Müller began to pray for the conversion of five men. The first was saved after eighteen months, the second five years later, the third was converted six years after that, the fourth was saved just before Müller's death, and the fifth came to Christ a few years later.[5] And we must face the fact that in some cases, for reasons we cannot know, God may not save certain persons despite our prayers.

In other instances, prayers may receive no answer for long stretches because of the timing of God's sovereign plans, as with Abraham. We see

---

5 Roger Steer, *George Müller: Delighted in God* (Ross-shire, Fearn, Scotland: Christian Focus, 1997), 193–194.

the same pattern in the lives of Zechariah and Elizabeth, who for decades prayed for a child, no doubt with deep sadness over their childlessness. Unknown to them, they would have to wait for God's precise timing so that John the Baptist could serve as the forerunner of Jesus (Luke 1). In some situations, God must arrange the circumstances necessary for the prayer to be answered—for example, opening a currently filled job position, or bringing a house onto the market that has not yet gone up for sale, or bringing the right person into the picture for marriage. At times, answers to prayers for change in our personal lives may seem to come slowly because of some deep, inscrutable work God must do in us first.

Mary and Martha give another instructive example of a delayed answer to prayer. They were praying earnestly for their sick brother Lazarus and sent an urgent message to Jesus to come heal him. But Jesus deliberately delayed, and Lazarus died. We are told that "Jesus loved Martha and her sister [Mary] and Lazarus" (John 11:5). Why would He delay? Because by doing so, He would be able to raise Lazarus from the dead and thereby much bring greater glory to God than by simply healing him. In other words, Jesus delayed answering because He had a better plan, and that is sometimes true with us as well.

In certain circumstances, demonic opposition can cause delays to God's answers to prayer, as with the Old Testament prophet Daniel. God granted His answer when Daniel prayed, but its manifestation was delayed for three weeks by the interference of a powerful demonic being (Dan. 10:1–14). Paul reports a similar demonic hindrance in his ministry plans (1 Thess. 2:18). In these situations, we can appreciate even more why Jesus tells us to keep asking, keep seeking, and keep knocking. Receiving the answer occurs as we continue to pray with faith. Like a marathon runner, we must not quit before reaching the finish line.

In some cases, the deep communion with God that grows as we persevere in waiting, pondering, questioning, and wrestling with

God in prayer becomes as much or more of a blessing than the answer itself, when it finally comes.

Delays for other reasons can also occur, including, for example, the harboring of intentional sin, as we saw in the previous chapter. In the book of Isaiah, God says, "Behold, the LORD's hand is not shortened, that it cannot save, or his ear dull, that it cannot hear; but your iniquities have made a separation between you and your God, and your sins have hidden his face from you so that he does not hear" (59:1–2). Similarly, the psalmist writes, "Come and hear, all you who fear God, and I will tell what he has done for my soul. I cried to him with my mouth, and high praise was on my tongue. If I had cherished iniquity in my heart, the Lord would not have listened. But truly God has listened; he has attended to the voice of my prayer" (Ps. 66:16–19). We therefore must be sure to confess and repent of any known sins, especially any grudges or unforgiveness. This includes any sins we continue to practice and/or excuse by telling ourselves that "God understands my weakness." God does understand our weakness. But His response is not to overlook or excuse our sin; rather, He gives us His Holy Spirit, who empowers us to overcome sin.

Another potential problem is half-heartedness or lack of earnestness. Or, God may want to teach us other important lessons to help grow our faith while we await His answer.

When we must persevere in prayer over a long and drawn-out period, can we ask God about the delay? Yes, but He may or may not give us answers. God has no obligation to explain Himself to us. Still, it's appropriate to seek to know why an answer has taken such a long time, especially when doing so renews our attention to Him and enables us to further discern His wisdom and ways.

Paul prayed three times for deliverance from a "thorn … in the flesh" that he found difficult to bear. God said "no." But the Lord also explained that He had designed the apostle's suffering for a higher purpose, to protect him from pride (2 Cor. 12:7–9).

When to Reexamine Our Requests

When we must deal with an especially long delay, we may want to reexamine our prayer to determine whether we have properly grounded it in God's Word and will. It may be that the request needs to be brought into full conformity with His will. Or that our motivation has some defect that requires correction, as James said: "You ask and do not receive, because you ask wrongly, to spend it on your passions" (James 4:3).

With the best of intentions, we may be praying for something that God has no intention of granting: for example, the healing of someone whose sickness is God's appointed way for them to die (see the case of Elisha in 2 Kings 13:14–20) or salvation for a lost person whom God knows will resist the gospel to his last breath. The counsel of a pastor or mature believer who has walked with God for a long time and has a solid grounding in the Bible can help us as we seek to discern possible reasons for long delays in prayer.

What about "Unanswered" Prayer?

Referring to certain of our prayers as "unanswered" is not quite right. It is more accurate to describe them as prayers that were answered, but not in the way we wished or expected. God sometimes says "no" to our petitions, as we just saw with Paul and his thorn in the flesh. C. S. Lewis explains, "Prayer is request. The essence of request, as distinct from compulsion, is that it may or may not be granted. And if an infinitely wise Being listens to the requests of finite and foolish creatures, of course He will sometimes grant and sometimes refuse them."[6] Lewis also wrote that, in hindsight, he could at times see the benefit of hearing "no": "I must often be glad that certain past prayers of my own were not granted."[7]

---

6 C. S. Lewis, "The Efficacy of Prayer," in *The World's Last Night and Other Essays* (New York: Harcourt, Brace, and Co., 1960), 4–5.

7 C. S. Lewis, "Petitionary Prayer: A Problem without an Answer," in *Christian Reflections,* ed. Walter Hooper (Grand Rapids, MI: Eerdmans, 1967), 144.

Those who have walked with God over many years will echo the same thing. Missionary Amy Carmichael says it well: "Do not forget that the answer to many prayers is 'Wait,' or sometimes, 'No, not that, but something else, which when you see Me, you will know was a far better thing.'"[8]

God knows what is best for us. And when He answers "no," however difficult it may feel, we must trust that it comes from His wisdom and love and that there is a higher purpose. We just saw such a situation with Paul's thorn in the flesh. And we see it with Jesus Himself, who prayed three times to escape the cross—but His loving Father denied the request (Matt. 26:39–44). Where would we be if God had granted that request?

Finally, it can sometimes help to do a postmortem on unanswered prayers with the aim of growing in faith and perseverance. If we build up a record of many unanswered prayers and have no idea why they remain unanswered, this can gradually undermine our faith and our prayer life. Seeking God through prayerful reflection and the counsel of wise, godly people can assist in this process. Perhaps the apparent lack of answer and the mandate to persist is an indication that God intends to use our prayer to change our own hearts and better align them with His will.

What If You Don't Feel Like Praying?

From time to time, all believers have the experience of not feeling like praying. When this happens, it is important to resist the natural temptation to stop praying. Evangelist, scholar, and author R. A. Torrey speaks for many when he says:

> Oftentimes when we come to God in prayer, we do not feel like praying. What shall one do in such a case? cease praying until

8 Amy Carmichael, *Edges of His Ways: Selections for Daily Reading* (Fort Washington, PA: Christian Literature Crusade, 1955), 113.

> he does feel like it? Not at all. When we feel least like praying is the time when we most need to pray. We should wait quietly before God and tell Him how cold and prayerless our hearts are, and look up to Him and trust Him and expect Him to send the Holy Spirit to warm our hearts and draw them out in prayer. It will not be long before the glow of the Spirit's presence will fill our hearts, and we will begin to pray with freedom, directness, earnestness and power. Many of the most blessed seasons of prayer I have ever known have begun with a feeling of utter deadness and prayerlessness; but in my helplessness and coldness I have cast myself upon God, and looked to Him to send His Holy Spirit to teach me to pray, and He has done it.[9]

Torrey's teaching is a good reminder that if we find ourselves frustrated or stuck, the answer is not to stop praying. Rather, we should recognize that God is with us and *keep praying*. Even if our prayer is just, "Lord, help me pray."

Pray with Faith

Prayer is a wonderful privilege from our Father in heaven, and all disciples should seriously pursue a stronger, more faith-filled prayer life. I encourage you to do a study of the topic of prayer in the Bible and also recommend that you read at least one or two respected books on prayer. A classic, this one focusing more on growing in faith, is *George Müller: Delighted in God* by Roger Steer.

Most of all, though, *pray*. We learn to pray by praying. And prayer really is our lifeline to the Creator of the universe.

---

9 R. A. Torrey, *How to Pray* (Old Tappan, NJ: Fleming H. Revell, 1900), 59–60.

Questions to Ponder

1. How confident are you that God is willing to answer your prayers?
2. Why is faith so foundational to a disciple's prayer experience?
3. How does our view of God influence our expectation that He will grant our requests?
4. Several passages of Scripture make unwavering promises about God's intention to grant our prayer requests (John 14:12–14; 15:7; 1 John 5:14–15). In light of these Scriptures, how would you explain the relationship between God's will and His granting us what we ask for?
5. Describe Jesus' teaching that perseverance is a necessary part of our prayer life. What are some discouragements or encouragements to persevering in prayer?

9

Forgiving Others

Forgive us our debts, as we also have forgiven our debtors.

Matthew 6:12

Immediately after the Lord's (or Disciples') Prayer, Jesus gives an addendum of sorts on forgiveness. His selecting this one theme out of the entire prayer sends a significant message. As if to underline His teaching in red, He says, "For if you forgive others their trespasses, your heavenly Father will also forgive you, but if you do not forgive others their trespasses, neither will your Father forgive your trespasses" (Matt. 6:14–15).

What strong words! They signal that forgiveness will be a major issue for us in our lives of discipleship.

If it were possible, Jesus later uses even stronger words. In response to Peter's question about how often believers must forgive other believers (Matt. 18:21–35), Jesus tells a story of a servant who was forgiven an enormous debt by his master. That servant, however, refused to forgive a fellow servant who owed him a small amount by comparison. Jesus continues:

> [The servant's] master summoned him and said to him, "You wicked servant! I forgave you all that debt because you pleaded with me. And should not you have had mercy on your fellow servant, as I had mercy on you?" And in anger his master delivered him to the jailers, until he should pay all his debt. *So also my*

> *heavenly Father will do to every one of you, if you do not forgive your brother from your heart.* (Matt. 18:32–35, my emphasis)

This is a very sobering statement, and all the more so because the context is a relationship with a fellow believer (vv. 21–22). Being delivered to the jailers is a terrifying prospect in view of the fact that the Greek word means "torturers."[1] The idea is that God will impose severe discipline on any believer who refuses to forgive another believer from his or her heart. The inner torment of a bitter, unforgiving heart, which grieves the Holy Spirit, is a common example of such discipline and is a heavy burden to bear. Whatever form God's discipline takes, we must remember that it is corrective and redemptive, intended to bring the sinner back to God.

At first glance, this severe discipline may seem draconian. But consider: to offer forgiveness seems relatively painless when it involves a minor offense—but a major offense can be a very different story. Forgiveness of a spouse who commits adultery or of a rapist who violated a woman[2] or of a close friend who has betrayed us is really difficult. Deep wounds feel much more difficult to deal with and often take longer to resolve. Sooner or later, a deep wound may come our way, and it is essential to know that refusing to forgive is not an option.

For instance, a pastor I know discovered that his wife, the mother of their four children, was having an affair. The news devastated him and left him disoriented. Despite his pleas to repent, she continued the affair.

The pastor's spiritual mentor urged him to remember that, as a disciple of Jesus, he was called to forgive her and harbor no bitterness toward her. "You must not speak ill of her to your children," the man added. The pastor found none of this easy, but by God's grace he did forgive her and refused to harbor any ill will toward her—initially, as a sheer act of

---

1 Although Jewish jailers didn't practice torture, Roman jailers did.

2 It is important to note that in cases such as rape or abuse, it is often not safe or wise to forgive perpetrators in person, or to communicate or try to restore the relationship in person. Nor does forgiveness preclude bringing a perpetrator to legal justice.

the will. God blessed his obedience and sustained him and his children through the ordeal and blessed their lives in the years following, though his wife refused to repent, and they divorced. This betrayal was indeed a major offense, and the process of forgiving was painful.

One of the most powerful stories of forgiveness I have ever heard came from Corrie ten Boom, a follower of Jesus who endured the horrors of World War II. She and her godly family lived in Holland and, despite the Nazi occupation, sought to hide Jewish people. The Gestapo discovered their activities, arrested them, and sent them all to concentration camps. All died there, except for Corrie. Her story of forgiveness, hard as it was, demonstrates the main lessons we all need to learn if we are to deal with the difficult issues of forgiveness we face.

The story is found in her book, *The Hiding Place*, in which Corrie ten Boom recounted her agonizing struggle to forgive a guard who worked at the concentration camp where she was imprisoned and her sister, Betsie, died.[3]

> It was in a church in Munich that I saw him, a balding heavyset man in a gray overcoat, a brown felt hat clutched between his hands. People were filing out of the basement room where I had just spoken, moving along the rows of wooden chairs to the door at the rear.
>
> It was 1947 and I had come from Holland to defeated Germany with the message that God forgives.
>
> It was the truth they needed most to hear in that bitter, bombed-out land, and I gave them my favorite mental picture. Maybe because the sea is never far from a Hollander's mind, I liked to think that that's where forgiven sins were thrown.
>
> "When we confess our sins," I said, "God casts them into the deepest ocean, gone forever."

---

3 This excerpt used by permission of Chosen Books LLC, Mount Kisco, NY. From *The Hiding Place* by Corrie ten Boom with John and Elizabeth Sherrill, copyright 1971.

The solemn faces stared back at me, not quite daring to believe. There were never questions after a talk in Germany in 1947. People stood up in silence, in silence collected their wraps, in silence left the room.

And that's when I saw him, working his way forward against the others. One moment I saw the overcoat and the brown hat; the next, a blue uniform and a visored cap with its skull and crossbones.

It came back with a rush: the huge room with its harsh overhead lights, the pathetic pile of dresses and shoes in the center of the floor, the shame of walking naked past this man. I could see my sister's frail form ahead of me, ribs sharp beneath the parchment skin. Betsie, how thin you were!

Betsie and I had been arrested for concealing Jews in our home during the Nazi occupation of Holland; this man had been a guard at Ravensbrück concentration camp where we were sent.

Now he was in front of me, hand thrust out: "A fine message, fräulein! How good it is to know that, as you say, all our sins are at the bottom of the sea!"

And I, who had spoken so glibly of forgiveness, fumbled in my pocketbook rather than take that hand. He would not remember me, of course—how could he remember one prisoner among those thousands of women?

But I remembered him and the leather crop swinging from his belt. It was the first time since my release that I had been face to face with one of my captors, and my blood seemed to freeze.

"You mentioned Ravensbrück in your talk," he was saying. "I was a guard in there." No, he did not remember me.

"But since that time," he went on, "I have become a Christian. I know that God has forgiven me for the cruel things I did there, but I would like to hear it from your lips as well. Fräulein"—again the hand came out—"will you forgive me?"

And I stood there—I whose sins had every day to be forgiven—and could not. Betsie had died in that place—could he erase her slow, terrible death simply for the asking?

It could not have been many seconds that he stood there, hand held out, but to me it seemed hours as I wrestled with the most difficult thing I had ever had to do.

For I had to do it—I knew that. The message that God forgives has a prior condition: that we forgive those who have injured us. "If you do not forgive men their trespasses," Jesus says, "neither will your Father in heaven forgive your trespasses."

I knew it not only as a commandment of God, but as a daily experience. Since the end of the war, I had had a home in Holland for victims of Nazi brutality.

Those who were able to forgive their former enemies were able also to return to the outside world and rebuild their lives, no matter what the physical scars. Those who nursed their bitterness remained invalids. It was as simple and as horrible as that.

And still I stood there with the coldness clutching my heart. But forgiveness is not an emotion—I knew that too. Forgiveness is an act of the will, and the will can function regardless of the temperature of the heart.

"Jesus, help me!" I prayed silently. "I can lift my hand. I can do that much. You supply the feeling."

And so woodenly, mechanically, I thrust my hand into the one stretched out to me. And as I did, an incredible thing took place. The current started in my shoulder, raced down my arm, sprang into our joined hands. And then this healing warmth seemed to flood my whole being, bringing tears to my eyes.

"I forgive you, brother!" I cried. "With all my heart!"

For a long moment we grasped each other's hands, the former guard and the former prisoner. I had never known God's love so intensely as I did then.

And having thus learned to forgive in this hardest of situations, I never again had difficulty in forgiving: I wish I could say it! I wish I could say that merciful and charitable thoughts just naturally flowed from me from then on. But they didn't.

If there's one thing I've learned at 80 years of age, it's that I can't store up good feelings and behavior—but only draw them fresh from God each day.

Maybe I'm glad it's that way. For every time I go to Him, He teaches me something else. I recall the time, some 15 years ago, when some Christian friends whom I loved and trusted did something which hurt me.

You would have thought that, having forgiven the Nazi guard, this would have been child's play. It wasn't. For weeks I seethed inside. But at last I asked God again to work His miracle in me. And again it happened: first the cold-blooded decision, then the flood of joy and peace.

I had forgiven my friends; I was restored to my Father.

Then, why was I suddenly awake in the middle of the night, hashing over the whole affair again? My friends! I thought. People I loved! If it had been strangers, I wouldn't have minded so.

I sat up and switched on the light. "Father, I thought it was all forgiven! Please help me do it!"

But the next night I woke up again. They'd talked so sweetly too! Never a hint of what they were planning. "Father!" I cried in alarm. "Help me!"

His help came in the form of a kindly Lutheran pastor to whom I confessed my failure after two sleepless weeks.

"Up in that church tower," he said, nodding out the window, "is a bell which is rung by pulling on a rope. But you know what? After the sexton lets go of the rope, the bell keeps on swinging. First ding then dong. Slower and slower until there's a final dong and it stops.

"I believe the same thing is true of forgiveness. When we forgive someone, we take our hand off the rope. But if we've been tugging at our grievances for a long time, we mustn't be surprised if the old angry thoughts keep coming for a while. They're just the ding-dongs of the old bell slowing down."

And so it proved to be. There were a few more midnight reverberations, a couple of dings when the subject came up in my conversation. But the force—which was my willingness in the matter—had gone out of them. They came less and less often and at last stopped altogether.

And so I discovered another secret of forgiveness: that we can trust God not only above our emotions, but also above our thoughts.

And still He had more to teach me, even in this single episode. Because many years later, in 1970, an American with whom I had shared the ding-dong principle came to visit me in Holland and met the people involved. "Aren't those the friends who let you down?" he asked as they left my apartment.

"Yes," I said a little smugly. "You can see it's all forgiven."

"By you, yes," he said. "But what about them? Have they accepted your forgiveness?"

"They say there's nothing to forgive! They deny it ever happened. But I can prove it!" I went eagerly to my desk. "I have it in black and white! I saved all their letters and I can show you where—"

> "Corrie!" My friend slipped his arm through mine and gently closed the drawer. "Aren't you the one whose sins are at the bottom of the sea? And are the sins of your friends etched in black and white?"
>
> For an anguishing moment I could not find my voice. "Lord Jesus," I whispered at last, "who takes all my sins away, forgive me for preserving all these years the evidence against others! Give me grace to burn all the blacks and whites as a sweet-smelling sacrifice to Your glory."
>
> I did not go to sleep that night until I had gone through my desk and pulled out those letters—curling now with age—and fed them all into my little coal-burning grate. As the flames leaped and glowed, so did my heart.
>
> "Forgive us our trespasses," Jesus taught us to pray, "as we forgive those who trespass against us." In the ashes of those letters I was seeing yet another facet of His mercy. What more He would teach me about forgiveness in the days ahead I didn't know, but tonight's was good news enough.
>
> When we bring our sins to Jesus, He not only forgives them, He makes them as if they had never been.

Corrie ten Boom is a powerful example of a disciple of Jesus Christ who paid a high price for her faithfulness to Him and later went on to have a fruitful worldwide ministry. Forgiveness was essential to her experiencing God's blessing in such a remarkable way. And it is essential for you and me if we are to experience all that God has for us. Her book, *The Hiding Place*, and the 1975 movie by the same title (directed by James F. Collier) will inspire and encourage anyone wanting to follow Jesus.

Questions to Ponder

1. Why do you think Jesus placed so much emphasis on forgiving others when they wrong us?
2. What is the relationship between God's forgiveness of us and our forgiveness of others?
3. How do you react to the story about the pastor forgiving his wife? To the Corrie ten Boom story?
4. As you were reading this chapter or spending time with God in prayer, did someone come to mind whom you need to forgive? If so, what action will you take?
5. Do you know someone who is struggling to forgive an offense? How can you support that person in seeking to forgive?

10

Meditating on God's Word

On the glorious splendor of your majesty,
and on your wondrous works,
I will meditate.
Psalm 145:5

As we have seen in the chapters above, God uses His Word as a major instrument of our transformation. This is why serious believers read and study the Bible and regularly listen to solid Bible teaching. These days, however, far fewer *meditate* on the Bible, even though previous generations emphasized meditation as a vital practice for maturing in the Christian life.

I have read and studied the Scriptures daily since my conversion in 1970, but only in recent years have I learned to meditate on them. Had I learned this earlier, I could have grown much deeper and stronger in the Lord than I have thus far. Knowing about God intellectually is not the same as knowing God personally; we need both. My experience with reading the Bible illustrates the fact that, as theologian Robert Saucy notes:

> *For the Word to have a transformative effect in our life, it must reach the depth of the heart and touch our whole person. Knowing it in our mind is not enough. …*

> Spiritual transformation does indeed come from knowing God through his Word, but the knowledge is a personal experiential knowledge. …
>
> Change comes only when the truth of Scripture is truly heard in the biblical sense of "hear" or "heed." …
>
> According to Scripture, the "hearing" that receives the Word of God into the heart does not come simply through reading or even studying the Word but through *meditating* on it.[1]

Many Bible-believing Christians I have known and helped to grow as disciples of Jesus have, like me, neglected meditation. But that doesn't have to be true of you if you will learn to meditate on God's Word even now!

If you have tried in the past to learn to meditate and not found it helpful, consider this true story. In the mid-1800s, Rufus Upchurch Darby joined many others in the Colorado Gold Rush. He staked a claim, began mining, and found gold. But before long, the gold vein disappeared. Darby became discouraged and sold his equipment to someone else. That person later discovered that the gold vein had simply shifted—just three feet from where Darby stopped digging. This illustrates something true for everyone who wants to learn to meditate: it takes perseverance. Meditation isn't learned quickly, nor are its riches harvested right away. It takes time. But with perseverance comes success.

Or consider this true story. Pastor Hoffmann is a gifted minister with a doctorate from Oxford University, but he felt something was missing and longed for greater intimacy with Christ. In the course of his times spent with a spiritual mentor, it became evident that while he regularly read and studied Scripture, he spent little time meditating on it. His mentor suggested a particular book on the subject, which he immediately began to read and ponder. Over the months that fol-

---

1 Robert Saucy, *Minding the Heart: The Way of Spiritual Transformation* (Grand Rapids, MI: Kregel Publications, 2013), 147–149. Emphasis original.

lowed, his intimacy with the Lord began to deepen, and his ministry has become more vibrant and fruitful. He now sees meditation as a vital part of the Christian life he had been neglecting.

Throughout history, godly leaders have testified to the transforming effects of meditation. Consider a beautiful description by Thomas Brooks, a seventeenth-century church leader:

> Remember that it is not hasty reading but serious meditation on holy and heavenly truths that makes them prove sweet and profitable to the soul. It is not the mere touching of the flower by the bee that gathers honey, but her abiding for a time on the flower that draws out the sweet. It is not he that reads most but he that meditates most that will prove to be the choicest, sweetest, wisest and strongest Christian.[2]

The examples and quotations above give us a glimpse of the power of meditating on God's Word. But what do we mean by "meditating"?

What Is Biblical Meditation?

In the Old Testament, there are two Hebrew words that are typically translated with the English word "meditate." One word (*hagah*) suggests a low-pitched murmuring sound (see Joshua 1:8, "you shall meditate … day and night"). The other (*siyach*) more commonly means to be taken up or absorbed with something (Psalm 77:6, "let me meditate in my heart"). Considering these two terms in tandem, we get the idea of pondering, carefully reflecting on a biblical word, verse, or story in one's mind, and quietly and repeatedly vocalizing it until it becomes a lens through which we see and live our lives. Memorizing the text is a great aid to the process of meditation.

Christian meditation focuses on God's Word (Ps. 1:1–2), seeing through it the glorious splendor of His majesty and His wondrous works and ways (Ps. 145:5–6), especially in and through Jesus, His

2 Thomas Brooks, *Precious Remedies against Satan's Devices* (Carlisle, PA: Banner of Truth, 2011), 21.

Son. Meditation shapes both the inner life and outward behavior. J. I. Packer describes it this simple way:

> Meditation is the activity of calling to mind, and thinking over, and dwelling on, and applying to oneself, the various things that one knows about the works and ways and purposes and promises of God ... It is an activity of holy thought, consciously performed in the presence of God, under the eye of God, by the help of God, as a means of communion with God.[3]

Thus, meditation is a *devotional* practice that we engage in with God's help to better know Him and to enjoy closer communion Him.

Meditation differs from formal, analytical study of the Bible; we must not confuse the two. "Meditation and study differ," said the Puritan preacher Thomas Watson. He further explained:

> Study is a work of the brain, meditation of the heart; study sets the attention on work, meditation sets the affection on work. Study is the finding out of a truth, meditation is the spiritual improvement of a truth; the one searches for the vein of gold, the other digs out the gold. Study is like a winter sun that has little warmth and influence: meditation leaves one in a holy frame: it melts the heart when it is frozen, and makes it drop into tears of love.[4]

Watson was keen to encourage disciples of Jesus to let their reading of Scripture not only inform them but inflame them through meditation. Although study can be a helpful preparation for meditation on a truth, it is not a substitute. He goes on to say:

> Without meditation the truth will not stay with us; the heart is hard and the memory slippery, and without meditation all is lost; meditation imprints and fastens a truth in the mind.

3 J. I. Packer, *Knowing God* (Downers Grove, IL: InterVarsity Press, 1973), 23.

4 Thomas Watson, *A Christian on the Mount* (Prescott, 1862), V.1.

> Without meditation the truths which we know will never affect our hearts. How can the word be wrought in the heart unless it be wrought in by meditation? As a hammer drives a nail to the head, so meditation drives a truth to the heart. Without meditation, the word preached may increase notion [knowledge], not affection. Meditation fetcheth life in a truth. There are many truths which lie, as it were, in the heart dead, which when we meditate upon, begin to have light and heat in them."[5]

We should hasten to say that biblical meditation is not related to New Age or Eastern meditation, fear of which has caused some believers to avoid the practice altogether. The following explanation from theologian Peter Toon illustrates the great difference between Eastern and biblical meditation:

> The simplest way to highlight the difference is to say that for the one, meditation is an inner journey to find the centre of one's being, while for the other, it is the concentration of the mind/heart upon an external Revelation. For the one, revelation/insight/illumination occurs when the inmost self (which is also the ultimate Self, the one final Reality) is reached by the journey into the soul, while for the other, it comes as a result of encounter with God in and through his objective Revelation, to which Holy Scripture witnesses.[6]

We should avoid Eastern meditation, whether Hindu, Buddhist, Transcendental, or various other forms of New Age meditation. But we should fully embrace biblical meditation, described above, as a valuable means of knowing God more intimately, growing in grace, becoming more Christlike, and fulfilling God's purposes for our lives.

---

5 Watson, *Christian on the Mount*, VII.2.

6 Peter Toon, *Meditating as a Christian: Waiting upon God* (London: HarperCollins, 1991), 18–19.

What Does the Bible Say about Meditation?

The Bible often urges God's people to meditate.

When God commissioned Joshua to lead the Israelites into the Promised Land, the Lord said, "This Book of the Law shall not depart from your mouth, but you shall *meditate on it day and night*, so that you may be careful to do according to all that is written in it. For then you will make your way prosperous, and then you will have good success" (Josh. 1:8; my emphasis).

For Joshua to succeed in what God had called him to do, he needed to immerse himself in God's Word and faithfully put it into practice. This helped him grow in the knowledge of God, through which he experienced divine enablement. This ancient truth applies as much to us today as it did to Joshua then. As James tells us, "Be doers of the word, and not hearers only, deceiving yourselves" (James 1:22). Meditation will help us succeed at whatever God has called us to do and to rest in Him when our progress seems scant.

The theme of meditation occurs often in the book of Psalms, which begins with Psalm 1 declaring the blessedness of the one "who walks not in the counsel of the wicked … but his delight is in the law of the Lord, and on his law he meditates day and night. He is like a tree planted by streams of water that yields its fruit in its season, and its leaf does not wither. In all that he does, he prospers" (vv. 1–3). This paints a picture of someone devoted to God who delights in saturating himself in God's Word and applying it in daily life, which results in a life of fruitfulness. Such a person prospers in whatever God has appointed him or her to do.

Psalm 119 extols God's Word and repeatedly refers to meditation (see, for example, vv. 6, 11, 15–16, and many more). In Psalm 145:5, David highlights the specific points of meditation: "On the glorious splendor of your majesty, and on your wondrous works, I will meditate."

Jesus saturated Himself in Scripture and constantly quoted it. He illustrates for us the vital importance of meditating on God's Word in preparation to succeed in fulfilling God's purposes. We see a similar kind of saturation in Scripture in the life of the apostle Paul, who quoted Scripture constantly in his epistles and encouraged believers to "let the word of Christ dwell in you *richly*" (Col. 3:16, my emphasis).

A careful study of how Jesus and Paul used Scripture reveals that they had not simply read, or even memorized, scattered Bible verses as some believers do today. Rather, they had gone beyond casual reading to meditate deeply on the meaning of these verses in context. That treasury of truth in their hearts enabled them to use God's Word in an accurate and effective way in whatever situations they encountered.

We need such a Spirit-empowered, solid, and ready grasp of God's Word if we are to be transformed and successfully navigate life in a fallen world, where every day our own flesh and the schemes and temptations of the devil challenge us. Meditation provides us with essential resources for a wise and godly life, enabling us to "above all else, guard your heart, for everything you do flows from it" (Prov. 4:23 NIV). More importantly, it helps us to know God more intimately and enjoy communion with the Father, Son, and Holy Spirit. Failure to meditate on God's Word, to learn from and commune with Him, leaves our hearts unguarded, spiritually impoverished, and shallow. No amount of knowledge *about* God can make up for lack of intimacy *with* God.

How Do We Learn to Meditate?

The Bible gives no hint that meditation requires instruction by gurus or utilizing special techniques such as controlling one's breathing, repeating mantras, or descending inward. Rather, the Bible pictures a straightforward activity readily accessible to every believer.

Although Scripture does not give any specific instructions or models to guide us, the Hebrew words for meditation, along with Packer's definition above, give us enough to find our way into the practice.

Below I describe two similar but slightly different approaches to biblical meditation recommended by Bible-believing, evangelical leaders. These are not intended as formulas but as examples of methods that others have found helpful. George Müller gives a simple, less structured account of how he learned to meditate, with examples of its positive impact. J. I. Packer describes an adapted version of a slightly more structured approach used since ancient times called *lectio divina* (divine reading).

Finding Nourishment in the Word

George Müller (1805–1898) was a man of prayer who founded over one hundred schools for Christian education and provided for the care of over ten thousand orphans during his lifetime. Müller's approach to meditation is less structured than Packer's adaptation of *lectio divina* and gives more attention to the affective dimension of the practice, illustrating the variety that is possible. In 1841, he reported a transformation in his understanding and practice of meditating on God's Word:

> While I was staying at Nailsworth … I saw more clearly than ever that the first great and primary business to which I ought to attend every day was to have my soul happy in the Lord. The first thing to be concerned about was not how much I might serve the Lord, how I might glorify the Lord; but how I might get my soul into a happy state and how my inner man might be nourished.
>
> Before this time my practice had been … to give myself to prayer, after having dressed in the morning. Now I saw that the most important thing I had to do was to give myself to the reading of the Word of God and to meditation on it, that thus my heart might be comforted, encouraged, warned, reproved, instructed; and that thus, whilst meditating, my heart might be brought into experiential communion with the Lord. I began

therefore to meditate on the New Testament, from the beginning, early in the morning. The first thing I did, after having asked in a few words the Lord's blessing upon His precious Word, was to begin to meditate on the Word of God; searching, as it were, into every verse, to get blessing out of it ... for the sake of obtaining food for my own soul. The result I have found to be almost invariably this, that after a very few minutes my soul has been led to confession, or to thanksgiving, or to intercession, or to supplication; so that though I did not, as it were, give myself to prayer, but to meditation, yet it turned almost immediately more or less into prayer.

When thus I have been for awhile making confession, or intercession, or supplication, or have given thanks, I go on to the next words or verse, turning all, as I go on, into prayer for myself or others, as the Word may lead to it; but still continually keeping before me, that food for my own soul is the object of my meditation. The result of this is, that there is always a good deal of confession, thanksgiving, supplication, or intercession mingled with my meditation, and that my inner man almost invariably is even sensibly nourished and strengthened and that by breakfast time, with rare exceptions, I am in a peaceful if not happy state of heart.

For my heart being nourished by the truth, being brought into experiential fellowship with God, I speak to my Father, and to my Friend (vile though I am, and unworthy of it!) about the things that He has brought before me in His precious Word.

As the outward man is not fit for work for any length of time, except we take food, and as this is one of the first things we do in the morning, so it should be with the inner man. We should take food for that, as everyone must allow. Now what is the food for the inner man: not prayer, but the Word of God:

and here again not the simple reading of the Word of God, so that it only passes through our minds, just as water runs through a pipe, but considering what we read, pondering over it, and applying it to our hearts …

By the blessing of God I ascribe to this mode the help and strength which I have had from God to pass in peace through deeper trials in various ways than I had ever had before; and after having now above forty years tried this way, I can most fully, in the fear of God, commend it.[7]

Lectio Divina *(Modified Version)*

During the sixth century in what is modern-day Italy, the Christian monk Benedict of Nursia and his followers formalized a way of meditating on Scripture called *lectio divina* ("divine reading"). This approach to meditation and prayer helps believers focus attention on one section of God's Word, approach it from several angles, and pray with it to draw out God's message. Though there are several ways to engage in *lectio divina*, the steps outlined here show one way this approach to meditation on the Bible can be used by the Holy Spirit to illuminate your mind and help you absorb the meaning and application of a chosen text. Or, put differently, it is a way for God to address you personally through His Word. (Prior to practicing *lectio divina*, you may want to do some basic study of the chosen passage to ensure that you understand its meaning in context. This will help guard against untethered subjectivism.)

This description, first published in *Never Beyond Hope* by J. I. Packer and Carolyn Nystrom, places somewhat more emphasis on cognitive engagement than the typical practice of *lectio divina*:

---

7 George Müller, *Autobiography of George Müller*, ed. G. Fred Bergin (London: J. Nisbet, 1906), 152–154.

Silence

Take time to be silent: prepare to communicate with God as He expresses Himself to you in [the] passage of Scripture [before you]. After a period of quiet, ask God's help as you enter this session of meditative prayer.

Read

Read [a short passage of Scripture] aloud several times slowly. Allow its words and meanings to sink into your soul.

Meditate

Meditation is a little like chewing. It is slow and thorough. Write notes about what you see in this passage. Make connections between the various sections. Ask yourself, "What do these words from God say?" "What do they mean?" Place who you are and what you do next to this passage and ask God to examine you. Continue to write your findings. [Here Packer and Nystrom lean more toward study than meditation.]

Prayer

Pray using the passage as an outline for your prayer. Read the passage phrase-by-phrase, responding to God after each.

Contemplation

Wait in stillness once more. Ask that God bring to your mind any areas of your life that you need to shape more closely to His design as revealed in this passage. Contemplate God's love and power as it is revealed [in this portion of His Word].

Live It Out

What precisely ought you to be believing, thinking, and doing as a result of this passage? Make notes about how you hope to bring these words from Jesus into your current practice.[8]

As the "Live It Out" step suggests, the purpose of meditation on Scripture doesn't end when you stop meditating; what you glean in meditation should, in turn, influence your discipleship to Christ.

Recommendations for Your Own Meditation

Consider a few concluding suggestions to help you pursue your own meditation on God's Word.

Meditation is not inductive Bible study.

To summarize, though meditation involves reflection on the meaning of a passage, it is not inductive study or preparation for teaching or preaching. Meditation is a *devotional* reading of the Scripture with the goal of drawing closer to God and Jesus. While both approaches give attention to the meaning of the text and are valuable for spiritual growth, they are not the same. Study focuses much more on understanding the meaning of the text, while meditation focuses more on pondering the personal application of the text before God.

Meditation will have limited value unless pursued with right motivation.

David guides us here when he writes, "I remember the days of old; I meditate on all that you have done; I ponder the works of your hands. I stretch out my hands to you, *my soul thirsts for you* like a parched land" (Ps. 143:5–6; my emphasis). This psalm reveals that David's heart thirsted for God. He had a strong desire for close communion

8 J. I. Packer and Carolyn Nystrom, *Never Beyond Hope: How God Touches & Uses Imperfect People* (Downers Grove, IL: InterVarsity Press, 2000), 134–135.

with God through His Word. If we do not share that orientation, we can ask God to make it so.

Meditation encourages communion with God as mediated by the Holy Spirit's inward illumination of the Word.

Although communion with God through His Word involves focused thought, prayer for the Spirit's help is a vital part of the practice. Some days you may experience an elevation of feelings; other times, you won't. Remember that one's feelings cannot measure the depth or intensity of one's communion with God.

It takes time to reap the benefits of meditation.

Look up the biblical passages that speak of meditation and ask God to help you see its importance and strengthen your desire to practice it. Then discipline yourself to stick with it over time to gain its enormous benefits. You may also find it helpful to talk with other Christians who meditate regularly on God's Word in order to learn about their approaches, experiences, and motivations.

Profitable meditation requires waiting on God.

Blaise Pascal observed that "all the troubles of life come upon us because we refuse to sit quietly for a while each day in our rooms."[9] In this, he echoed David, who said, "For God alone, O my soul, wait in silence, for my hope is from him" (Ps. 62:5). Meditation requires a measure of discipline to sit quietly before God in silent worship, but it yields blessings not available in any other way.

Before you begin meditation proper, it can be helpful to first quiet your heart in the presence of God and focus your attention on Him, remembering that we live *coram deo*, that is, before the face of God (Ps.

---

9 Blaise Pascal, *Pensees* #139, trans. W. F. Trotter (New York: The Modern Library, 1941), 48. The quote cited above is a very common paraphrase of the original wording: "I have discovered that all the unhappiness of men arises from one single fact, that they cannot stay quietly in their own chamber."

56:13). The words of teacher and pastor Andrew Murray give us helpful guidance in preparing to meditate:

> Take time to be separate from all friends and all duties, all cares and all joys; time to be still and silent before God. Take time not only to secure stillness from man and the world, but from self and its energy. Let the Word and prayer be very precious; but remember, even these may hinder the quiet waiting. The activity of the mind in studying the Word, or giving expression to its thoughts in prayer, the activity of the heart, with its desires and hopes and fears, may so engage us that we do not come to the still waiting on the All-glorious One. Though at first it may appear difficult to know how thus quietly to wait, with the activities of the mind and heart for a time subdued, every effort after it will be rewarded; we shall find that it grows upon us, and a little season of silent worship will bring a peace and a rest that give a blessing not only in prayer, but all the day.[10]

Don't let busyness stop you.

For many of us, busyness hinders our ability to meditate. In today's fast-paced, stress-filled, high-pressure world, life is hectic; time is at a premium. Meditation takes time out of our already overloaded schedule. But as pastoral writer A. W. Tozer wisely said,

> We Christians must simplify our lives or lose untold treasures on earth and in eternity. Modern civilization is so complex as to make the devotional life all but impossible. It wears us out by multiplying distractions and beats us down by destroying our solitude, where otherwise we might drink and renew our

10 Andrew Murray, as quoted in *Joy and Strength*, ed. Mary Tileston (New York: Grosset & Dunlap, 1901), 41.

> strength before going out to face the world again. The need for solitude and quietness was never greater than it is today.[11]

The busyness of our lives isn't really a reason *not* to meditate; actually, it's one of the main reasons we should! Finding time to meditate means *making* time to meditate and setting ourselves apart from the pressing needs of the day so that we do not feel rushed, hurrying to move on to the next thing.

Here are a few practical steps to guide your time of meditation.

- Find a quiet place where you will not feel distracted. Allow fifteen to twenty minutes for meditating.
- Bring your Bible, a notebook, and a pen. Record important insights if they come; jot down any tasks or memories that pop into your mind and may distract you.
- To keep from becoming drowsy, avoid beds, overstuffed chairs, or sofas; sit in a chair with an upright back.
- Select your text from your daily Scripture reading or a passage that speaks to an important need or concern in your life.
- Select anywhere from one verse to several, or possibly a brief parable or story of Jesus.
- Open your time with prayer and ask God to meet you.
- If you have not tried meditation before, start small, perhaps one time a week, and live with one text for the whole week, recalling and pondering it periodically.
- Most people find it helpful to memorize the text and read it aloud several times; this ancient practice is still widely used today.
- Read the selected verses several times, as noted above.
- Attend to anything that applies to your life and resolve to make whatever changes seem necessary.
- Conclude your meditation by giving thanks to God.

---

11 A. W. Tozer, *Of God and Men* (Harrisburg, PA: Christian Publications, 1960), 103.

The book *Meditating on the Word* by Dietrich Bonhoeffer has been a helpful guide to many people, as has Edmund Clowney's *Christian Meditation: What the Bible Teaches about Meditation and Spiritual Exercises.*

Questions to Ponder

1. Describe your exposure to and experience with the practice of meditation on Scripture. Are you inclined to appreciate or question the value of meditating on God's Word? Explain your answer.
2. List some benefits of consistently meditating on Scripture as mentioned in this chapter.
3. Compare and contrast biblical meditation and Eastern or New Age meditation.
4. Also compare and contrast biblical meditation and Bible study.
5. Name some of the challenges to practicing biblical meditation in our day. How will you begin to overcome these challenges?
6. Are you ready to set a time and place to begin learning to meditate on Scripture? If not now, when?

11

Pursuing Daily Communion with God

Draw near to God, and he will draw near to you.

James 4:8

God tells us that our communion with Him will grow and flourish as we intentionally seek and pursue Him—and He has given us several means by which to do so. Meditation, as discussed in the previous chapter, is one of these, but there are others. Through the diligent use of these means and the work of the Spirit, we can grow *much* closer to God—if we really desire to. A. W. Tozer said that "every man is as close to God as he wants to be."[1]

Generally speaking, God intends that we pursue communion with Him in the context of active engagement in a congregation of His redeemed people. This means following the example of believers in the early church, who "devoted themselves to the apostles' teaching and the fellowship, to the breaking of bread and the prayers" (Acts 2:42). God offers no substitute for regularly gathering to worship Him, sing His praises, listen attentively to the preaching of His Word, share our lives with one another, pray together, celebrate communion, and rejoice in the baptism of new believers.

1 A. W. Tozer, *That Incredible Christian: How Heaven's Children Live on Earth* (Harrisburg, PA: Christian Publications, 1964), 64.

Three of these corporate practices also have a private, personal dimension that we can experience by setting aside time each day to quietly read and reflect on God's Word, lift our prayers to Him, and give thanks and praise to Him for who He is and for His goodness to us. We can see believers seeking God daily as far back as the Psalms (see 5:3; 119:147), many of which were written around 1000 BC. We also see God urging His people to learn and love His Word in the Pentateuch (see Deuteronomy 6:4–9, for instance). And, as we've already noted, Jesus often took time to get away from others and spend time in prayer (Mark 1:35; Luke 5:16; 6:12), a pattern of engagement and withdrawal. Those who have known God most intimately have devoted themselves to prayer, worship, and meditation on His Word.

I think of "Trevor," a brilliant young philosophy professor and faithful follower of Jesus who often speaks to others about Christ. In the course of our times of spiritual counsel, he expressed a desire to draw closer to Christ. Further conversation indicated the need for a deeper and more consistent devotional life. He began to regularly read his New Testament (in Greek), savoring its richness, and soon found his prayer life growing fuller and more earnest, leading to deeper fellowship with Christ. No one who hungers and thirsts for Christ and seeks Him in His Word and prayer will be sent away empty!

And you don't need to read Greek to do this yourself!

Helpful Counsel for a Daily Time with God

Consider several helpful suggestions designed to aid you in developing your own daily time with God to know Him better and love Him more.

Set a specific time and place to meet with God each day.

Most people choose the early morning because they feel alert and can start the day with God before the busyness begins. But the morning doesn't work for everyone. God made both larks and owls, so learn which you are and operate accordingly. If you have a lot of responsibilities in the morning and thus will always feel rushed, choose another time that works best for you. Select a place that is familiar, quiet, comfortable, free of distractions, and regularly available. Do what you can to make entry into this space simple. Put your Bible, notebook, and pen in easy reach. Remove any obstacles that might prevent you from getting started or might distract you once you begin. This includes your cell phone; turn it off and put it in a different room.

Make your daily time with God a top priority.
Consider your devotional time a key part of putting God first in your life. As your loving Father, He wants to spend time with you and help you—and this is why He speaks to you through His Word. What could be more important in your life than meeting with God? Many years ago, I realized that putting God first each day meant praying and reading His Word before reading the newspaper. Listening to God before listening to man. That made a significant difference in the quality of my time with God. Today, it means spending time with God before checking my cell phone in the morning. This choice will require desire, commitment, discipline, and planning.

And what if your reading in the Bible becomes dry and prayer grows stale? That has happened to me many times over the years. Other believers report the same thing. Do not stop reading and praying! Continue on, telling God of your weariness and asking Him to reveal any hindrances and restore you. Seek advice and encouragement from others in your congregation. Our continuing faithfulness in arid times pleases God, who sees that we do not simply seek the gift of good feelings in our devotional exercises, but the Giver of good gifts—God Himself (James 1:17).

Other recommendations are more practical: for instance, make sure that you get adequate sleep so you can meet with the Lord while alert. Research has shown that, for optimal health, most adults need to sleep seven hours or more each night.[2] Attempts to operate on significantly less sleep will have a negative physical and mental impact, and for most people, this is not sustainable. It will also hinder your ability to pray, concentrate, and profit from reading Scripture.

Set a reasonable duration for your daily devotional time.

Although the Bible gives no directions here, you might start with twenty or thirty minutes a day, spending half of this time reading Scripture and half in prayer. Once that becomes an established pattern, you may want to try increasing to a longer period. Any expansion should grow out of a heartfelt desire for more time in Scripture and prayer, not out of a spirit of legalism, performance, or competition with others. Start from wherever you are, even if it's only five minutes a day. Then let your appetite increase. Let *God* increase your appetite.

Pick an approach that works for you.

Although there is no such thing as "the best approach to Bible reading and prayer," you may find it helpful to begin by reading the Bible, then praying, as George Müller did. Scripture teaches us truth about God, His works, His ways, ourselves, and the world, and thus can prepare our hearts and minds for fellowship with Him. When we prepare our hearts in this way, we will find that sometimes God highlights a truth in a way that brings special blessing and prompts us to offer specific prayers and praise. Others may find it more helpful to start with prayer, and in doing so prepare their hearts to receive the Word.

---

2 Eric Suni, "How Much Sleep Do You Need?" Sleep Foundation, July 11, 2025.

Before starting to read, ask God to illuminate your mind through the Holy Spirit so that you might rightly understand His Word and how it applies to your life.

As you prepare to read God's Word, make sure you have a clean heart. Confess any sins of which you are aware, and ask God's forgiveness (1 John 1:9). Unconfessed and unrepented sin will hinder your prayer (Ps. 66:18), so ask God to bring to mind anything that requires confession and repentance. You should also pray for God's illumination and guidance as you read. Psalm 119:17–19 is a good starting point if you don't have a prayer of your own.

When reading the Bible, slow is better than fast, and aloud is better than silent.

If you rush through your reading of Scripture, you will miss much of the benefit. Take time to ponder and reflect. Listen for what the Spirit may want to say to you, pausing to pray or praise or give thanks whenever appropriate. Reading aloud, the common practice of God's people until recent times, adds a second sensory channel and will enhance your reading. You may also want to explore listening to Scripture read aloud.

Pick a place in the Bible to read.

Where in the Bible should you read? Many people like to read straight through from beginning to end, moving ahead at a comfortable pace. This approach has a long history and also has the virtue of showing the big picture of Scripture. Others prefer to focus on areas that address a present need or interest, or perhaps a section such as the Gospels or the Epistles, or the Pentateuch or the Psalms. Still others take a less structured approach. Each approach has its place, depending on one's age, maturity, and present needs.

Many Bible reading plans[3] or study Bibles are available; you may want to find one that seems right for you and try it out. Whichever plan you choose, do not tie yourself down to completing it in one year unless you have ample time for reading each day. Otherwise, you can feel pressured to complete the daily portion and read it too fast, which can lead to a dry exercise of self-discipline with little spiritual benefit.

Meditate on what you read.

Reading the Bible without meditating on it can increase your knowledge but leave you with a shallow faith. As we saw in the previous chapter, Scripture places a strong emphasis on meditation—the prayerful, slow reading (ideally *aloud*) and pondering of selected Bible verses, passages, or stories. Through this practice, we gain deeper understanding and find ourselves increasingly transformed. Practicing meditation as part of your daily communion with God can be valuable if you have the time. But many people (for instance, those who typically have thirty minutes or less for reading the Word and praying) probably do not. In such cases, thoughtful reflection and pondering on a verse or two in the course of your reading is good option. Later, when you have a slightly longer period of time, you can do the kind of focused meditation described in Chapter 10.

To grow spiritually, apply whatever you learn from Scripture.

Approach reading God's Word with the settled intention of obeying whatever you discover to be His will. Failure to obey God leads to self-deception (James 1:22–25) and hardens your heart. Many people have found the following questions helpful to ask as they try to discern how to respond to what they read:

---

3 Reading through the Bible from start to finish is one option; another is the One-Year Bible reading plan of Robert Murray M'Cheyne, available free on the internet from a variety of sources. And there are many other plans.

- In this section of Scripture, what is God revealing about Himself—Father, Son, and Holy Spirit?
- What does God teach me about myself?
- What does God teach me about life in this world?
- What response do these verses require of me?

Be sure to have a notepad or journal and a pen handy to jot down any special insights (and any "to-do" items that come to mind, so they don't distract you).

Use a version of the Bible that you can easily understand, translated by scholars who believe in the full trustworthiness of the Scriptures.

Some people find it helpful to read one version that takes a more literal approach to translating the Scriptures (such as ESV or NASB) alongside another that takes a more dynamic-equivalent approach (such as NIV or NLT). Comparing the two can sometimes clarify the meaning of passages that are fuzzy to you. Also, you can find answers to many questions in the notes included in good study Bibles, such as the *ESV Study Bible*, the *NIV Study Bible, Fully Revised Edition*, and the *New Living Study Bible*. All are reliable and cover the main issues, but some have notes that are more practically helpful or spiritually insightful, so check them out to find the one that is best for you. If you aren't sure where to start, ask your pastor or a teacher at church.

Choose a specific approach to prayer.

Many people pray about whatever comes to mind, perhaps prompted by what they have just read or even personal concerns. While this can work in some cases, we should not neglect Jesus' teaching in the Disciples' Prayer (see Chapter 7). Ask Jesus to teach you to pray as you try this approach; doing so will put you into the Jesus School of Prayer.

Learning to pray this framework or pattern for prayer has greatly blessed God's people over the centuries.

Another helpful and simple approach is to pray the Scriptures. Simply turn the Bible's words into a prayer that you offer back to God. Many biblical passages are well suited to this approach, especially in the Psalms, Gospels, and Epistles. As mentioned above, Psalm 119:18 is a fitting prayer before you open God's Word: "Open my eyes, that I may behold wondrous things out of your law." Or James 4:17 could serve as the basis of a prayer for right understanding and right action. It reads, "So whoever knows the right thing to do and fails to do it, for him it is sin." This could become a prayer such as "Lord, show me the right thing to do," or "Lord, I know this is right; please give me the will and the power to do it." A book by Donald Whitney called *Praying the Bible* provides additional guidance for turning Scripture into prayer.

Record in a journal any insights you gain from your Bible reading and meditation.

This practice has a long history and has proven beneficial for some, though others have not felt drawn to it. While using a journal isn't necessary, you may want to give it a try. Writing things down can help crystallize and clarify your thoughts. If done regularly, taking notes (or recording audio notes) can also provide a record of milestones in your spiritual life, markers that enable you to see the pattern of God's dealings with you over time. You might also consider keeping a prayer list, which records the date of requests and answers. This can help you remember specific prayer concerns and build your faith as you see answers come. The use of a journal to nurture your spiritual life can take many forms; it doesn't require recording your inmost thoughts. Some people keep a jot list of theological questions or observations, or they reflect on the meaning of sermons they hear or Bible passages they read.

Remember that anything you do repeatedly can become routine and boring.

If you notice this happening, first, tell God, and ask Him to help you. Ask Him to show you what has gone wrong and to restore your hunger and thirst for Him. Also remember that sin will interrupt your fellowship with God and make your devotional times empty and hollow. Do you have any unconfessed sin, broken relationships, unforgiveness, or other hindrances? Pray Psalm 139:23–24, asking God to search you and show you what has gone off course.

Sometimes, of course, when God seems distant, we cannot find any reason except that He has chosen to remain silent with us for a time. In such cases, ask Him to help you learn any lessons He wants to teach you through His silence.

Because none of us is yet perfected, we can lose sight of God's grace and drift into a joyless legalism in our devotional lives.

This is not uncommon. If it happens to you, ponder anew God's love for you and how He has poured out His grace on you in salvation and call to mind the many other ways He has blessed you (Ps. 103:1–5). Remind yourself from time to time that prayer and Bible reading are not ends in themselves but means to an end. We read the Bible to personally know the One who spoke it. Sometimes we need to remind ourselves that knowing God is not simply intellectual but also experiential. We come to know Him more intimately through experience. He is not a thesis statement but a living Being.

Bible reading and prayer play a vital part in nurturing personal intimacy with the Father and the Son. At times, we may need to remind ourselves that neither our love for God nor our good works can earn His acceptance, because we can do nothing to increase or decrease His love for us. He calls us to holiness, but He loves us the same regardless of how well we are living the Christian life—even when we disappoint or seriously fail Him. God has made us acceptable to Himself through the atoning work of Jesus His Son, who took upon Himself at the cross the penalty for all our sins. God saves us by His grace alone, through faith in Jesus alone and His finished work on the cross alone. And He blesses us and makes us fruitful by that same grace.

Questions to Ponder

1. What do you think of A. W. Tozer's comment, "Every man is as close to God as he wants to be"?
2. Briefly discuss the one or two suggestions regarding a "devotional life" mentioned in this chapter that you would most like to integrate into your daily routines.
3. Describe some of the potential challenges to be aware of as we develop a daily devotional life. Have you experienced any of these in the past? How might you respond to these challenges when you encounter them in the future?
4. What have you found helpful in dealing with times of spiritual dryness or feelings of condemnation for an irregular pattern of devotional life? Are there any parts of Scripture that have become particularly meaningful to you during these times?
5. What steps do you need to take to have a more consistent and fruitful devotional life with God?

12

Becoming a Disciple-Maker

Go therefore and make disciples of all nations, baptizing them in the name of the Father and of the Son and of the Holy Spirit, teaching them to observe all that I have commanded you. And behold, I am with you always, to the end of the age.
Matthew 28:19–20

A major part of Jesus' work on earth was to make disciples and train them to carry on His work of making disciples and spreading God's kingdom. At the threshold of His departure from this world:

> Jesus came and said to them, "All authority in heaven and on earth has been given to me. Go therefore and make disciples of all nations, baptizing them in the name of the Father and of the Son and of the Holy Spirit, teaching them to observe all that I have commanded you. And behold, I am with you always, to the end of the age." (Matt. 28:18–20)

The disciples took Jesus' words to heart. As they went to the ends of the earth, they knew He was with them and was empowering them by His Spirit to have an extraordinary impact on the world of their day.

History records other people who were called to serve Christ in distant lands and saw extraordinary fruit in making disciples. Few know John Geddie today, but God used him in a remarkable way with dangerous islanders in the South Seas in the 1800s. A memorial raised in his honor reads: "In memory of Rev. John Geddie, D.D., born in Scotland 1815, minister in Prince Edward Island for seven years, missionary sent from Nova Scotia to Aneiteum for twenty-four years. When he landed in 1848, there were no Christians here, and when he left in 1872 there were no heathen."[1]

Even as He has called his church to spread the gospel to all nations, God calls relatively few of His children to serve Christ in faraway missions posts as these individuals did. Rather, He calls the vast majority of us to serve and glorify Him in the families, workplaces, and communities where we already live. But this requires the same obedience we see in those who are called to distant places, and it may require the same sacrifice.

One example of sacrifice from the last century is John Harper (1872–1912), a Scottish evangelist who sadly died in the sinking of the *Titanic* on April 15, 1912. Harper had been invited to serve as a guest preacher at The Moody Church in Chicago, Illinois, but did not survive the journey from Scotland. Erwin Lutzer, pastor emeritus of The Moody Church, gives the following account of Harper's final moments:

> John Harper, his sister, and his six-year-old daughter (his wife had died) found themselves on the great ship, the *Titanic*. Survivors later reported that as *Titanic* began to sink, Harper admonished people to be prepared to die. He made sure his sister and daughter were in a lifeboat even as he continued to share the Gospel with whoever would listen. And when he found himself in the icy water with a life jacket, floating near another man, Harper asked, "Are you saved?"
>
> "No, I'm not saved!" the desperate man replied.

---

1 Eugene Myers Harrison, *Blazing the Missionary Trail* (Chicago, IL: Scripture Press Book Division, 1949), 58. See also Craig Sheppard, "Who Was John Geddie?" Missionary Biographies Collection, *Ligonier Ministries* (learn.ligonier.org), accessed January 13, 2026.

> "Believe on the Lord Jesus Christ and you will be saved!" Harper shouted.
>
> One report says Harper, knowing he could not survive long in the icy water, took off his life jacket and threw it to another person with the words, "You need this more than I do!" Moments later, Harper disappeared beneath the water.[2]

A more recent extraordinary example of making disciples in the process of glorifying God in family, work, and community appears in the lives of "James" and "Cindy," a quiet, humble, unassuming couple. We met many years ago through a discipleship program at the C. S. Lewis Institute. James and Cindy were clearly a team; they loved each other and served God wherever they went. For James, that included a twenty-year career in the armed forces, followed by teaching at the United States Naval Academy, then cofounding and helping build a large, successful business; and for Cindy, a career in elementary education and raising four children who know and love the Lord, and nurturing all of her grandchildren, who have also grown up to know and love the Lord. All of this along with teaching women's Bible study groups.

Throughout their long marriage, James and Cindy have sought to serve others and help them grow as disciples of Jesus, through Officers' Christian Fellowship, local churches, and the C. S. Lewis Institute. As retirement age approached, they built a very large home on the family farm (comfortably accommodating thirty people) as a gathering place for their scattered children and grandchildren, and also as a retreat center for pastors and ministry leaders. Now in their eighties, they both lead weekly discipleship groups, James with men and Cindy with women from around the local area. They have always been generous stewards of God's blessings, and recently they placed their farm into an irrevocable trust and provided finances to ensure its continued use

---

2 Erwin W. Lutzer, "John Harper's Last Convert," *Moody Church Media* (www.moodymedia.org), 2012.

for family and for making disciples—even as they continue to carefully disperse their remaining assets to trusted ministries that are bearing fruit in God's kingdom. James and Cindy provide a good example of making disciples in the course of everyday work and family life.

Most Bible-believing Christians hold dear the command to "go … and make disciples of all nations" (Matt. 28:19), whether or not we personally travel to other nations. Most of us also assume that we understand what it means. But after many years of life in the church and in ministry, I have concluded that while some do, many do not.

As we explore the two phrases "go and make disciples" and "all nations," you can determine for yourself how well you grasp the full scope of their meaning.

Making Disciples

In the American evangelical church, the command to "go and make disciples" has for many decades been understood to mean "go and make converts." In other words, go out to evangelize nonbelievers and help them come to faith in Jesus Christ. *Gospel proclamation* is the primary focus.

This understanding is good, so far as it goes.

We definitely need to "go" and evangelize nonbelievers. Clearly, we must share the gospel message with the lost and help them come to faith in Christ. And clearly, we must encourage them to publicly affirm their faith by being baptized into the fellowship of the church.

But that isn't the end of the matter; in fact, it is just the beginning. The Great Commission doesn't stop with the command "Go therefore and make disciples …, baptizing them." It includes *gospel transformation* when it adds: "teaching them to observe [that is, to obey] all that I have commanded you."

Let's look at the Great Commission again. The Greek word we translate "disciple" is *mathetes*, which in Jesus' day meant a learner and adherent—that is, one who accepts the teaching of a master and follows him in daily life. It is the root of the main verb, *matheteuo*, which means "to make disciples," and appears as an imperative, a command. The three supporting participles—going, baptizing, and teaching—have imperative force and indicate different aspects of the multifaceted process of making disciples. "Going" indicates going out into one's world with the intention of sharing the gospel message with nonbelievers. "Baptizing" refers to baptizing those who profess faith in Christ into the community of disciples—the fellowship of the church. "Teaching" refers to the last and longest part of the discipleship process, teaching believers by word and deed to obey Jesus' teachings.

Thus, the phrase "teaching them to observe [obey] all that I have commanded you" expands the focus from gospel proclamation and membership in the community to *gospel transformation*, which lasts a lifetime! But unfortunately, this is where things often break down.

For various reasons, many churches and believers have neglected this part of Jesus' commission or have refocused the command from teaching disciples to obey the specific teachings of Jesus to general Christian education. To be sure, some in history have understood the command accurately and taken it seriously; but in many settings, it remains largely neglected or misapplied. When this happens, believers are not grounded in all that Jesus instructed as He taught His disciples how to obey and be transformed into Christlikeness. We lack basic training. As a result, many of us fare poorly in our battle with the world, the flesh, and the devil, like soldiers who have never received combat training.

"Wait," you say. "My church has a six-week new-member class and also a class on the basics of the faith." That's certainly helpful! But do these alone encompass what Jesus meant by "teach them to observe [obey] all that I have commanded you"? That is the question.

Discipleship for the Ages

Let's look at what Jesus meant by *all that I have commanded you*, as well as the outcome He intends from our obeying this command. Our Lord does not leave us to figure this out for ourselves.

We find *all that He commanded* in the Gospels—beginning with Matthew, which has five major teaching sections. As we noted in Chapter 4, Matthew actually appears to have been designed as a discipleship manual. In fact, from the early second century, "among all the New Testament writings and especially among the Gospels, Matthew seems to have been the only one to have had a normative role and to have created the climate of Christianity at large." And "it is a fact that mainstream Christianity was, from the early second century on, to a great extent Matthean Christianity."[3] So we should make Matthew one of our main resources for Jesus' teachings, and it is a good starting place as well.

We should not, however, limit "all that I commanded you" to Jesus' specific commands in Matthew, even though that is the primary context of the words of the Great Commission. The verb "commanded" (*entellomai*) in this context "has a more all-inclusive sense. Jesus is not pointing to particular commands but rather to the full explication of His life and ministry for disciples. All that Jesus commanded by word of mouth is included in His commands, whether they are teachings, proverbs, blessings, parables or prophecies. Indeed, all of Jesus' life is included."[4] Thus, when Jesus refers to "all I have commanded," He has in mind not just the Gospel of Matthew, but everything He taught during the three years He was with the disciples in person. For us today, that means His teachings as recorded in Matthew and the other Gospels, as well as His life.

---

3 R. T. France, *Matthew, Evangelist and Teacher* (Downers Grove, IL: InterVarsity Press, 1989), 20.

4 Michael J. Wilkins, *Matthew*, The NIV Application Commentary (Grand Rapids, MI: Zondervan, 2004), 957.

It is important to note that while the learners in view here are typically assumed to be new believers, the command applies to more mature believers as well, for we never learn all that there is to know about Jesus. And in any event, spiritual growth is not linear; throughout life, we need to circle back to certain things and learn them again at a deeper level. We never graduate from Jesus' school of discipleship; there is always more to learn and the potential for more growth.

Further, the learning Jesus commends is not simply a matter of mastering of facts, though surely that must happen. Rather, as we learn what Jesus taught, we must go on to internalize and put it into practice, for in biblical thinking, what we *do* is the real measure of what we *know*. Jesus' moral and ethical instructions, as well as His example, must become a practical guide to living, creating a life that bears fruit and glorifies God. Giving priority to the teaching of Jesus certainly does *not* minimize other parts of the Bible. In fact, it will send us back to the Old Testament, which He frequently quoted, and push us forward elsewhere in the New Testament as we seek further understanding. Only as we see the rest of the Bible through the lens of Jesus and His teaching can we read it aright.

How do we help other believers learn what Jesus taught? Jesus demonstrates the basic approach. He began by creating a community in the form of twelve disciples who wanted to follow and learn from Him. He initiated a process of discipleship with them that included large group teaching, small group processing, one-on-one counsel and guidance, and supervised on-the-job training in how to practice what they were learning in their daily lives. We can adapt these elements—some or all—into effective discipleship training programs today.

What goal or outcome did Jesus intend for this process? In a word, transformation. He wanted His followers to become like Him. "A disciple is not above his teacher, nor a servant above his master," He said. "It is enough for the disciple to be like his teacher and the servant like his master" (Matt. 10:24–25). As the disciples saw Jesus' example each day, grew to know and love Him increasingly and began to more fully understand and obey His teachings, they would become more like Him. But not instantly—it took time, and they made mistakes along the way. For them, discipleship was the work of a lifetime. And so it will be for us. A few weeks in a Christian basics class can provide a helpful start to this journey, but this is only a start).

One of Jesus' most noteworthy disciples, the apostle Paul, made Christ-centered transformation his lifelong work (though he never used the word "disciple"). "For no one can lay a foundation other than that which is laid, which is Jesus Christ" (1 Cor. 3:11). "Him we proclaim," he wrote of Jesus, "warning everyone and teaching everyone with all wisdom, that we may present everyone mature in Christ. For this I toil, struggling with all his energy that he powerfully works within me" (Col. 1:28–29). Paul was passionately devoted to discipling believers! To this end, Paul patiently labored with the Galatians "until Christ be formed in you," (Gal. 4:19). And as part of this process, the apostle frequently said to believers in his churches, "I urge you, then, to be imitators of me" (1 Cor. 4:16), and "be imitators of me, as I am of Christ" (1 Cor. 11:1), and "join in imitating me, and keep your eyes on those who walk according to the example you have in us" (Phil. 4:16). Paul urged people to follow him *as he followed Christ.* And he said this not because he was a narcissist, but because he knew from Jesus the importance of personal example in changing character. This is just as true today as it was then, which underscores our need to have faithful disciples of Jesus in our lives who reflect Him and influence us to become more like Him. Although he overstated his case, Albert Schweitzer made an important point when he said, "Example is not the main thing in influencing others. It is the only thing."[5] Though not the

---

5 Albert Schweitzer, *Brothers in Spirit: The Correspondence of Albert Schweitzer and William Larimer Mellon, Jr.* (Syracuse: Syracuse University Press, 1996), 18.

only thing, it is certainly a *major* thing, because becoming like Jesus is caught as well as taught.

Observing the disciple-making practices of Jesus and Paul can give us insight in how to develop disciples. In the church today, growing as a disciple requires regular Bible teaching from the pulpit and in the classroom. Biblical preaching, teaching, and pastoral counseling are major elements of the process of making disciples. But there is more, and that is the relational element. Learning in relationship involves meeting with a small group of other believers to develop friendships and to discuss and process the lessons taught. In addition, it requires more mature believers (disciplers) and less mature believers (disciples) to develop Christ-centered, growth-oriented friendships. In such a friendship, the less mature believer is mentored and coached about how to understand and apply the teachings of Jesus in his or her daily life.[6]

The maturation process begins with learning the teachings of Jesus, but it doesn't end there. It comes to fruition in practical application—when the truths learned by instruction become a part of the disciple's lived experience. The disciple becomes "a doer of the word, and not a hearer only" (James 1:22). And thus, little by little he or she becomes more like Jesus and eventually begins to disciple others as well.

In the early stage of the process, the discipler will take the disciple with him or her to observe ministry firsthand. In the next stage, the discipler will have the disciple help in the ministry. Then the roles switch, and the disciple take the lead, and the discipler will help. With continued growth, the disciple will be ready to go out on a mission taking the lead role while the discipler observes. The discipler must see this process as a labor of love, recognizing that it takes commitment and time. And the learning often goes both ways: the more mature believer may gain fresh perspective from listening to and teaching someone who is younger in the faith. Ongoing progress depends on a desire to

6 Once the person is grounded in the main teachings of Jesus, other areas of Scripture should be engaged.

grow, a teachable spirit, and a willingness to obey. This methodology can be used in a wide spectrum of activities, ranging from cleaning toilets and floors in the church building to personal witnessing to sharing the gospel in public venues and more.

Because of the time commitment, larger churches sometimes see this approach to disciple-making as impossible to provide. And they would be right, if it were only the *pastor's* job to work at making disciples. But if a pastor will start small, disciple a core of capable disciple-makers (ideally the elders and other church leaders), and then commission and coach them to disciple others in the congregation, who in turn make other disciples, over time even a large church can develop a culture of disciple-making. I know of several that are doing this, and Perimeter Church in the Atlanta area, which has about five thousand parishioners, is a good example. Such discipleship transforms everything it touches. But it cannot be done overnight. It takes time, and many pastors do not have a vision for the longer-term effort that is required. Hopefully, that will change.

The failure of many churches to teach, train, and nurture their members to maturity in Christ helps to explain why so many believers today seem so spiritually childish, entangled in the sins of the flesh, immersed in worldliness, and not much different from nonbelievers. Is it any wonder that the church appears neither credible nor attractive to the watching world? Surely this grieves God.

But just as surely, God will enable and empower *any* person or church that elevates disciple-making to the priority He gives it. He has already shown us the way in Scripture.

Of All Nations

Another phrase we must explore for disciple-making is "of all nations." This phrase spells out the scope of the disciple-making mandate. The English words "all nations" are a translation of the Greek phrase *panta ta ethne*. That last word, *ethne*, provides the root of the English word "ethnic." The idea here is of ethnic or people groups.

The Bible doesn't speak in terms of "races," because from the biblical perspective only one race exists: the human race. The Scriptures teach that all human beings originated from one couple, making them all part of the single human race. They have, however, differentiated into various ethnic groups (Gen. 1:26–28; Acts 17:26). Thus, when Jesus says "all nations," this means, "Make disciples from among all ethnic groups"—whether Africans, Asians, Caucasians, Latinos, or whatever other subgroups may exist. This vastly expands His earlier commission to go only "to the lost sheep of the house of Israel" (Matt. 10:6).

This all-inclusive command further fulfills God's promise to Abraham that "in you all families of the earth shall be blessed" (Gen. 12:3). The Jews of Jesus' day found this expansion to "all nations" very difficult to accept. They saw themselves as God's chosen people, which indeed they were, but unfortunately, they also looked down on all non-Jews. They typically despised and avoided Gentiles—especially Samaritans, who were of ethnically mixed ancestry and held heterodox beliefs.

Although Jesus focused His ministry almost exclusively on Jews, He did give hints of the coming commission to all ethnic groups through His interactions with Samaritans. For instance, on one occasion He rebuked James and John when they wanted to call down fire upon the Samaritans (Luke 9:51–56). On another, He confronted the Jews (and His disciples) with their own religious and ethnic pride by making the Good Samaritan the hero in His teaching about loving one's neighbor (Luke 10:25–37). He sent a clear message: Do not hate and try to destroy Samaritans, but rather love and win them! As recorded in John 4, Jesus also foreshadowed the coming Gentile mission by deliberately engaging a Samaritan woman in conversation and leading her to faith in Him as the Messiah.

How did the commission to make disciples from all ethnic groups unfold once Jesus returned to heaven? In the book of Acts, Jesus says, "But you will receive power when the Holy Spirit has come upon you, and you will be my witnesses in Jerusalem and in all Judea and Samaria, and to the end of the earth" (1:8). This is exactly what happens throughout Acts.

Peter, John, Stephen, and others preached the gospel around Jerusalem (Acts 2–7). Philip went to Samaria, where he preached Christ and saw many come to faith (8:4–8). An angel then sent him to explain the gospel to a high-ranking Ethiopian court official who was on his way back home after a visit to Jerusalem (8:26–38). That official carried the faith with him to Africa. From Acts 13 to the end of the book, we see Paul preaching the gospel to people of various ethnicities in the Roman world, from Antioch, through Asia Minor, to Greece and Rome.

Peter had a more difficult time grasping what seemed so clear to Paul. Even though Peter had received the Great Commission directly from the lips of Jesus, and even though he served as the leader of the apostles, he remained blind in certain areas. He felt comfortable taking the gospel to the Jewish people, but it required a supernatural vision from God, followed by a supernatural confirmation, to free him from his blindness and prejudice toward the Gentiles. That story takes up the entire tenth chapter of Acts, which is worth reading in full.

One might think that after this clear revelation from God, Peter would have grasped the point of God's acceptance of those from every ethnic group on equal terms with Jews—but old thinking and patterns of behavior sometimes take time to change. This became evident when Peter came to Antioch, where Paul ministered to a mixed congregation of Jews and Gentiles. Paul describes how Peter reverted to his Jewish elitist mentality in Galatians 2:11–14.

This sobering story challenges us today to examine ourselves and see if we harbor prejudice against people of any ethnic group. Do we behave hypocritically by not warmly embracing them in love as fellow heirs of the grace of God through faith in Christ?

Paul clearly explained how the work of Jesus the Messiah destroyed the wall of separation between Jews and Gentiles. To the Gentile church in Ephesus, he wrote:

> Therefore remember that at one time you Gentiles in the flesh, called "the uncircumcision" by what is called the circumcision, which is made in the flesh by hands—remember that you were at that time separated from Christ, alienated from the commonwealth of Israel and strangers to the covenants of promise, having no hope and without God in the world. But now in Christ Jesus you who once were far off have been brought near by the blood of Christ. For he himself is our peace, who has made us both one and has broken down in his flesh the dividing wall of hostility by abolishing the law of commandments expressed in ordinances, that he might create in himself one new man in place of the two, so making peace, and might reconcile us both to God in one body through the cross, thereby killing the hostility. And he came and preached peace to you who were far off and peace to those who were near. For through him we both have access in one Spirit to the Father. (Eph. 2:11–18)

Christ's revolutionary dismantling of the wall of separation between Jews and Gentiles was intended to abolish the divisions that fractured and fragmented human relationships and community in that time. Paul made this clear, not just to the Ephesian believers, but everywhere he ministered.

To the church in Galatia, he wrote, "For as many of you as were baptized into Christ have put on Christ. There is neither Jew nor Greek, there is neither slave nor free, there is no male and female, for you are all one in Christ Jesus" (Gal. 3:27–28). Similarly, he assured the church in Colossae that "here there is not Greek and Jew, circumcised and uncircumcised, barbarian, Scythian, slave, free; but Christ is all, and in all" (Col. 3:11). Our new identity in Christ supersedes all these identity markers in the natural world. In God's kingdom, we are bound together in a new humanity with all other believers, through Christ, regardless of ethnicity.

This multiethnic evangelizing and disciple-making, and the multiethnic congregations that resulted after the church broke out of its Jewish cocoon, show us the outworking of the Great Commission in New Testament times (and for some time afterward). These churches help explain why the early Christian movement grew so quickly and became so strong. Empowered by the Holy Spirit, churches became communities of love in which the barriers of ethnicity, social class, economic status, and literacy (which normally divide people) had been transcended. And that love spilled over to their nonbelieving neighbors in the form of caring for the sick, feeding the hungry, rescuing abandoned infants, and many other ways. Such things were unheard of and stimulated widespread curiosity and openness to explore what lay behind such amazing behavior. In addition, physical healings and deliverances from demonic spirits experienced by nonbelievers who sought help from the Christian God served to fuel the growth.[7]

In today's world of strife, hatred, division, and widespread movement of people around the globe, Jesus' command and commission to make disciples from people of all ethnic groups is just as important now as it was in the early days of the church. When the world sees communities of Christians living as the new humanity and loving one another across the barriers that normally separate people, it takes notice (see Matt. 5:14–16; John 13:34–35). Opportunities to explain the reason for that love will open up, and we can share the message of Christ's redeeming love, highlighting the wonderful destiny of all who trust

---

7 Ramsey McMullen, *The Christianizing of the Roman Empire* (New Haven: Yale University Press, 1984).

and follow Christ. Outsiders can share in that destiny, becoming a part of that great multitude clothed in white robes that no one can number, from every nation, from all tribes and peoples and languages, standing before the throne and before the Lamb. Waving palm branches in their hands, they will cry out, "Salvation belongs to our God who sits on the throne, and to the Lamb!" (Rev. 7:9–10).

Your Personal Response?

How can you personally respond to this call to make disciples? The first step is to become a growing disciple yourself. You must be a disciple in order to make a disciple.

As we consider what it means to be Jesus' disciple and to raise up other disciples, ideally our local church will hold *together* gospel proclamation and gospel transformation so that those led to faith in Christ also receive help to grow into the likeness of Christ. We must find our specific role within that context, which we probably best discern in a disciple-making team of several people. While we must remain ready for whatever opportunities God brings to us, some of us will gravitate more to proclamation, and others to transformation. Some of us may more naturally serve in support roles such as prayer or hospitality rather than in frontline engagement. Whatever our role may be, we must remember that, like all other believers, we are witnesses of the Risen Jesus.

Commit yourself to sharing the gospel with anyone and everyone regardless of ethnicity and to helping them grow in Christlikeness. Many people get stuck right here. Because they do not have the gift of evangelism or an outgoing personality, they imagine they cannot lead others to Christ. But while God calls relatively few to be evangelists, He calls every believer to be a witness for Christ. Jesus said, "You will receive power when the Holy Spirit comes upon you, and you will be my witnesses" (Acts 1:8). That simply means you and I are to be filled with the Spirit daily and share what Christ has done for us and what

He means to us, which should include the foundation of our faith, the gospel message. Our motivation to share will be helped if we remind ourselves that the nonbeliever with whom we speak (family, friends, coworkers, neighbors, strangers) will spend eternity in either heaven or hell—and that God is "not wishing that any perish, but that all should reach repentance" (2 Pet. 3:9).

Other people get stuck when they think about helping new believers grow, since they lack seminary training. But such training has never been a requirement. People with little or no education have been making disciples since the first century, and well before that among the people of God in the Old Testament era! Truth gained from oral instruction and committed to memory can give anyone a sound foundation for him- or herself as well as for others. Thus, any believer with a grasp of key biblical truths and a healthy (not perfect) Christian life can share with interested individuals about the teachings of Jesus and how to follow Him—providing, of course, that they are doing so themselves.

If you have no experience, start small. Pray for God to bring you one person and simply do whatever you can. Remember the story of the woman who anointed Jesus with a very costly ointment just before He was crucified. His disciples scolded her for the waste of such a valuable resource, but Jesus commended her. He said, "She has done what she could" (Mark 14:8). That is what we should do.

And do not feel discouraged if you are working with only one person. There is wisdom in the old saying, "Each one reach one, and each one teach one, until all are taught." What if every believer took up this call and worked with just one other person? The impact for God's kingdom would be staggering.

Take encouragement from the well-known story of the boy and the starfish. As an older man walked along the seashore in the early morning mist, a boy was picking up starfish and gently throwing them back into the ocean. The man came near and asked, "Son, what are you doing?" The boy said, "Throwing starfish back into the ocean. The surf is up, and the tide is going out. If I don't throw them back, they'll die." The man replied, "There are miles of beach and hundreds of starfish. You can't make any difference." The boy picked up another starfish and threw it into the sea and said, "I made a difference to that one!"

So it is with us. Many believers are in desperate need of discipling. Disciples are made one by one. Each is precious in the eyes of God, and our investment in their lives, small or large, makes a real difference!

Does this commission still sound daunting to you? If so, take comfort. It felt daunting to Jesus' original disciples too! And take even more comfort in His promise to them, which applies equally to us: "I am with you always, to the end of the age" (Matt. 28:20).

He is with us through the Holy Spirit, who is the Spirit of Christ. And He will be with us every step of the way. Now is the time to step out in reliance on Him!

Questions to Ponder

1. What is the difference between interpreting the Great Commission (Matt. 28:16–20) as a command to make converts and interpreting it as a command to make disciples? How does the second perspective change the way we go about fulfilling the Great Commission?
2. What three actions does the Great Commission mention, and why are they all important for experiencing transformation? How do these three work together in the life of a disciple of Christ?
3. In addition to biblical teaching, what other contexts has God designed to facilitate personal and corporate transformation into the image of Christ? Where do you see this happening in your local church or context?
4. Why is it important to recognize the scope ("all nations," Matt. 28:19) of Christ's commission? How has that scope been interpreted in biblical times and today?
5. What is the significance of Jesus' promise, "Behold, I am with you always, to the end of the age" (Matt. 28:20)? What difference does this make for how you respond to His command?

Part 2

Becoming a Fruitful Disciple of Jesus

13

Learning about the Holy Spirit from Jesus

And I will ask the Father, and he will give you another Helper, to be with you forever, even the Spirit of truth . . . . [H]e dwells with you and will be in you.
John 14:16–17

You cannot become a faithful disciple of Jesus Christ without understanding and embracing the truths of discipleship that He taught, including in the Sermon on the Mount. But knowing what you must do, and even committing yourself to doing it, often reveals significant shortcomings. You and I need power if we're going to live out such a commitment. And when we lack it, we become discouraged, then disillusioned, and finally we settle into a life of spiritual mediocrity.

This is not the abundant life Jesus offers us. He invites us to live hopeful and expectant lives and has provided the means to do so by the Holy Spirit.

Two dear friends of mine, a physicist and his historian wife, were career government workers. They were respectable citizens who, with their kids, regularly attended a liturgical church that had grown somewhat sleepy. They sensed something missing in their spiritual lives but couldn't identify it. They lived with spiritual mediocracy and sluggishness.

When a seminary professor was invited to teach a series on the book of Acts, my friends and several others in the congregation who felt a similar spiritual hunger finally discovered what they lacked. They committed themselves afresh to the living Christ, were filled with the Holy Spirit, and found their lives filled with power, purpose, joy, and a deeper love for Jesus, for others, and for the Bible—along with a greater passion to serve Him. And serve Him they did, for the rest of their lives, whether in the church, workplace, community, or mission outreaches. Over many years, I witnessed in them a truly amazing transformation and fruitfulness for Christ.

How do we get such life-changing power? Where does it come from?

Jesus declares that only the Holy Spirit gives us that power; on this point, Protestants, Roman Catholics, and Eastern Orthodox believers all agree.[1] Somehow, however, many believers continue to struggle in their spiritual lives, settling for a weak and anemic discipleship.

In this chapter, we will look at who the Holy Spirit is and what He does, based primarily on what Jesus taught in John's Gospel. In later chapters, using primarily Paul's teaching, we will explore the Spirit's work in our daily lives: what it means to be filled with the Spirit, to walk in the Spirit, to bear the fruit of the Spirit, and to manifest the gifts of the Spirit.

Why are we going to devote so much attention to the Holy Spirit? Because He is the one who empowers and directs us to glorify Christ! After Jesus accomplished our redemption on the cross and was raised from the dead, He returned to heaven, where He now intercedes for us, seated at the right hand of the Father (Rom. 8:34; Heb. 1:3). Although He is no longer physically here to help us, that doesn't mean we are left alone! Jesus and the Father have poured out the Holy Spirit to be with us, to apply all the benefits of Christ's work in our lives,[2] and to

---

1 However, the Protestant and Roman Catholic Churches disagree with the Eastern Orthodox Church on whether Jesus or the Father poured out the Spirit on the church.

2 John Murray gives a classic account of this truth in his *Redemption Accomplished and Applied* (Grand Rapids, MI: Eerdmans, 1955), 79–181.

carry forward the work of making disciples, which Jesus began while on earth.

A Little Background

The Old Testament prophets, weary of hardhearted Israelites, looked forward with great anticipation to the end of the "present evil age" and the dawning of the "age to come."[3] The Messiah, a Spirit-anointed Davidic king with a ministry that would pour out God's Spirit in life-changing power on all God's people and establish a new covenant (Isa. 11:2; 44:3–5; Jer. 31:31–34; Ezek. 36:25–27; Joel 2:28–29), would inaugurate that new age.

We saw earlier how God sent John the Baptist to announce the Messiah's arrival and to call Israel to prepare for it through repentance and baptism. "I baptize you with water for repentance," he said, "but he who is coming after me is mightier than I, whose sandals I am not worthy to carry. He will baptize you with the Holy Spirit and fire" (Matt. 3:11). When God revealed to John the identity of the coming one, John proclaimed:

> Behold, the Lamb of God, who takes away the sin of the world! … I saw the Spirit descend from heaven like a dove, and it remained on him. I myself did not know him, but he who sent me to baptize with water said to me, "He on whom you see the Spirit descend and remain, this is he who baptizes with the Holy Spirit." And I have seen and have borne witness that this is the Son of God. (John 1:29, 32–34)

No one can enter God's kingdom apart from the work of the Holy Spirit, as Jesus explained to a religious ruler named Nicodemus: "Truly, truly, I say to you, unless one is born of water and the Spirit, he cannot

---

3 "Present evil age": see 1 Cor. 2:6; Gal. 1:4. "Age to come": see Mark 10:30; Luke 18:30; Eph. 2:7. Prophets looked forward: see 1 Pet. 1:10–12.

enter the kingdom of God. That which is born of the flesh is flesh, and that which is born of the Spirit is spirit" (John 3:5–6).

How does this spiritual rebirth happen? John explains: "God so loved the world, that he gave his only Son, that whoever believes in him should not perish but have eternal life" (John 3:16). To be born anew, we must believe and trust in Jesus as God's Son and in His atoning death on the cross—not just for the whole world, but for us personally. Such faith comes as the Holy Spirit works, either instantaneously or over time, to draw us to Jesus through hearing and embracing the gospel message.

An element of mystery exists here, Jesus says, like the movement of the wind, but we can see its reality through its effects:

> Do not marvel that I said to you, "You must be born again." The wind blows where it wishes, and you hear its sound, but you do not know where it comes from or where it goes. So it is with everyone who is born of the Spirit. (John 3:7–8)

Regenerated by the Holy Spirit, we go from being dead in sin to being alive in God. Spirit-given belief in Jesus is more than bare intellectual assent. John signals this by using the verb believe (*pisteuo*) with the preposition *eis*, literally "believe in" or "believe into" (John 3:16: "whoever believes in him"). This emphasis contrasts with that of another common Greek phrasing, *pisteou hoti*, meaning "believing that."[4] As theologian Millard Erickson has observed, the Greek word *pisteuo* can mean either to accept a statement as factually true or to indicate personal trust "as distinct from mere credence or belief." He concludes that

---

4 See Leon Morris, *The Gospel According to John*, rev. ed., The New International Commentary on the New Testament (Grand Rapids, MI: Eerdmans, 1995), 296. Morris explains that *pisteuo* ("believe") + *eis* ("into") is a construction unique to the Gospel of John and proposes that John created this phrasal verb in order to emphasize the dynamic nature of faith in Jesus and "the moral element of personal trust" and commitment of one's life to Him (p. 297). As Morris elsewhere says, "We are to see faith, as John understood it, as a wholehearted commitment to Christ so that the believer became one with Christ and came to be within Christ" (*New Testament Theology* [Grand Rapids, MI: Zondervan, 1986], 274).

"the type of faith necessary for salvation involves both 'believing that' and 'believing in,' that is, assenting to facts and trusting in a person."[5]

The active trust in Jesus that John speaks of involves commitment to Him and His Word. This is seen quite clearly in John 3:17–21, where we read that whoever trusts Jesus and is born of the Spirit turns from the darkness of sin to the light of Christ and a new life. And what does such life look like? Jesus gives us a tantalizing hint in this scene from John 7:

> On the last day of the feast, the great day, Jesus stood up and cried out, "If anyone thirsts, let him come to me and drink. Whoever believes in me, as the Scripture has said, 'Out of his heart will flow rivers of living water.'" Now this he said about the Spirit, whom those who believed in him were to receive, for as yet the Spirit had not been given, because Jesus was not yet glorified. (vv. 37–39)

Those who believe in Jesus will find "rivers" of living water flowing out of their heart (their innermost being)! The source of these rivers "of living water" is Jesus, through the indwelling Holy Spirit. He first satisfies the thirst of the one who believes and then uses that person to carry His message to other thirsty souls. And the Spirit doesn't produce a mere trickle; He produces rivers—a torrent of living water.

This is the heritage of all who savingly believe in Jesus. It became available after Jesus' glorification at the cross and when God poured out the Holy Spirit at Pentecost. The late pastor Stephen Olford, who had a great influence on me, often said the normal Christian life is characterized by being "consciously, continuously, and conspicuously filled with the Holy Spirit."[6] May it be so for you and me and all God's people!

---

5 Millard Erickson, *Christian Theology*, 3rd ed. (Grand Rapids, MI: Baker Academic, 2013), 870.

6 Dr. Olford stated this many times, especially in his frequently preached sermon on John 7:37–38.

Who Is the Holy Spirit?

Who or what *is* the Holy Spirit? From my observations over the years, it appears that many in the church have little understanding of the Bible's teaching about the Holy Spirit. One often hears professing believers, for example, refer to the Holy Spirit as "it." Others think of the Spirit in vague terms, not much different than an impersonal power such as electricity or "the Force" in the *Star Wars* universe. We see this in the *2025 State of Theology Survey*, which found that 53% of evangelicals agree with the statement, "The Holy Spirit is a force but is not a personal being."[7]

In the first of five passages on the Spirit in John 14–16, Jesus makes it clear that the Holy Spirit is a *personal being*. "If you love me," he says, "you will keep my commandments. And I will ask the Father, and he will give you another Helper, to be with you forever, even the Spirit of truth, whom the world cannot receive, because it neither sees him nor knows him. You know him, for he dwells with you and will be in you" (John 14:15–17). When Jesus spoke of "another Helper" to take His place, he used a Greek word that means "another of the same kind"—that is, another divine person just like Jesus (though without a physical body). This Helper would carry on the work of Christ and make Him personally present to the disciples (and by extension, to all His subsequent followers).

Jesus referred to the Helper as "the Spirit of truth." Just as Jesus spent much of His ministry teaching truth, so would the Helper dedicate Himself to teaching truth to Jesus' followers. Although the Helper had been with the disciples during their three years with Jesus, empowering them in ministry, soon He would come to dwell in them—a momentous change.

---

7 Chris Larson, "The Results from Our 2025 State of Theology Survey Are In," Ligonier Ministries, www.ligonier.org, September 19, 2025, par. 2.

In the second passage, John 14:26, Jesus further describes the Helper and His work: "But the Helper, the Holy Spirit, whom the Father will send in my name, he will teach you all things and bring to your remembrance all that I have said to you." Here Jesus describes the Helper as the "Holy" Spirit, reminding the disciples of God's command, "For I am the LORD your God. Consecrate yourselves therefore, and be holy, for I am holy" (Lev. 11:44). A major part of the Holy Spirit's work, as His name implies, is to help God's people become holy—that is, to become increasingly sanctified or Christlike.

Jesus also spoke here again of the teaching ministry of the Spirit. The Spirit will "teach you all things" (no doubt with holiness high on the list). But He also would remind them of everything Jesus taught, ensuring (for example) that they would accurately recall and record Jesus' words and works in the Gospels for future generations. The Spirit would ensure that Jesus' disciples had the right words at the right time as they taught and preached about Jesus, which by extension applies to future disciples (see also Matt. 10:19–20).

In the third passage, Jesus again refers to the Helper as "the Spirit of truth": "But when the Helper comes, whom I will send to you from the Father, the Spirit of truth, who proceeds from the Father, he will bear witness about me. And you also will bear witness, because you have been with me from the beginning" (John 15:26–27). Becoming equipped and transformed by truth paves the way for mission. The Spirit will bear witness to Jesus, causing the truth about Jesus and His work to be made known and lifted high. The disciples would join this great work of speaking truth about the Son of God, full of grace and truth (John 1:14), who called Himself the way, the truth, and the life (John 14:6) and said, "I have come into the world … to bear witness to the truth" (18:37). All who have received grace by the Spirit bear witness to Christ and His salvation.

Jesus' fourth saying must have shocked the disciples, because it declared that His departure would result in great blessing. This blessing would come because by leaving them and returning to the Father, Jesus (in union with the Father) would pour out upon them the Holy Spirit, who would empower their witness about Him and bring conviction upon those who didn't yet follow Jesus:

> Nevertheless, I tell you the truth: it is to your advantage that I go away, for if I do not go away, the Helper will not come to you. But if I go, I will send him to you. And when he comes, he will convict the world concerning sin and righteousness and judgment: concerning sin, because they do not believe in me; concerning righteousness, because I go to the Father, and you will see me no longer; concerning judgment, because the ruler of this world is judged. (John 16:7–11)

The fact that only the Spirit can bring conviction to the hearts of sinners gives great encouragement to those of us who witness to others about Christ. *We* cannot save anyone. And that isn't our job. We must speak the truth about Christ and point people to Him. But it is the Spirit who does the work of conversion.

The fifth and final passage assures the disciples that Jesus will not leave them helpless. The Spirit will guide them after Jesus departs. Again referring to the Spirit as "the Spirit of truth," Jesus says the Spirit will reveal to His disciples things they cannot yet grasp, as well as future events:

> I still have many things to say to you, but you cannot bear them now. When the Spirit of truth comes, he will guide you into all the truth, for he will not speak on his own authority, but whatever he hears he will speak, and he will declare to you the things that are to come. He will glorify me, for he will take what is mine and declare it to you. All that the Father has is

> mine; therefore I said that he will take what is mine and declare it to you. (John 16:12–15)

The Spirit will impart to the disciples truth about Jesus that will enable them to glorify Him. The Spirit seeks to glorify Jesus; He does not seek to glorify Himself. We need to reemphasize that point in today's Christian world, where in some circles the Spirit is so emphasized that Jesus is overshadowed.

Jesus did not speak exhaustively in His teaching on the Holy Spirit in John's Gospel. He did not say all that could be said. But He gave these foundational truths to comfort and strengthen His disciples in their mission and for all who would follow them.

Summarizing, we have seen that the Holy Spirit is not an impersonal force but both divine and a personal being, like Jesus. He dwells in true believers, helping them become holy, teaching them about Jesus, bringing truth to their minds whenever needed, empowering them to bear witness to Jesus and to glorify Him, and convicting those without Him of sin, righteousness, and judgment (see John 16:8).

More to Come

Jesus left much unsaid about the Spirit's work in our lives, such as the Spirit's filling and the fruit and gifts of the Spirit, rivers of living water that spring forth from Pentecost onward. Those things fell to the apostle Paul (from whom we'll hear later). Paul will give us additional practical teaching on how to experience the fullness of the Spirit in our daily lives.

Questions to Ponder

1. Why is it so important for us as disciples of Jesus to clearly understand and experience the ministry of the Holy Spirit?
2. Where in the Gospels does Jesus describe the Holy Spirit in personal terms?
3. Of the five sets of verses reviewed above, which one stands out to you the most? Which one would you like to look into further?
4. What is significant about the personal nature of the Spirit? What's wrong with thinking of the Spirit in impersonal terms, as "it" or a "force"?
5. Why is it significant that the Spirit points us to Jesus?
6. Where do you see the Spirit at work in you? Through you?

14

Living in the Spirit-Filled Community

I will build my church, and the gates of hell shall not prevail against it.

Matthew 16:18

In his action-packed story of the early church, Luke introduces his second biblical book (The Acts of the Apostles) by saying that in his first book (the Gospel of Luke) he dealt with "all that Jesus *began* to do and teach" from the beginning up to His return to heaven (Acts 1:1; my emphasis). He implies that Jesus now *continued* to do His work of making disciples in the early church, through the Holy Spirit.

The episodes in Acts take us back to the roots of the church and call all believers to join in the disciple-making, kingdom-spreading work Jesus has continued to do through the centuries and is still doing now. To gain renewed vision and encouragement for that work, in this chapter we will focus our attention on the church of Acts and on how the broader church developed during the three centuries that followed and beyond. Our aim? To recover the apostolic vision that has inspired many hungry souls and renewal movements since the days when Jesus walked the earth.

The Great Commission

After His resurrection, Jesus gave His eleven disciples a charge; we call it "the Great Commission" (Matt. 28:18–20). The eleven were first Jesus' disciples, but He also had designated them as apostles (Luke 6:12–16)—that is, disciples sent out on a special mission (the Greek term *apostoloi* literally means "sent ones"). These men became the church's first leaders, and they carried forward on a global scale the work that Jesus had begun in Israel. Jesus instructed them to make disciples not just of Jews, but of all ethnic groups around the globe. He wanted them to spread God's kingdom to the ends of the earth (see Acts 1:8).

Their earlier training as disciples and "fishers of men" (Matt. 4:19; Mark 1:17) had laid the foundation for this additional role. In that period, Jesus had sent them out to proclaim the kingdom of heaven to the lost sheep of Israel (Matt. 10:5–6), an exciting but potentially dangerous assignment. Later, He commissioned seventy-two others for the same task (Luke 10:1–12). But now, speaking to them in His final moments on earth, He enlarged the scope of their mission field to reach out to all people, not just Jews.

We must remember that Jesus did not call perfect men, but flawed, broken people (like us) still plagued by areas of ignorance, blindness, and prejudice. Pastor and author Greg Ogden makes this point in a somewhat humorous but telling way. It takes the form of a memorandum to Jesus from Jordan Management Consultants:

> Dear Sir,
>
> Thank you for submitting the resumes of the twelve men you have picked for management positions in your new organization. All of them have now taken our battery of tests; we have not only run the results through our own computer but also arranged personal interviews for each of them with our psychologist and vocational aptitude consultant.

> It is the staff opinion that most of your nominees are lacking in background, education, and vocational aptitude for the type of enterprise you are undertaking. They do not have the team concept. We would recommend that you continue your search for persons of experience in managerial ability and proven capability.
>
> Simon Peter is emotionally unstable and given to fits of temper. Andrew has absolutely no qualities of leadership. The two brothers, James and John, the sons of Zebedee, place personal interest above company loyalty. Thomas demonstrates a questioning attitude that would tend to undermine morale.
>
> We feel that it is our duty to tell you that Matthew has been blacklisted by the Greater Jerusalem Better Business Bureau. James, the son of Alphaeus, and Thaddaeus definitely have radical leanings, and they both registered high on the manic-depressive scale.
>
> One of the candidates, however, shows great potential. He is a man of ability and resourcefulness, meets people well, has a keen business mind, and has contacts in high places. He is highly motivated, ambitious, and responsible. We recommend Judas Iscariot as your controller and right-hand man. All of the other profiles are self-explanatory.
>
> We wish you every success in your new venture.[1]

Isn't this fictional memo an excellent reminder that God sees the hearts of people? As God said to Samuel, "The Lord sees not as man sees: man looks on the outward appearance, but the Lord looks on the heart" (1 Sam. 16:7). Jesus saw their hearts and didn't wait until these men were perfect before He called and commissioned them. He would need to work on their sins and flaws, but He took them as He found them,

1 Greg Ogden, *Transforming Discipleship* (Downers Grove, IL: InterVarsity Press, 2003), 77. This is an excellent book on discipleship that should be read by everyone who is interested in the subject.

"warts and all," as people say, and the disciples devoted themselves to Jesus and committed to serving Him. They illustrate for us what we see all through the Bible: God builds His kingdom using broken tools.

Before the apostles could take up their work, however, they needed power for the enormous and dangerous task ahead. Thus, Jesus commanded them to remain in Jerusalem until the Father had poured out the promised Holy Spirit upon on them (Acts 1:4–5). During this time, He continued to teach them about God's kingdom and the crucial role of the Holy Spirit in the advance of that kingdom.

The apostles felt eager for the kingdom to come and asked if it would arrive soon (Acts 1:6). They had in mind the restoration of Israel's political kingdom. They still had not fully grasped that God's kingdom, first, means His rule and reign in the lives of His people, not an earthly regime. Jesus deflected their question and reminded them of their chief priority, which was to fulfill the Great Commission: "You will receive power when the Holy Spirit has come upon you, and you will be my witnesses in Jerusalem and in all Judea and Samaria, and to the end of the earth" (Acts 1:8). As they (and those who came after them) focused on faithfully bearing witness to Jesus in the Spirit's power and making disciples of all nations, they could do so with divine assurance that many souls would enter God's kingdom and that the final, cataclysmic in-breaking of the kingdom in its fullness would come … in God's appointed time (Acts 1:7).

The Birth of the Church

Acts 2 tells the electrifying story of the Spirit's birthing of the church. At the end of Acts 1, we learn that the apostles and many other disciples, about 120 in all, had devoted themselves to prayer in a spirit of unity (vv. 12–15). When the Day of Pentecost arrived, Peter explained that Jesus, having received the promise of the Father, has poured out the Holy Spirit on them with extraordinary power and remarkable signs, such as a mighty rushing wind, tongues of fire resting on each one of them, and speaking in unlearned human languages. This miracle attracted a large crowd of bewildered Jews from all over the Roman Empire who had gathered in Jerusalem for the feast of Pentecost (see Acts 2:1–13, 33).

Peter, who not long before had denied that he even knew Jesus (Matt. 26:69–75), suddenly became as bold as a lion and preached fearlessly to the crowd, some of whom may have joined in condemning Jesus. In a passionate sermon, Peter recounted the life, death, and resurrection of Jesus and confronted the crowd for the sin of crucifying Him (Acts 2:14–36). Many believed the message, were convicted and repented of their sins, and were baptized. Three thousand people became disciples of Jesus that day, the first recorded fruit of the Great Commission (vv. 37–41).

Believing the good news about Christ, repenting of their sins, getting baptized into the fellowship of the church, and receiving the Spirit marked the beginning of these new converts' discipleship (and all others in Acts). Now they would need to learn all that Jesus taught His original disciples, including how to "observe all that [he] commanded" them (Matt. 28:19–20). Suddenly alive to God through the Spirit, they eagerly

> devoted themselves to the apostles' teaching and the fellowship, to the breaking of bread and the prayers. And awe came upon every soul, and many wonders and signs were being done through the apostles. And all who believed were together and had all things in common. And they were selling their possessions and belongings and distributing the proceeds to all, as any had need. And day by day, attending the temple together and breaking bread in their homes, they received their food with glad and generous hearts, praising God and having favor

> with all the people. And the Lord added to their number day by day those who were being saved. (Acts 2:42–47)

If we and our churches are to experience all that God calls us to be, and to do all that He has for us to do, we need to follow the example of these first believers.

Devotion to the four Spirit-inspired practices for growing in grace discussed above shaped and propelled these new Christians' personal and community formation as disciples and was crucial to their abiding in Christ. This, in turn, formed the church into a critical mass that radiated spiritual light and power for all to see. The result? Extraordinary love and generosity in their corporate life, which proved both attractive and contagious. As these new disciples of Jesus became more like Him, growing in visible love for one another, outsiders were drawn to Him.

This is the purpose of the church.

As C. S. Lewis said, the churches "exists for nothing else but to draw men into Christ, to make them little Christs. If they are not doing that, all the cathedrals, clergy, missions, sermons, even the Bible itself are simply a waste of time. God became man for no other purpose."[2] Let's look together at these four foundational practices and how we can live them out today.

Four Foundational Practices

As we saw above, Acts 2:42 tells us that in the early days, Jesus' disciples "devoted themselves" to four things. The Greek word used here for "devoted," *proskartereo*, means more than casual involvement; it means steadfast commitment and faithfulness. Devotees are persistent and tenacious; they persevere and do not slack off. This high level of intensity governs each of the four practices described in Acts 2:42.

---

2 C. S. Lewis, *Mere Christianity* (New York: Touchstone Books, 1996), 171.

They devoted themselves "to the apostles' teaching."

Disciples are learners; that's one of their main characteristics. These new believers devoted themselves to learning all that the apostles could teach them about Jesus, including all that Jesus had taught them by word and action (these are the teachings recorded for us in the Gospels). Central are Jesus' teachings from the Sermon on the Mount and the Upper Room, as well as the significance of His life, death, and resurrection. In many instances, Jesus' lessons pointed them back to the Old Testament, so their study would have encompassed all of Scripture.

They devoted themselves to "the fellowship."

The word translated as "fellowship" here is the Greek term *koinonia*, from which English words such as "communion" or "common" are derived. In the context of Acts 2, "the fellowship" referred to how believers shared the overflow of the new life they experienced in Christ, manifested in close involvement with, support of, and care for one another—in other words, in community. "Fellowship" meant love in practical terms, including the sharing of material resources when needed (vv. 44–45). This common bond in the Spirit was obviously much deeper and stronger than what we typically understand as "fellowship" in most of our churches today, which often indicates something more like "greeting one another" or "having a casual conversation with acquaintances." It is vital that we recover the original sense and experience of Spirit-led "fellowship" in all of its richness and depth.

They devoted themselves to "the breaking of bread."

People who are close to one another frequently express their *koinonia* by sharing a meal. In these early days, the church celebrated the Lord's Supper in conjunction with a community meal, similar to the first one celebrated by Jesus and the Twelve (Luke 22:14–23). Some scholars thus understand the phrase "breaking of bread" to mean a meal only, while others believe it refers to a meal plus Communion, or even to

Communion alone. The fact that Luke lists it along with teaching, fellowship, and prayer lends credence to the latter two viewpoints.[3] These Christians gathered to carry out the Lord's commands, including His command to "do this in remembrance of me" (Luke 22:19).

They devoted themselves to "the prayers."

Whether this refers to the formal prayers offered at set times during the day at the Temple or to informal prayers in home groups, we see here a praying church! Prayer made up a major part of their personal lives and of their corporate life. The book of Acts vividly describes how God regularly and powerfully answered their prayers.

A Paradigm for the Church

The life of the early church and the practices which shaped it were not simply the religious components of otherwise busy lives. Church historian Gerald Bray notes that in the early decades after Christ's resurrection, "Churchgoing was not just one activity among many others but an essential part of the identity of individual Christians. The church was their primary community, in which all the serious business of life was conducted. Joining it was almost like moving to another country, so different from the wider world was it and so demanding were its norms."[4]

The dramatic launch of the church as a Spirit-filled community of Jesus' disciples, all of them devoted to these four foundational practices and committed to spreading God's kingdom, provides the basic paradigm for the life of the church in *all* generations.

As is obvious here, the essence of the New Testament church is not a building. Nowhere in the New Testament is the church described as

3 Robert Banks has given a captivating extended description of such a meal in *Paul's Idea of Community: Spirit and Culture in Early House Churches*, 3rd ed. (Grand Rapids, MI: Baker Academic, 2020), 173–192.

4 Gerald Bray, *The Church: A Theological and Historical Account* (Grand Rapids, MI: Baker Academic, 2016), 249.

a building. Nor is it an institution. Rather, the church's essence is that it is a community of the King—a group of people whom the Spirit has drawn out of the fallen world to salvation in Christ through the gospel and into life together in God's kingdom. In the New Testament, such groups are described with the term *ekklesia*, that is, a local congregation or gathering of disciples in a given area, or all such groups in that area.[5]

As these early believers embarked on this new life of discipleship—of denying self, taking up their cross, and following Jesus daily in costly obedience—they soon discovered that "through many tribulations we must enter the kingdom of God" (Acts 14:22). Thus, another mark of the church, as Luther would later say, was suffering.[6]

Ignorance of these foundational truths and their implications is one of the main reasons for the weak and anemic spiritual lives of many Christians today, and a major reason we need to recover our identity as disciples of Jesus.

What Was the Church Like in the Apostolic Era?

After Jesus' resurrection, the disciples met together in the temple precincts and in homes (Acts 2:46). Tensions with Jewish authorities, however, quickly rendered them *personae non gratae* on the temple grounds, forcing them to meet only in homes.

In Rome, Priscilla and Aquila hosted a church in their house (Rom. 16:3–5), just as they did earlier when they lived in Corinth (1 Cor. 16:19). In Colossae, the church met in Nympha's home (Col. 4:15), and Philemon also hosted a church in his home (Philem. 2–3). As in Jerusalem, "Most likely, only ten to a dozen believers, plus chil-

5 The term *ekklesia* can also have a broader usage, as in Ephesians 1:22 ("And [the Father] put all things under [Christ's] feet and gave him as head over all things to the church").

6 Martin Luther, "On the Councils and the Church," in *Luther's Works*, vol. 41, ed. Eric Grisch (St. Louis: Concordia, 1966), 164–166, 172–173. Suffering was the seventh of Luther's seven marks of the true church.

dren, met in typical households like that of Priscilla and Aquila."[7] The larger homes of more affluent believers could accommodate several such groups, perhaps forty or so.[8] They may have met in the early morning or after dark. We might consider this the original "house church movement"! Churches met in private homes into the fourth century. These small venues encouraged the development of close relationships and community among believers.

What kind of ethnic composition did these gatherings have? In Jerusalem, they consisted predominantly of Jews. But at the cross, Christ had "broken down in his flesh the dividing wall of hostility" between Jew and Gentile (Eph. 2:14). In the church, everyone's fundamental identity had changed through faith in Jesus; they had become children of God and disciples of Christ. As the gospel spread to Samaria and then to the wider Greco-Roman world, Gentiles of every description trusted in Christ and entered the church. This family had "no Greek and Jew, circumcised and uncircumcised, barbarian, Scythian, slave, free; but Christ is all and in all" (Col. 3:11). Thus, the word "catholic," in the sense of "universal," would become one of the marks of the church.

In his letters to these house churches, Paul often used the descriptive term "the body of Christ," that is, a living organism headed by Christ Himself (Eph. 1:22–23; Col. 1:18). This metaphor reinforces the idea of the church as a group of people who have come to faith in Christ and who relate to one another like various parts of a body, over which Jesus is the head and rules through His Spirit. In its local manifestations, the church is to visibly express His example of truth, grace, and love in its internal relationships and operations and to carry out His mission to the world. Daily filling with the Holy Spirit made this beautiful supernatural life possible.

---

7 Robert Banks, *Paul's Idea of Community: Spirit and Culture in Early House Churches*, 3rd ed. (Grand Rapids, MI: Baker Academic, 2020), 32.

8 Banks, *Paul's Idea of Community*, 32.

But there's more. Paul also referred to the church in terms of a family—"the household of God" (Eph. 2:19) and "the household of faith" (Gal. 6:10)—and reinforced this with warm relational words such as "brothers," "sisters," fathers," "mothers," "children of God," and "household." The image of a family suggests love, peace, warmth, and care for one another.

The content of Paul's epistles, however, shows that these images of "the body of Christ" and "family of God" did not mean local churches were always grace-filled, loving, peaceful communities active in mission and free of doctrinal aberrations. In fact, none of them were perfect. Each had its own set of problems; some major (Corinth), others relatively minor (Philippi). The church as Christ's body and God's family is the place where God's glory is to be manifested concretely in the darkness of this fallen world, which explains why it is the prime target of the devil's relentless attacks.

Nor did Paul's images mean that everyone in an assembled congregation was truly born again. No doubt most were when he planted a church, but not necessarily all. In fact, Paul urges the Corinthians, "Examine yourselves, to see whether you are in the faith. Test yourselves" (2 Cor. 13:5). This reality eventually led to the recognition of a distinction between the visible church (all who verbally profess faith) and the invisible church (those in the visible church, known only to God, who are truly regenerate).

Seven Features of the Church

The example of the Spirit's work in the early church raises an obvious and important question. How do we recognize a faithful church, a church true to the apostolic faith and practice? We can start by asking what features the worldwide church shares across the centuries. The description found in the Nicene Creed, an early summary of essential doctrine, helps us here: the church of Christ as a whole is *one*, *holy*, *catholic*, and *apostolic*. Very briefly,

> *One* refers to the unity of one body (Eph. 4:4ff.).
> *Holy* refers to the church as a holy nation (1 Pet. 2:9).
> *Catholic* refers to universality of peoples in the church (Gal. 3:28).
> *Apostolic* refers to faithfulness to the teaching of the apostles (2 Tim. 1:13).

In his book *Christian Basics: An Invitation to Discipleship*, John Stott describes how the whole church is connected:

> In one sense the church is not divided and cannot be. Even our outward divisions do not tear it asunder, since the one Spirit indwells it. Piers in a harbour may divide it into sections, so that boats are cut off from each other, but the same sea flows and swells underneath. Our man-made denominations also separate us outwardly and visibly, but inwardly and invisibly the tide of the Spirit unites us.[9]

He goes on to define the four features of the church mentioned in the Nicene Creed in this succinct summary:

> The Nicene Creed characterizes the church as "one, holy, catholic and apostolic," which are the four classical "marks" or "notes" of the church. And they are true. The church is both one and holy because the Holy Spirit has united and sanctified it, setting it apart to belong to God, even though in practice it is often disunited and unholy. The church is also catholic (embracing all believers and all truth) and apostolic (affirming the teaching of the apostles and engaging in mission),

---

9 John Stott, *Christian Basics: An Invitation to Discipleship* (Grand Rapids, MI: Baker, 1991), 83.

> even though in practice it often denies the faith it should profess and the mission it should pursue.[10]

Appreciating these aspects of the church is a good starting place for understanding what a faithful church looks like.

In addition to these four common attributes articulated by the ancient church (the Nicene Creed was formally recognized by the church in the fourth century), church leaders during the Protestant Reformation (sixteenth century) regarded three more as noteworthy. Theologian Edmund Clowney observes, "The Reformation made the gospel, not ecclesiastical organization, the test of the true church … . Three marks were defined in distinguishing a true church of Christ: true preaching of the word, proper observance of the sacraments; and faithful exercise of church discipline."[11]

Does the local church you attend exhibit the seven marks of a faithful church? If so, how does your involvement in that church help you to follow Christ more fully and love Him more deeply? If not, can you do something to help make things better?

Always a Remnant

When we get discouraged about the state of the church, it is sometimes helpful to remind ourselves that the church exists in a fallen world whose seductive culture is a source of constant temptation to believers; the devil exploits this to ensnare our flesh. In this battle, the church goes through cycles of advance and decline that stretch as far back as Old Testament times, when Canaanite Baal worship was the great snare.

But despite bleak, even seemingly faithless epochs in church history, God has always preserved a remnant of His people, even in the worst of times. In one of the darkest periods of Israel's history, God gave the discouraged prophet Elijah a reason to hope, promising that "I will leave

10 Stott, *Christian Basics*, 83.

11 Edmund P. Clowney, *The Church* (Downers Grove, IL: InterVarsity Press, 1995), 101.

seven thousand in Israel, all the knees that have not bowed to Baal, and every mouth that has not kissed him" (1 Kings 19:18). Though we may not immediately see His hand at work in challenging times, God does not abandon His people or His plans.

We need to remind ourselves that such bleak times are temporary. In due course, God will come in fresh power to restore His church. Throughout history, He has poured out His Spirit in periodic renewals and revivals to save unconverted church members, cleanse and empower true believers, draw them back to the fundamentals of the apostolic church and sound doctrine, fuel missions, and advance His kingdom of love.[12] How glorious such advances are when they come!

We can see such renewal in the impact of Augustine's work as the Roman Empire crumbled around him; Benedict of Nursia and the Benedictine movement; the Irish missionary monks; Francis of Assisi and the Franciscan movement; Bernard of Clairvaux and the Cistercian reform movement; Thomas à Kempis and the Devotio Moderna; John Wycliffe, the morning star of the Reformation; William Tyndale, father of the English Bible; the magisterial Reformers (Martin Luther, Huldrych Zwingli, and John Calvin); John Knox; Thomas Cranmer; and many others up to our own day. None was perfect, and none had perfect doctrine, but all were devoted to Christ and His kingdom, and He used them to build His church despite their sins, flaws, and errors—as He does us today.

Yet the efforts of these groups and individuals eventually faded. Why do such revivals not last? There are several reasons.

First, as church historian Richard Lovelace explains, the flesh and the world always introduce distortions and confusion.[13] And simultaneously, sustained demonic opposition also arises to meet revivals,

---

12 For more on this topic, see Richard Lovelace, *Dynamics of Spiritual Life: An Evangelical Theology of Renewal* (Downers Grove, IL: InterVarsity Press, 1979), 239–261.

13 Richard Lovelace, *Dynamics of Spiritual Life* (Downers Grove, IL: InterVarsity Press, 1979), 244–254.

introducing doctrinal errors, excesses, confusion, division, and other aberrations.[14] In addition, a common cycle recurs: after a season of revival in which the church grows stronger and spreads, new converts become more honest, responsible, hardworking, and prosperous; then, worldliness begins to increase, the fires eventually grow cold, and the church again becomes weak and in need of fresh revival. Along with this, many of those converted do not adequately disciple their children into the faith, if they do it at all. A couple of generations of such decline takes a big toll on the church, as the ranks of truly converted and committed believers dwindle. At that point, revival is needed again.

Cotton Mather, the leading clergyman in the American colonies, summed up the decline of true religion in America from its founding in the early 1600s to 1699 by observing that "piety begat prosperity, and the daughter consumed the mother."[15] Near the end of his life, John Wesley made a similar observation about the Methodist movement:

> Wherever riches have increased, the essence of religion has decreased in the same proportion. Therefore I do not see how it is possible in the nature of things for any revival of religion to continue long. For religion must necessarily produce both industry and frugality, and these cannot but produce riches. But as riches increase, so will pride, anger, and love of the world in all its branches.
>
> How then is it possible that Methodism, that is, a religion of the heart, though it flourishes now as the green bay tree, should continue in this state? For the Methodists in every place grow diligent and frugal: consequently, they increase in goods. Hence, they proportionately increase in pride, in anger, in the desire of the flesh, the desire of the eyes, and the pride of life.

---

14 Lovelace, *Dynamics*, 254–270.

15 Cotton Mather, *Magnalia Christi Americana, The Ecclesiastical History of New England*, vol. 1 (Hartford, CT: Silas Andrus and Son, 1855), 63.

> So, although the form of religion remains, the spirit is swiftly vanishing away.
>
> Is there no way to prevent … this continual decay of pure religion?[16]

By the early 1700s, the churches of New England had become dry and rife with formalism and were being challenged by the rationalism of the Enlightenment. Times were bleak. But several decades later, in response to prayer for revival, God responded to this dismal situation by sending the Great Awakening, a mighty outpouring of the Holy Spirit that brought many into God's kingdom. This cycle of advance and decline goes all the way back to the period of the judges in the book of Joshua.

We can see the same pattern of spiritual decline today in rapidly secularizing Europe, Canada, and America—a sad decline of church and culture from a more faithful and fruitful era. Spirit-led revival and reform of the church is the greatest need of the hour in these lands, and earnest intercessory prayer is our only hope. At the same time, we can feel encouraged over the thrilling work of the Spirit in kingdom advances now taking place in Asia, Africa, and South America, despite persecution.

Looking further back, we see that the Holy Spirit had been deeply grieved by the church's steep spiritual decline from the fourteenth to the sixteenth century. This was due to a number of factors, including worldliness, widespread corruption, internal political strife, uneducated and morally corrupt clergy, the sale of indulgences, and resistance to reform. Although the Spirit was at work in lay movements like the Devotio Moderna, corruption in the church hierarchy was too deeply entrenched for the few reform-minded cardinals to effect change.

The Protestant Reformation took a great step forward, beginning in 1517 when Martin Luther nailed his 95 Theses to the door of Wittenberg Chapel, a major advance in restoring the church to

---

16 John Wesley, *The Works of the Rev. John Wesley*, vol. 10 (New York: J. & J. Harper, 1827), 150.

its apostolic foundations. These foundations were understood not as the apostolic succession of clergy but apostolic teaching of the Bible. Edmund Clowney observed that "above all, the Reformers emphasized the meaning of apostolicity. To be apostolic, the church must be built on the doctrine of the apostles."[17] And apostolic doctrine clearly taught that salvation was by grace alone, through faith alone, in Christ alone, and not earned through good works. Along with Scripture alone and to God's glory alone, these became known as the "Five Solas"[18] and were core principles of the Reformation.

Neither Luther nor Calvin wanted to split from the Roman Catholic Church. They wanted to correct abuses and reform the church in areas where it had seriously strayed from apostolic teaching and life. Sadly, that didn't happen. Luther was declared a heretic and excommunicated from the church. And the unintended consequence of the Reformation was that the church split into smaller groups such as denominations. The Reformation did, however, bring much-needed reform in both doctrine and practice. Salvation and all its blessings again were understood to come, as Paul had taught, by grace alone, through faith alone in the finished work of Christ alone—and not by works (Eph. 2:8–9)—but also not *without* works, which are the fruit of true saving faith (v. 10).

Despite these and many other doctrinal and structural reforms, Luther, Calvin, and other Reformers lamented that the church experienced so little *reformation of life* among its people, and so little true personal revival. In time, it came to be understood that the church is always in need of reform: *ecclesia reformata, semper reformanda*, "the church reformed, always reforming."

---

17 Clowney, *The Church*, 101.

18 In Latin, these are: *Sola Gratia, Sola Fide, Solus Christus, Sola Scriptura*, and *Soli Deo Gloria.*

What To Do Now?

In light of all this, how do we make sense of the church today? We must always remember that Jesus said, "I will build my church, and the gates of hell shall not prevail against it" (Matt. 16:18). Jesus also prayed for His disciples "that they may all be one … that the world may believe that you have sent me" (John 17:21). Jesus works through the Holy Spirit to bring these things to pass, and the Spirit works through us.

We might find these realities hard to imagine due to the church's fragmentation into such a great variety of denominational forms (for example, Eastern Orthodox, Roman Catholic, Lutheran, Reformed, Anabaptist, Anglican, Baptist, Methodist, Pentecostal, nondenominational). But though the forms of worship and certain doctrinal beliefs might differ, Jesus has continued to build His church in congregations that welcome Him and hold fast to His Word. And one day, all true believers will unite again in truth and love in the world to come, and possibly sooner on earth, though it may take the fires of tribulation and persecution to bring that about!

Paul proclaimed, "Christ is the head of the church, his body, and is himself its Savior … . [He] gave himself up for her, that he might sanctify her, having cleansed her by the washing of water with the word, so that he might present the church to himself in splendor, without spot or wrinkle or any such thing, that she might be holy and without blemish" (Eph. 5:23, 25–27). This, too, we may find difficult to imagine, given the present moral and theological compromise in many contemporary churches. But it will definitely come to pass! For nothing is impossible with God (Matt. 19:26; Luke 1:37), and the fires of revival and persecution can have a powerful purifying effect on the church.

Truth is perpetually under assault as the devil and his minions work through false teachers and heresies, seeking to deceive even the elect, if that were possible (Matt. 24:24). But Luther said it well in the hymn "A Mighty Fortress Is Our God": "And though this world, with devils filled, should threaten to undo us, we will not fear, for God hath willed his truth to triumph through us."[19]

If we are disciples of Jesus, who "loved us and gave himself up for us" (Eph. 5:2), we will believe what He taught, love what He loves, and stay committed to His church in every circumstance. We will stay in the battle, even when it gets hard. This means loving and staying committed to a theologically sound local church despite its imperfections and, through all its ups and downs, actively seeking its health and flourishing, supporting the leadership, faithfully praying for its revival and reform, and using our spiritual and material gifts to advance its life and mission of glorifying Christ by making disciples and spreading the kingdom of God. Faithfulness can also, of course, mean leaving a church or denomination that has abandoned orthodox belief.

As we press on, we can take encouragement from the words of another great hymn:

> Though with a scornful wonder men see her sore oppressed,
> By schisms rent asunder, by heresies distressed,
> Yet saints their watch are keeping, their cry goes up, "how long?"
> And soon the night of weeping shall be the morn of song.
>
> 'Mid toil and tribulation and tumult of her war,
> She waits the consummation of peace forevermore;
> Till with the vision glorious her longing eyes are blest
> And the great church victorious shall be the church at rest."[20]

Let's pray for God's blessing, not only on our own local church, but also on other faithful churches, and for the continuing advance of God's kingdom as we await the return of Jesus and the consummation of all things. Jesus promised that He would build His church (Matt. 16:18), and He is doing so even now.

---

19 Martin Luther, "A Mighty Fortress Is Our God" (1529). Translated by Frederic Henry Hedge (1852).

20 Samuel J. Stone, "The Church's One Foundation" (1866).

Questions to Ponder

1. Considering the early disciples' devotion to the four foundational practices mentioned in Acts 2:42, how would you evaluate your experience in the contemporary church? Which of these are most visible, and which less so?
2. After reading about the ongoing work of the Holy Spirit in lives of early disciples, what characteristics of the early church stand out to you?
3. Name the four marks of a faithful church that are stated in the Nicene Creed. To what extent does the church you attend exhibit these marks?
4. What are the three additional marks noted by the leaders of the Protestant Reformation? Which of these is most and least familiar based on your experiences in local churches?
5. As a faithful follower of Christ, name some reasons why it is important to stay connected to a local church.

15

Experiencing Life in the Spirit

But you will receive power when the Holy Spirit has come upon you,
and you will be my witnesses in Jerusalem and in all Judea and Samaria,
and to the end of the earth.
Acts 1:8

The outpouring of the Holy Spirit and new birth marks only the beginning of the Spirit's work in a believer. New life from the Spirit brings power for new obedience, imparts gifts for ministry, and leads us into mission. And throughout our lives, the Spirit works to bring us to increasing maturity in Christ.

All of these good things have their starting point when Jesus baptizes us in the Holy Spirit. In this chapter, we will expand on our understanding of the Holy Spirit and His work and then look at how Jesus baptizes or immerses us in the Spirit.

A Blessed Life

Wendy Hatcher, a woman I knew for many years, provides a good example of how the Holy Spirit can empower and change an ordinary person's life. She was the wife of a circuit court judge in Cleveland, Mississippi, and a Sunday school teacher at First Presbyterian Church, where she sat under an abundance of sound teaching. But something seemed missing in her life.

Early one morning while alone and praying in the family room, she had an encounter with the Holy Spirit that made Jesus real to her, brought deep inner change, and imparted a passion to tell the world about Him. She became a committed, fearless disciple of Jesus and a lifelong student of the Bible and theology. And she shared her learning with anyone who expressed an interest.

Though she had no formal training in ministry, through her church's prison outreach she began to volunteer at the nearby Parchman State penitentiary, said to be one of the worst in the nation. She worked tirelessly with the female prisoners. Her ministry of grace and love had such a profound effect that the prison soon hired her as their first female chaplain, and she served in that role for over thirty years. At her retirement, top prison officials recognized her for having made a major impact on the entire prison system—inmates and staff alike—through her Christlike life and ministry.

It had not been easy, of course. She had faced many hardships and challenges along the way. But God sustained her and brought her through them all. Even in retirement, she continued to share the gospel and the Scriptures with people in her church and community who sought her out for counsel and encouragement.

An important part of how God makes us like Jesus is by using us to serve Him, as He did Wendy Hatcher. Regardless of our station in life, God has things for us to do, good things that glorify Him. God calls every believer to be filled with the Holy Spirit continually so He can guide and empower them to fulfill His purposes through their life.

If that is what we desire, we will do well to study what Scripture tells us about the person and work of the Spirit and to seek to deepen our experience with Him. Whenever this happens, we become more fruitful.

Out of the Shadows

The Holy Spirit is not as prominently highlighted in the Old Testament as He is in the New Testament. But do not mistake "less prominent" for "nonexistent." The Spirit was present and active at creation, inspired the prophets who authored much of the Old Testament, and anointed and empowered various leaders of Israel, including judges and kings, to perform specific roles and tasks. The Spirit also imparted special gifts to certain individuals such as Bezalel and Oholiab, artisans called and gifted to serve in the construction of the tabernacle (Exod. 35:30–35).

Before Jesus' incarnation and ascension, what role did the Spirit play in the life of the ordinary Israelite living under the Old Covenant? The Bible does not give us as clear a picture as we might like, so opinions differ at points. But we know that God promised to change the hearts of believing Israelites so they and their children could know, love, and serve Him (Deut. 30:6) and that the Spirit would have been the agent of such a change. We can also say with confidence that God was present to His people in the tabernacle (and later, in the temple) through His Spirit and that the faithful could draw near to Him there (see Exod. 25:8; 1 Samuel 3). And we know that God illuminated, taught, and guided His people in daily life (Ps. 25:9; 31:3; 32:8; 37:23–24; 119:18, 33, 105, 135; Prov. 3:5–6) through His Spirit. Clearly, the Holy Spirit was *with* true believers in the Old Testament era, as He was *with* Jesus' first disciples, but it is not clear that He dwelt *in* them until Pentecost (John 14:17; Ezek. 34:26).

Though the Spirit was certainly active throughout the Old Testament period, His personhood remained in the background, with His work often described in ways that might suggest impersonal divine power or agency. Despite His lower profile, however, many Jewish people looked forward to the outpouring of the Spirit in connection with the coming of the Messiah and the new age He would usher in (Isa. 11:1–2; 32:15; Joel 2:28–29). Many also longed for the new heart and transformed life the Spirit would beget in God's people (Ezek. 36:25–27).

In the New Testament, the Holy Spirit's person *and* work become increasingly visible. This begins when He brings about the miraculous conception of Jesus, the Messiah, and then later anoints and empowers Jesus for ministry (Matt. 1:20–21; Luke 1:34–35; 3:21–22). Just before His ascension, Jesus promised His disciples the Spirit's empowerment for their mission: "Behold, I am sending the promise of my Father upon you. But stay in the city until you are clothed with power from on high" (Luke 24:49).

At Pentecost, as we considered briefly in Chapter 14, the Holy Spirit broke forth in blazing intensity, empowering, launching, and guiding the church and its mission of making disciples of all nations. Let's look at this passage again:

> When the day of Pentecost arrived, they were all together in one place. And suddenly there came from heaven a sound like a mighty rushing wind, and it filled the entire house where they were sitting. And divided tongues as of fire appeared to them and rested on each one of them. And they were all filled with the Holy Spirit and began to speak in other tongues as the Spirit gave them utterance. (Acts 2:1–4)

Peter proclaims that this mighty outpouring of the Holy Spirit inaugurated the era of the Spirit, which was prophesied centuries earlier by the prophet Joel. Peter says:

> But this is what was uttered through the prophet Joel: "And in the last days it shall be, God declares, that I will pour out my Spirit on all flesh, and your sons and your daughters shall prophesy, and your young men shall see visions, and your old men shall dream dreams; even on my male servants and female servants in those days I will pour out my Spirit, and they shall prophesy. And I will show wonders in the heavens above and

> signs on the earth below, blood, and fire, and vapor of smoke; the sun shall be turned to darkness and the moon to blood, before the day of the Lord comes, the great and magnificent day. And it shall come to pass that everyone who calls upon the name of the Lord shall be saved." (vv. 16–21)

From that day forward, not just leaders but *all* of God's people—male and female, old and young, masters and servants—would receive the Holy Spirit's indwelling presence, and "everyone who calls upon the name of the Lord [would] be saved" (v. 21). Through the life, death, resurrection, and ascension of the Messiah and the outpouring of the Holy Spirit at Pentecost, the new age of the Spirit's work began, and the church was established. With the people of God guided and empowered by the Spirit dwelling within them, God's kingdom would continue to advance.

The "Third Person" of the Trinity

The Bible teaches us that there is one God (Deut. 6:4) in three persons: the Father, the Son, and the Holy Spirit. This terminology can be confusing, because we don't mean that God is three "persons" in the same way that we would say "three persons remained in the room," where each of the three human beings in question was wholly separate from the other two. Similarly, it is also customary to speak of the Father as the "first person" of the Trinity, the Son (Jesus Christ) as the "second person," and the Holy Spirit as the "third person." But again, the use of "first," "second," and "third" doesn't indicate an ordering by rank or a hierarchy as it might in common speech regarding human beings. Rather, the three persons might be thought of like three cords braided together to make one rope. Each of the three is identifiable but is not separable from the others within the context of the rope. (The analogy is, of course, imperfect, yet some may still find it helpful.)

Jesus declared in His Upper Room discourse that the Holy Spirit, the third person of the Trinity, was a person like Himself (but without a physical body) who would take His place with the disciples. The Holy Spirit's personhood and crucial role in discipleship and the work of the kingdom become clear in the fuller light of Jesus, the church, and the new era.

The personhood of the Spirit is also obvious in Acts, where we read that the Spirit speaks (10:19; 11:12; 13:2; 21:11), confers (15:28), forbids (16:6), and can be lied to (5:1–11). Impersonal forces do none of those things. In Paul's epistles we read that "the Spirit intercedes for us" (Rom. 8:26) and wills/decides (1 Cor. 12:11); He can be experienced in fellowship (2 Cor. 13:14), grieved (Eph. 4:30), and quenched (1 Thess. 5:19). These are the actions of a personal being, not an impersonal force.

The Holy Spirit is divine. The Scriptures make this plain in several places, including the familiar baptismal formula of Matthew 28:19 ("baptizing them in the name of the Father and of the Son and of the Holy Spirit") and Paul's benediction in his second letter to the Corinthians ("The grace of the Lord Jesus Christ and the love of God and the fellowship of the Holy Spirit be with you all" [13:14]). By mentioning the Holy Spirit alongside God the Father and Jesus the Son, the Scriptures confirm that the Spirit is also God.

Discovering that the Holy Spirit is not merely an impersonal force but a divine Person dwelling within the believer has revolutionized the lives of many over the centuries. If you have an unclear or vague understanding of the Spirit, ask God to give you clarity as you read this chapter and ponder the relevant scriptures. And in prayer, ask the Holy Spirit to fill you, teach you of Himself, and let you know His indwelling presence.

The Person and Work of the Holy Spirit

When we survey the New Testament, we see that Jesus Christ secured our redemption through His life, death, resurrection, and ascension. After He finished everything the Father had given Him to do on earth, He returned to heaven and sat down at the Father's right hand (Heb. 10:12). From there He now intercedes for us and will one day return as God's appointed judge of all humankind and bring God's eternal kingdom to its consummation (Acts 17:30–31; Rom. 8:34).

As we await that glorious day, Jesus continues the kingdom mission He began on earth; He does so through the Holy Spirit. The Spirit glorifies Jesus by applying in His people's lives all the benefits He secured for them through His work on earth. Theologian Herman Ridderbos writes,

> What this life by the Spirit involves further in its outworking and realization is expressed in Paul's epistles in a great many ways and in richly shaded terminology … . From all this it is clear how great the span of the work of the Spirit is and how much Paul ascribes the whole of the new life, in its origin as well as its realization and consummation, to the Spirit, to his operations, powers and gifts.[1]

On the personal level, this includes drawing us to trust Christ, giving us new birth, dwelling within us, teaching us, empowering us, imparting gifts to us, transforming us, sending us out on mission, and using us to extend God's kingdom throughout the earth—in other words, the full spectrum of our life in this world.

I have observed that many believers feel surprised when they see a list of things the Bible says the Spirit does. Here are a few examples:

- convicting unsaved individuals of sin, righteousness, and judgment (John 16:8–11)

1 Herman Ridderbos, *Paul: An Outline of His Theology* (Grand Rapids, MI: Eerdmans, 1975), 222–223.

- bringing spiritual regeneration (or new birth) to those who trust Christ (John 3:5–6)
- incorporating new believers into the body of Christ (1 Cor. 12:13)
- adopting believers into the family of God and assuring them of sonship (Rom. 8:15–16)
- dwelling within believers (John 14:16–17; Rom. 8:9ff; 1 Cor. 6:19–20; Eph. 5:18; Col. 1:27)
- giving believers a deep knowledge of Christ and His love (Eph. 3:19)
- illuminating the truth of Scripture (1 Cor. 2:6–13; Eph. 1:16–20)
- empowering believers to put to death the works of the body/flesh (Rom. 8:13; Gal. 5:16)
- producing the character of Jesus (fruit of the Spirit) in believers' lives (Gal. 5:22–23)
- imparting gifts for ministry (1 Cor. 12:11)
- guiding in ministry (Acts 13:1–3; 16:6–10)
- empowering God's people to proclaim the good news about Christ (Acts 1:8; 4:31; 1 Cor. 2:1–5; 1 Thess. 1:4–5).

The Spirit does His work in these areas not by making Himself the center of attention, but by focusing attention on Christ and glorifying Him (John 16:13–14). The Spirit is emphatically Christ-centered in His work. From the time we are first drawn to Christ until the day we get actively engaged in kingdom ministry and beyond, the Holy Spirit works in us to make all these things happen.

Where do you see the Spirit working in your life? If you aren't sure or just would like to learn more about the Holy Spirit, I encourage you to read Gregg R. Allison's *God, Gift and Guide: Knowing the Holy Spirit* or J. I. Packer's *Keep in Step with the Spirit: Finding*

Fullness in Our Walk with God. For a deeper look, try the most recent scholarly treatment, Gregg R. Allison and Andreas Köstenberger's *The Holy Spirit*, which is part of a series called *Theology for the People of God* published by B&H Academic.

Baptism with the Holy Spirit

Clearly, the Holy Spirit is at the heart of the disciple's life, start to finish. Only He can empower our transformation into Christlikeness, the goal of discipleship. And only He can supply the gifts, power, and guidance we need for fruitful ministry as disciples of Jesus.

How do we experience His life-changing work in our lives? Holy Scripture, which the Holy Spirit inspired and illuminates, shows the way and helps us interpret our experiences. This means that we must seek to understand any experiences of the Spirit we have had (or not had) through the lens of Scripture. In other words, we should not read our experiences into the Scripture but rather let the Scripture teach us the meaning of our experiences. That is what we will try to do ahead, and it will require some focused thinking.

With this in mind, let's now look at the phrase "baptize with the Holy Spirit," a term that has been understood in differing ways over the years by Christ-loving, Bible-believing Christians from diverse backgrounds. We start here because John the Baptist, the forerunner and herald of the Messiah, used this phrase as an overall characterization of Jesus' ministry (see Matt. 3:11; Luke 3:16). As we proceed, it will be helpful to keep in mind a central question over which opinions have differed: Does "baptize with the Holy Spirit" refer to receiving the Holy Spirit at the beginning of the Christian life (that is, the new birth, which all true believers experience), or to an experience of the Spirit subsequent to the new birth that empowers for service and/or holy living and which only some believers enjoy? Clarity about this will strengthen the foundations of our Christian life. A brief sketch is all we can provide here, but it will lay out the basics.[2]

Regardless of our views on this question, we do well to start our inquiry by giving thanks and praise to God for the gift of the Holy Spirit and His empowering and transforming work in our lives. Without His work in us, we would not have been born again, nor would we be able to overcome sin, become like Jesus, serve Him in ministry to others, be His witness, or help spread His kingdom. And we also do well to give thanks for the Spirit's empowering work in other believers, even if their experience differs from ours or if we would not explain it as they do. We are, after all, members of the same family.

In recent decades, Bible-believing scholars have made significant advances in the field of biblical studies, and this includes a refined understanding of the meaning of the phrase "baptize with the Holy Spirit."[3] I have found John Stott's explanations in *Baptism and Fullness: The Work of the Holy Spirit Today* to be clear and helpful and well worth reading. Similarly, Professor Gregg Allison's more recent discussion, quoted below, is also quite concise and illuminating:

> I will use an example—water baptism—to illumine Spirit baptism. Water baptism consists of four elements; the agent who baptizes (the pastor), the one who is baptized (the new believer), the medium of baptism (water), and the purpose of baptism (e.g., association with the triune God [Matthew 28:19] …). Baptism with the Spirit similarly consists of four elements: the agent who baptizes (Jesus Christ), the one who is baptized (the new believer), the medium of baptism (the Holy Spirit), and the purpose of baptism (incorporation into the body of Christ [1 Corinthians 12:13]) … . I define baptism with the Spirit as

2 Those wishing to explore this subject in greater depth should consult *Perspectives on Spirit-Baptism: Five Views*, edited by Chad Owen Brand and R. Stanton Norman (B&H Academic, 2004).

3 The word "with" translates the Greek preposition *en*, which can be rendered "in," "with," or "by," depending on the context.

> the work of Jesus Christ in which he pours out the Holy Spirit on new believers thereby incorporating them into his (Christ's) body, the church.[4]

There are a total of seven references to "baptizing with the Holy Spirit" in the New Testament: four in the Gospels, two in the book of Acts, and one in the writings of Paul, in 1 Corinthians.[5] If this is an area of Christian theology that you would like to learn more about, I recommend studying those passages in more depth while seeking out the guidance of trusted commentators and pastors.

The weight of biblical evidence does not support the view that the phrase "baptize with the Holy Spirit" refers to an experience of the Spirit subsequent to conversion, and only for some. Rather, it leans heavily in favor of understanding the phrase "baptize with the Spirit," which the Gospels use to characterize Jesus' ministry, as the proper term for His work of initiating the Christian life and incorporating believers into the body of Christ and God's kingdom.

However, this does not mean that post-conversion experiences of the Spirit, sometimes powerful ones, do not occur in the lives of believers. They certainly can and do occur and should be desired and welcomed. Many believers have testified to the blessings they bring; but they are properly described as being "filled with the Spirit." This is reinforced by the fact that Scripture nowhere commands believers to be baptized with the Holy Spirit, but it does command them to be filled with the Spirit, something which can occur on multiple occasions. One baptism, many fillings is the biblical pattern—thus, we say "yes" to a second, third, fourth, fifth blessing, and more!

A small but growing number of noted Pentecostal and Charismatic scholars (communities traditionally affiliated with the view

---

4 Gregg Allison, "Baptism with and Filling of the Holy Spirit," *Southern Baptist Journal of Theology* 16, no. 4 (2012): 5.

5 See Matt. 3:11; Mark 1:8; Luke 3:16; John 1:33; Acts 1:5; 11:16; 1 Cor. 12:13.

that there is a separate experience of the Spirit post-conversion) have recognized this and concluded that the phrase "baptize with the Spirit" does indeed refer to the initial reception of the Spirit at conversion, and that "filling" is the proper term for subsequent experiences with the Spirit.[6] Regardless, it is important to affirm that our discussion of differing views of this phrase is not meant to question the genuineness of any believer's experiences of the Holy Spirit, but only to provide more accurate understanding and terminology for them and help promote greater unity in the body of Christ. It cannot be emphasized too strongly that this is a family discussion among brothers and sisters in Christ and should never be allowed to divide us: "Unity in essentials, liberty in non-essentials, and love over all" should be our guiding principle.[7]

It remains to ask, what signs accompany Spirit baptism? This is another significant issue where opinions of faithful believers have differed, but some signs are widely agreed upon. Certainly, empowerment for ministry is one. As noted earlier, Jesus said, "You will receive *power* when the Holy Spirit has come upon you and you will be my *witnesses* in Jerusalem and all Judea and Samaria, and to the end of the earth" (Acts 1:8, my emphasis). In other words, they would be enabled to bear witness to the life, death, and resurrection of Jesus and thus begin to fulfill the Great Commission in some measure.

Power for new obedience and holiness of life is another sign. But Luke's primary concern in Acts is not the sanctification of the believer, but rather the missionary expansion of the church. Luke's main purpose in writing Acts is to describe the launching of the new era of the Spirit and the progress of God's kingdom, not the details of Christian

---

6 See Gordon Fee, *God's Empowering Presence: The Holy Spirit in the Letters of Paul* (Peabody, MA: Hendrickson, 1994), 864–865; Max Turner, *The Holy Spirit and Spiritual Gifts in the New Testament Church and Today* (Peabody, MA: Hendrickson, 1996), 147–165.

7 These words have been variously attributed to Augustine, Rupertus Meldenius, and Richard Baxter. They appeared in a tract on unity by Meldenius in 1627. See Philip Schaff, *History of the Christian Church*, vol. 7 (Grand Rapids, MI: Eerdmans, 1965), 650–653.

experience. By contrast, the topic of sanctification appears more frequently in Paul's letters to the churches, just where we would expect it to be.

Some believers hold that speaking in tongues is the sign of Spirit baptism. While it certainly was a sign for those gathered together at Pentecost (Acts 2:1–13), it is not mentioned at all regarding the three thousand people converted later that day (v. 41) or the two thousand others converted as reported in Acts 4:4 or 5:18. Neither is it mentioned in connection with the Ethiopian eunuch (Acts 8:26–40), Lydia (16:11–15), the Philippian jailer (16:25–34), or those converted on Paul's missionary journeys (with the exception of Ephesus). We simply do not know whether others in the early church spoke in tongues when they were baptized with the Spirit. They may have, but if they did, Luke, the author of Acts, did not think it important enough to mention in every case. In light of the examples above, it is also helpful to note that the actual experience of the Spirit in individual lives varied from the highly dramatic (such as on the day of Pentecost) to the quiet and gentle (such as with Lydia, Acts 16:14).

Concerning tongues, in fairness, we should note that even if speaking in tongues is not *the* sign of Spirit baptism, or a prominent gift, it is listed as one of the gifts of the Spirit that was given to some but not all in the church of Corinth (1 Cor. 12:30). Further, Paul valued the gift highly in his own life. He tells the Corinthians, "I thank God that I speak in tongues more than all of you" (14:18). And he saw sufficient value in this gift to warrant saying, "I want you all to speak in tongues" and "Do not forbid speaking in tongues. But all things should be done decently and in order" (14:5, 39–40). This last sentence suggests that the exercise of tongues could get out of hand. Despite potential abuses, however, there is no suggestion that it should be banned. Whether the gift of speaking in tongues is still available is a subject of lively ongoing discussion in the Christian world. We will look at it again in the chapter on spiritual gifts below (Chapter 18).

Through the Holy Spirit's presence and power, the church grew by leaps and bounds, even in the face of intense persecution. The Spirit enlarged the community of disciples, filling and refilling both the apostles and ordinary believers as circumstances required. These repeated fillings empowered them to endure persecution and to boldly, faithfully, and powerfully speak God's Word and spread His kingdom.

We see the effects of this mighty movement of the Spirit throughout the book of Acts. More and more people got swept into God's kingdom as it spread through the Roman Empire. Outside the secular West, many people today are being swept into the kingdom through the empowered ministry and witness of ordinary believers who are filled with the Holy Spirit. Every believer in the secular West needs to be likewise filled with the Spirit in order to live an empowered life that impacts the world in which they live for Christ. Are you?

Questions to Ponder

1. What effect did spotlighting the personal nature of the Holy Spirit in this chapter have on you?
2. Briefly comment on two or three of the listed actions of the Holy Spirit that you found most encouraging.
3. How would you describe the relationship between the "baptism with the Holy Spirit" and subsequent experiences involving the Holy Spirit (such as filling, coming upon, etc.)?
4. How do you respond to the thought of being personally filled with and empowered by the Spirit?
5. Do you hunger for a deeper and more personal experience with the Holy Spirit? If not, are you willing to ask God to give you a desire for all that He has for you?

16

Being Filled with the Spirit

Do not get drunk with wine, for that is debauchery,
but be filled with the Spirit.
Ephesians 5:18

Our new life in God begins when Jesus baptizes us with the Holy Spirit into the body of Christ. This can happen anywhere and anytime, as we see in the book of Acts. Prior to that moment, we are dead in sin, regardless of any formal religious involvements we may have. After that moment, we are alive to God through Jesus Christ by the Spirit (Rom. 6:11). Like the blind man whom Jesus healed, we can say, "One thing I do know, that though I was blind, now I see" (John 9:25).

This conversion may come suddenly, as it did with Paul on the road to Damascus (Acts 9:1–17), or it may come gradually, as with Timothy (2 Tim. 1:5; 3:15), who came to faith through the nurture of his mother and grandmother. It may look dramatic, as with Cornelius and his family and friends (Acts 10:34–48), or it may look quiet and gentle, as with Lydia (Acts 16:14). One thing will remain true in all cases, however: the man or woman who once was spiritually dead is now alive to God through Jesus Christ and becomes part of the new creation. He or she is a new creature in Christ. Paul put it this way: "If anyone is in Christ, he is a new creation. The old has passed away; behold, the new has come" (2 Cor. 5:17). Evangelist and author Leonard Ravenhill sums this up memorably: "Jesus didn't come into the world just to make bad men good. He came into the world to make dead men live."[1]

Live in the Fullness of God's Spirit

From new birth onward and throughout our life on earth, God calls us to live each day in the fullness of the Holy Spirit. The Spirit is the key to authentic Christian living—discipleship—and without His empowerment, teaching, and guidance, none of us can live faithfully or fruitfully.

To experience the fullness of the new life God has given us, we must learn how to live in the Spirit. This supernatural, Spirit-filled life is just as available to us today as it was to first-century believers. And what's more, the Scripture does not suggest or recommend, but *commands* us to seek it (Eph. 5:18). *This means that everyone who obeys the command can be full of the Spirit.* It also means that everyone who disobeys the command is not walking in the Spirit's fullness. Living in the fullness of the Spirit is essential for transformation, for as theologian John Murray said, "It is the Spirit who is the agent of sanctification."[2] Sanctification is that great, lifelong work of transformation into the image of Christ that the Holy Spirit carries on in everyone who has been justified by faith and born again.

How do we live such a life? Consider one important guiding principle from an unknown source: "Believe everything the Scriptures teach about the Holy Spirit and expect everything that the Scriptures promise from the Holy Spirit." Although this brief chapter cannot cover the full teaching of Scripture, we will look at one of the most important keys to living in the Spirit.

---

1 Leonard Ravenhill, "No Man Is Greater Than His Prayer Life," sermon, YouTube, posted June 28, 2023, by Sermons with G.

2 John Murray, *Redemption Accomplished and Applied* (Grand Rapids, MI: Eerdmans, 1955), 146; see also 147–150.

Be Filled with the Holy Spirit

The Holy Spirit comes to *reside* within us when we are baptized with the Holy Spirit and born again. If at that point we give ourselves over to the Spirit's leadership as we should, He can fill us and *reign* in us at once, allowing sanctification to advance. But for a variety of reasons, many believers do not make a full commitment at conversion, or they only do so for a short time. A striking example of this occurs among the believers in Corinth. Paul gave thanks to God for them "because of the grace of God that was given to you in Christ Jesus" and also because "you are not lacking in any [spiritual] gift" (1 Cor. 1:4, 7). And yet, he also said to them,

> But I, brothers, could not address you as spiritual people, but as people of the flesh, as infants in Christ. I fed you with milk, not solid food, for you were not ready for it. And even now you are not yet ready, for you are still of the flesh. For while there is jealousy and strife among you, are you not of the flesh and behaving only in a human way? For when one says, "I follow Paul," and another, "I follow Apollos," are you not being merely human? (3:1–4)

The Spirit resided in the Corinthians, but He could not reign in them; they had become stuck in prolonged spiritual infancy. The root cause of their stagnation was lack of wholehearted commitment to God, resulting in a proliferation of sinful attitudes and behaviors which apparently went unrecognized, unconfessed, and unrepented. This sad state of affairs effectively quenched the Spirit and denied Him control of these believers' lives. They had defaulted to human strength and wisdom and thus manifested little of the Spirit's fruit and the self-control He produces. This helps explain F. B. Meyer's observation: "In every born-again Christian the Spirit of

Christ is present; in some He is prominent; in only a few, alas, He is preeminent."[3]

Research has shown that most professing believers in the American church have never made such a surrender of themselves to God.[4] They have never taken a decisive stand against the flesh—their old, sinful self and its desires—and have never put God first in their lives. That is, they have never bowed to God as supreme in their lives and aimed to make everything else secondary to Him and His will and to live under the lordship of Christ. From my observation, this often fails to occur because Christians haven't been properly taught, and therefore they lack a clear understanding of what God wants of them. In other cases, believers do know what God wants but refuse His conditions. They say "no" to sin only so long as doing so doesn't conflict with what they want to do. They have one foot in the kingdom and one foot in the world, which means they live with a divided heart and a compromised life.

Such a situation may well have contributed to the arrested development of the people addressed in the book of Hebrews, who were told, "You have become dull of hearing. For though by this time you ought to be teachers, you need someone to teach you again the basic oracles of God. You need milk, not solid food" (5:11–14). Sadly, this appears to be the state of many in the American church.

What should we make of this? If such individuals have been truly converted, they are indwelled by the Spirit but not *filled* with the Spirit. Or, as we said earlier, the Spirit resides in them but does not reign in them. On the other hand, if they are not converted, then the Spirit does not dwell in them at all. An indication of the latter is a lack of spiritual interest, hunger, and growth over a long time; the absence of sanctification suggests the absence of justification.

---

3 This quotation is widely attributed to F. B. Meyer though not found in this form in modern editions of his works.

4 "Self-Described Christians Dominate America but Wrestle with Four Aspects of Spiritual Depth," *Barna Group* (www.barna.com/research), September 13, 2011.

How can we be filled with the Holy Spirit so that He reigns in us? The fundamental starting point is hunger for God, a desire for greater intimacy with the God who loves us and has done so much for us. This desire fuels an eagerness to do the things that please Him. If we lack this desire, we can ask God to give it to us, to stir up in us a hunger and thirst for Himself, His Son, His Spirit, and His glory. When we come to this stage, we are at the threshold of being filled with the Spirit.

Next, we must reckon with the decisive issue: Who will be in charge of our life? For being filled with God's Spirit is not about me having more of the Spirit, but about Him having more of me. This requires abdicating the throne of our self-rule and giving control to Him. Are we ready to renounce our autonomy and let Him rule over and lead our life, with all that this entails? This is the critical question we must answer in the affirmative. If we do not cede control to the Spirit, we block Him from filling us (Gal. 5:16–17). But if we do, the moment we surrender, He can begin to reign in us.

How Do We Surrender to God?

In the book of Romans, Paul wrote eleven chapters about God's grace and mercy, and then he shifted his focus to how we should respond: "I appeal to you therefore, brothers," he writes, "by the mercies of God, to present your bodies as a living sacrifice, holy and acceptable to God, which is your spiritual worship" (Rom. 12:1). Paul means that the only appropriate response to God for the totally undeserved grace and mercy He has lavished upon these disciples of Christ is for them to give themselves over to Him wholeheartedly and continually live under His lordship. To borrow a phrase from Oswald Chambers, they must "recklessly abandon themselves to God."[5]

To some, this may sound like a harsh demand. But it isn't. As Bible commentator William Barclay observed, "Christianity does not think of

5 This theme is prevalent throughout Oswald Chambers' classic devotional *My Utmost for His Highest* (Grand Rapids, MI: Our Daily Bread Publishing, 2011).

a man finally submitting to the *power* of God; it thinks of him as finally surrendering to the *love* of God. It is not that man's will is crushed, but that man's heart is broken."[6] God's love, manifested in grace and mercy at the cross, must grip our hearts and motivate our surrender.

This surrender is not passive in nature but active—a decisive act, a commitment which we must reaffirm daily, sometimes even moment by moment. It means freely giving ourselves, body and soul, to the loving Father who sent His only Son to rescue us from our sin and rebellion and lead us into what is "good and acceptable and perfect" (Rom. 12:2 KJV). This requires, as Paul said elsewhere, recognizing "that your body is a temple of the Holy Spirit within you, whom you have from God[.] You are not your own, for you were bought with a price," and that you are to "glorify God in your body" (1 Cor. 6:19–20). Thus, we present ourselves to God as children who want to please Him and be used for His purposes, no matter the cost, for as long as we live. (If you are not yet willing to make this commitment, ask God to help you become willing.)

Paul had already explained in Romans 6 that this is simply an implication of what it means to be united with Christ, to be truly converted. It is not something extra, not an optional, higher-level commitment made only by those who choose to be "all in." But apparently, not every believer in the Roman church understood this (otherwise, Paul would not have needed to stress it in Romans 6, especially verses 12 to 14, and in Romans 12:1). Many today seem to be completely unaware of this crucial truth—and their lives show it. But thanks be to God, once we learn this truth and hand over control of our life to God, His Spirit can fill, empower, and direct us into all that He has for us. And as our knowledge of Him grows, the expanding circle of light will illuminate areas to give Him that we did not recognize earlier; we will experience even deeper transformation as life unfolds.

---

6 William Barclay, *New Testament Words* (Philadelphia: The Westminster Press, 1974), 23.

How specifically do we, as born-again believers, give ourselves wholly to God if we have not already done so? By sincerely abandoning ourselves to God from the heart, prayerfully confessing and forsaking any known sin, and trusting Him to forgive us and accept our self-giving. This is not simply an emotional impulse but is first of all a principled decision, a choice and commitment to no longer live for self but *for* God and *with* God for His glory. Some people experience the Spirit's presence in an unusual way at the moment of commitment, but others do not. And to be clear, the nature of one's personal experience is not the issue. Regardless of what we experience or don't experience, what we feel or do not feel, the key is a decisive act of our will, made in faith.

Paul's instructions to the believers in Ephesus about the Spirit-filled life hold valuable practical insights for us today. Note first that he told this church, "You also, when you heard the word of truth, the gospel of your salvation, and believed in him, *were sealed* with the promised Holy Spirit" (Eph. 1:13; my emphasis). In Paul's day, a seal was a mark of ownership—a visible mark that, in essence, represented the person to whom the seal belonged (somewhat comparable to a person's signature in today's economy). The phrasing of this verse in Greek suggests that this seal, this mark of ownership, was placed on them at once when they placed their trust in Christ. Clearly, then, these people were born of God—they were His children—and the Holy Spirit was dwelling in them. But some of them were not *filled* with the Spirit—that is, not under His full control. Put differently, the Spirit resided in them, but He did not reign in them. We can say this because Paul goes on to command them, "Do not get drunk with wine, for that is debauchery, but be filled with the Spirit" (5:18). This exhortation shows us that being filled is not automatic. We have an essential part to play: we must give ourselves over to the Spirit continually.

The verb translated "be filled" has several characteristics that help us understand God's desire for us when it comes to life in the Spirit: the Greek verb is imperative, plural, passive, and present tense. Paul is commanding (imperative mood) the entire congregation (plural) to allow themselves (passive voice—they are not the primary actors) to be continually filled (present tense) with the Spirit and to follow His direction. This command is a loving call to continually enjoy all that is theirs in Christ by yielding to the Spirit of Christ, who resides in them. Herein lies the abundant life Jesus offers, the fullness of Christian life.

Being Filled with the Spirit in Daily Life

What does this look like in daily living? Some have pointed out that a glass filled to the brim with water has no room for anything else; the water fully possesses the glass. This is what life in the Spirit is like for us.

To be filled with the Holy Spirit is to give God full possession of our lives. We cannot live the Spirit-filled life without the wholehearted commitment described in Romans 12:1, without giving God full control. John Stott says of being filled with the Spirit: "There is no technique to learn and no formula to recite. What is essential is such a penitent turning from what grieves the Holy Spirit and such a believing openness to him that nothing hinders him."[7]

After Paul urges the Ephesians to "be filled with the Spirit" (5:18), he describes in practical terms some of the ways being "filled with the Spirit" shows up in the community of God's people. Stott points out four participles that appear in verses 19–21:

addressing one another in psalms and hymns and spiritual psalms (v. 19)
singing and making melody (v. 19)
giving thanks always (v. 20)
submitting to one another (v. 21).

7 John Stott, *God's New Society: The Message of Ephesians* (Downers Grove, IL: InterVarsity Press, 1979), 208.

Then Paul moves on to describe loving relationships between husbands and wives, children and parents, and slaves and masters. At times, these relationships can challenge us and cause difficulty. No wonder God calls us to be filled *continually*! Paul concludes with an exhortation for the Ephesian believers to "put on the full armor of God" (6:11), to prepare themselves for spiritual warfare, which he tells them to expect (v. 12).

Why must we be filled with the Spirit continually? Because the only alternative is for the flesh to be in control of our lives, resulting in our grieving or quenching the Spirit. Such a choice interrupts our communion with Him until we confess, repent, and seek to be filled afresh.

Our ability to consistently live in the Spirit grows stronger as we devote ourselves to the means of grace (the ways He communicates His grace to us) in a community of Jesus' disciples and learn how to let the Spirit have more and more control of our lives. As we do this, our life comes to be characterized by being full of the Spirit, like Stephen (Acts 6:5) and Barnabas (Acts 11:22–24).

Being Filled with the Spirit in Ministry

What does being filled with the Holy Spirit look like in ministry situations, as, for example, in Acts? At certain times, the Spirit can enable us to speak or act effectively to glorify Christ and/or minister to people. One example is when we present the gospel to those who don't yet know Jesus. When the Spirit filled Peter at Pentecost, Peter preached a sermon that God used to bring three thousand people to Christ (Acts 2:14–41).

The Spirit filled Peter again as he addressed a group of hostile Jewish rulers (Acts 4:8), giving him the right words to say just as Jesus had promised that the Spirit would (Luke 12:11–12). Soon after that, he was filled yet again when the Spirit was poured out on the church in response to prayer for boldness in the face of persecution (Acts 4:23–31). He was filled multiple times, as the need arose.

Likewise, in another extraordinary evangelistic encounter, the Spirit filled Paul and led him to place a curse of immediate blindness on a magician who was attempting to block his effort to share the gospel with a Roman proconsul (Acts 4:6–11). This dramatic demonstration of God's power so impacted the proconsul that he trusted Christ as Savior (v. 12).

How do we understand these and similar instances of someone being spiritually "filled"? They are instances of the Holy Spirit filling people in whom the Spirit already reigns and giving them special surges of power for specific mission situations. This seems especially common when believers are proclaiming God's Word. Anyone today can experience such special surges of the Spirit's power when needed (and not only for evangelism).

More broadly, we need the Spirit's fullness for ministry of every sort, even for distributing bread and serving tables (Acts 6:3)! Our ministry activities may or may not be dramatic, but that isn't the issue. What matters is the Spirit's special empowerment for the service we offer to God and others. As noted earlier, although we experience only one baptism of the Spirit, we can be (and should be) filled with the Spirit again and again. If this teaching is unfamiliar to you, prayerfully study the book of Acts and other passages mentioned in this and the previous chapter and ask God to bring you into the fullness of life in the Holy Spirit.

Do Not Grieve the Holy Spirit

In his letters, Paul issues two specific warnings about dangers that will hinder the Spirit's fullness in our life. The first appears in Ephesians 4: "Do not grieve the Holy Spirit of God, by whom you were sealed for the day of redemption" (v. 30). As one commentator observed, Paul's use of the formal description "the Holy Spirit of God" here makes this a very sober warning.[8]

The verses immediately before and after this verse focus on sinful speech and attitudes, teaching us to avoid "corrupting talk" (v. 29) along with "bitterness and wrath and anger and clamor and slander" (v. 31). Such warnings about the tongue appear throughout the Bible in one form or another, for words can be very destructive in people's lives. Paul would have known Proverbs 18:21, which says that "death and life are in the power of the tongue," but perhaps when writing to the Ephesians he also had in mind the sobering words of Jesus: "I tell you, on the day of judgment people will give account for every careless word they speak, for by your words you will be justified, and by your words you will be condemned" (Matt. 12:36–37). The tongue is one of the members of our body that we are to present to God as instruments of righteousness (Rom. 6:12–14).

In many churches today, people seem unaware of the seriousness of sins of the tongue or of the connection between sinful words and ongoing fellowship with the Spirit. We must always remember that the Holy Spirit is *holy* and therefore is naturally offended and grieved by sin. Our words reveal our heart, for "out of the abundance of the heart the mouth speaks" (Matt. 12:34). Unholy words arise from unholy attitudes of heart and can grieve the Spirit and interrupt our communion with Him. When this happens, we will not only have a diminished sense of His presence but also a diminished experience of His power. This, in turn, makes us less able to overcome other sins and temptations. As James 3:6 says, "The tongue is a fire, a world of unrighteousness. The tongue is set among our members, staining the whole body, setting on fire the whole course of life, and set on fire by hell."

What specific sins of the tongue does Paul have in mind when he says, "Do not grieve the Spirit"? From the context of Ephesians 4:30,

---

8 Peter Thomas O'Brien, *The Letter to the Ephesians*, The Pillar New Testament Commentary (Grand Rapids, MI: Eerdmans, 1999), 348.

it seems clear that he includes any form of unwholesome or corrupting talk, whether gossip, lies, cursing, dirty jokes, or critical comments about others. Speaking evil of others offends God, often corrupts those who hear it, and amounts to the sin of spreading an evil report (Exod. 23:1). Not least, it can trigger ripple effects that do great and sometimes lasting damage to the subjects of our sinful comments.

If we go through the day with a loose tongue, carelessly speaking words that grieve the Spirit, we are walking in the flesh and will not enjoy fellowship with Him (1 John 1:6–7). But if we want to walk in the Spirit and *not* grieve Him, if we would like to enjoy close fellowship with Him and experience His power to overcome sin, if we would like to grow in Christlikeness, if we would like to have fruitful ministry to others, we must bridle our tongue. As James said, "If anyone thinks he is religious and does not bridle his tongue but deceives his heart, this person's religion is worthless" (James 1:26), and, "Let every person be quick to hear, slow to speak, slow to anger" (v. 19). If we cannot speak well of another person, we should remain quiet. And when we do speak, we must be careful to "let no corrupting talk come out of your mouths, but only such as is good for building up, as fits the occasion, that it may give grace to those who hear" (Eph. 4:29).

As the Word of God teaches in these verses and elsewhere, we should always aim to speak in gracious ways to bless and lift up those with whom we speak, as befits people of grace and love. Prayer is vital: "Let the words of my mouth and the meditation of my heart be acceptable in your sight, O Lord, my rock and my redeemer" (Ps. 19:14). It is also important to set a guard or sentinel over our lips, as David prayed: "Set a guard, O Lord, over my mouth; keep watch over the door of my lips!" (Ps. 141:3). It can help to ask ourselves, before we speak, these questions suggested by the great missionary Amy Carmichael, which she calls "three sieves": "Is it true? Is it kind? Is it necessary?"[9] If it isn't all three, we should hold our tongues.

James says that if we will discipline our tongues, we can bridle our whole body (James 3:2). On the other hand, as we just saw, "If anyone thinks he is religious and does not bridle his tongue but deceives his heart, this person's religion is worthless" (1:26). This counsel is sometimes overlooked, but it provides an important key to walking in the Spirit. Sadly, many of us do sin with our tongues; many of us do it often as one of the "respectable" sins we regularly commit. But thanks be to God, confession and repentance open the door to forgiveness and restored fellowship with the Holy Spirit.

Misusing the tongue is only *one* way to grieve the Holy Spirit and impair our fellowship with Him. Harboring a range of other sinful attitudes, desires, and behaviors can have the same effect.

Do Not Quench the Spirit

Paul's second warning concerns "quenching" the Holy Spirit. In his closing instructions to the believers in Thessalonica, Paul writes, "Do not quench the Spirit. Do not despise prophecies, but test everything; hold fast what is good. Abstain from every form of evil" (1 Thess. 5:19–22).

In five of the six times the New Testament uses the word "quench," it refers to putting out a fire. Paul's basic meaning here, then, is "do not put out the Spirit's fire."

With respect to "prophecies" (v. 20), Paul is teaching that if a prophetic utterance is offered by someone in the congregation, it should not automatically be despised or disregarded; it might be from the Holy Spirit.[10] Because "prophetic utterances" have become more common in some churches today, mainly Pentecostal and charismatic,

---

9 Amy Carmichael, *Edges of His Ways: Selections for Daily Reading* (Fort Washington, PA: Christian Literature Crusade, 1955), 113.

10 See an example in 1 Corinthians 14:29–33.

this injunction perhaps has more relevance than in years past. Leaders and members of such churches must weigh and discern the content of a presumed prophetic word to evaluate whether it indeed came from God. The same applies to any other extraordinary manifestations of spiritual gifts in the church.

And how does one discern? By following the example of the Bereans, whom Luke commended. After listening to Paul preach, "they received the word with all eagerness, examining the Scriptures daily to see if these things were so" (Acts 17:11). Church members (and especially leaders) must test any message, sermon, lecture, or prophetic utterance by its agreement with what the Spirit has already said in Scripture. He is the Spirit of truth, who inspired the writing of the Scriptures and will never contradict Himself (John 16:13; 2 Pet. 1:21). When Scripture speaks, God speaks. What agrees with Scripture is to be embraced. What does not agree is to be rejected.

As we carefully study the Scripture and obey it as God's direction for our lives, we will mature in our ability to discern what is true and what is false. It is also useful to consult with others in your church or denomination to further learn about the work of the Spirit. The counsel given here is not exhaustive but rather is designed to set us on the right track toward deeper knowledge and appreciation of the Spirit.

The Empowering Presence

The life of discipleship is made possible only through the empowering presence of the Holy Spirit, the Spirit of Jesus Christ. Discipleship—the Christian life—does not work on any other basis.

Only as we daily allow the Holy Spirit to fill us by consciously yielding ourselves to His control and direction, and as we avoid grieving and quenching Him, can we walk as Jesus walked. Only in this way can we experience transformation into Christlikeness and fulfill the work He has called us to do. And only then will we be in a position to receive special surges of the Spirit's power for mission and ministry.

Questions to Ponder

1. How would you describe your daily expectation regarding the empowering presence of the Holy Spirit in your life?
2. Why is it so important that disciples of Jesus give themselves wholeheartedly to God and daily yield themselves to His will?
3. Name some characteristics of a community of Jesus' disciples who are being filled with the Holy Spirit.
4. Describe the relationship between the influence of the Holy Spirit and the use of the tongue. What are some ways that walking in the Spirit affects our speech?
5. Using language from some of Paul's teachings discussed above, write out some short prayers asking God to help you hunger and thirst for His Spirit's fullness. Pray these prayers every day for a week or more, perhaps at a certain time each day, and note any changes you see in your walk with God.

17

Walking by the Spirit

Walk by the Spirit, and you will not gratify the desires of the flesh.
Galatians 5:16

Being filled with the Spirit and walking in the Spirit are closely related. Once the Spirit fills us, we must walk by the Spirit and keep in step with Him. In his New Testament letters, Paul teaches us that walking by the Spirit is essential to faithfully living the Christian life each day.

Writing to the Galatian church, Paul says, "Walk by the Spirit, and you will not gratify the desires of the flesh" (Gal. 5:16). Just as he commanded the Ephesians to "be filled" with the Spirit, so here he commands the Galatians to "walk" by the Spirit. "Walk" is a present imperative verb, which typically indicates ongoing action: Paul means that we are to "continue to walk." The Bible commonly uses the metaphor of "walking" to refer to the way one conducts one's life, and that's what Paul means here. He is particularly concerned that the Galatians' moral lives be continually directed by the Holy Spirit and not by elements of the Old Testament law or by sinful, fleshly desires.

New Testament scholar F. F. Bruce sums it up beautifully: "Walking by the Spirit is the outward manifestation, in action and speech, of living by the Spirit. Living by the Spirit is the root; walking by the Spirit is the fruit, and that fruit is nothing less than the practical reproduction of the character (and therefore the conduct) of Christ in the lives of his people."[1]

Valuable Lessons for Today's Church

Believers today can learn valuable lessons by attending to what was going on in the Galatian church. Like the Ephesians, the Galatians had been converted and thus received the Holy Spirit (Gal. 3:3). But false teachers had infiltrated their ranks, insisting that in addition to faith in Christ, salvation required keeping elements of the law of Moses. This emphasis on law-keeping was a form of legalism, which teaches that salvation requires faith in Jesus *plus something else*. Professor Michael Kruger describes it this way: "At its core, legalism is when we base our justification on our own law-keeping rather than on the finished work of Christ. If we depend on our own merits, our own efforts, even our own rituals, to make us acceptable before a holy God, then we have become legalists."[2]

On the other hand, a kind of lawlessness or licentiousness was also present in the church. The term "antinomian"—formed from two Greek words, *anti* ("against") and *nomos* ("law")—is often used to describe this perspective. It is the opposite of legalism and proclaims the Christian's liberation from the requirements of the Old Testament law and freedom to do anything he or she wants. It insists that salvation requires nothing except faith in Jesus; moral change is not necessary. Rather than just clarifying that we are not *saved by* the keeping of the law, it rejects the idea that God's law should guide our conduct at all.[3]

---

1 F. F. Bruce, *The Epistle to the Galatians: A Commentary on the Greek Text*, New International Greek Testament Commentary (Grand Rapids, MI: Eerdmans, 1982), 257.

2 Michael Kruger, "What Exactly Is Legalism? It's More Complicated Than You Think," Canon Fodder, michaelkruger.com, August 12, 2020.

3 Two other "isms" that have long troubled the church are *formalism*, which involves external observance of religious practices and rituals that lack heartfelt devotion and is sometimes called "going through the motions"; and *rigorism*, which takes self-denial to extremes in strict adherence to moral rules and practices in pursuit of a holy life.

These two evils, legalism and lawlessness, have plagued the church from its earliest days. Paul responded to these twin threats by exhorting the Galatian believers to continue to live every day in the Spirit's fullness and power, which would produce righteous behavior, and to continue to resist the temptation to live under the law and the flesh.

The only thing that ultimately matters, he tells them, is "faith working through love" (Gal. 5:6). He urges them to "through love serve one another" (v. 13). He says they will do so as they are "led by the Spirit" (v. 18).

Here again we find a present passive verb in the word "led" (as we saw in Ephesians 5:18), indicating we are to allow the Spirit to direct us, voluntarily yielding ourselves to Him and His guidance. Such guidance normally comes as the Spirit brings applicable scriptures and principles to mind. If we yield to the Spirit, we will neither "gratify the desires of the flesh" (Gal. 5:16) nor live "under the law" (v. 18).

The result? The Holy Spirit can manifest His presence in our lives in the form of "love, joy, peace, patience, kindness, goodness, faithfulness, gentleness, self-control" (v. 22)—a good description of the character of Jesus, into whose image the Spirit seeks to shape all believers. As a result, we are increasingly characterized as people who are full of the Spirit, people in whom Christ is being formed (Gal. 4:19). Many have noted that each of these characteristics has both a personal and an interpersonal dimension. As these disciples walk by the Spirit, the relational life of the congregation also will reflect Christ to the watching world.

If we let the Spirit lead us, our lives will blossom and flourish. But if we neglect or refuse His leading, our lives will languish. It is just that simple.

Unfortunately, many believers misunderstand how the Spirit's leading relates to personal transformation. They use the term to refer to guidance in various life issues, not to moral life and spiritual transformation. A clearer grasp of the Spirit's leading will help us as we seek to grow in grace.

Led by the Spirit?

The phrase "led by the Spirit" is a common one today among many believers, yet it only occurs twice in the New Testament. Because of the widespread misunderstanding of this phrase, we do well to dig a bit deeper. What do these words mean in their context?

The first time this phrase appears is in Romans 8:13–14: "For if you live according to the flesh you will die, but if by the Spirit you put to death the deeds of the body, you will live. For all who are l*ed by the Spirit of God* are sons of God" (my emphasis). In the immediate context, Paul is speaking of the Spirit's empowerment of the believer to put to death the deeds of the body. The second occurrence comes, as we have just seen, in Galatians 5:16–18:

> But I say, walk by the Spirit, and you will not gratify the desires of the flesh. For the desires of the flesh are against the Spirit, and the desires of the Spirit are against the flesh, for these are opposed to each other, to keep you from doing the things you want to do. But if you are *led by the Spirit*, you are not under the law." (my emphasis)

Again, the immediate context highlights believers' battle with sin since they no longer live under the law. In both instances, Paul has a larger concern to show us how to live in a way that produces the beauty of holiness and thereby glorifies God. This all flows out of gratitude to God for His mercy and grace toward us through Christ as well as a desire to please Him.

To address the problems of legalism and licentiousness, Paul doesn't look to Aristotle's Golden Mean, aiming to find a mediating position between the two. Rather, as New Testament scholar Richard

Longenecker has said, he builds a highway above both.[4] As we saw, he does this by giving both a command and a promise: "Walk by the Spirit, and you will not gratify the desires of the flesh" (v. 16). To walk by the Spirit is to live one's daily life actively given over to the Holy Spirit's direction and empowerment (continually filled with the Spirit, as we saw in Ephesians 5:18) and thus manifesting the Spirit's fruit and not that of the flesh. Paul often uses the Greek word *sarx*, usually translated "flesh," to refer to fallen human nature and its self-centered attitudes, desires, and behaviors. To walk in the flesh is the opposite of walking in the Spirit and involves living according to the desires of our old self, a life characterized by various sins and selfish behaviors manifested in the works of the flesh.

Paul then notes how the flesh and the Spirit contend against each other, something every believer knows by experience. This struggle is part of our lifelong battle against the world, the flesh, and the devil, as the Holy Spirit works to make us progressively more like Jesus.

Sometimes we can grow weary and discouraged by this struggle and even doubt our salvation because of it. But, in fact, the struggle provides evidence of life. We overcome the desires of the flesh and live a holy life by keeping in step with the Spirit. What a great encouragement to know that we don't have to remain trapped in our sins in an endless, demoralizing cycle of defeat after defeat with no way of escape!

Practically speaking, how do we walk by the Spirit and overcome the desires of the flesh? This question puzzles many people. In essence, Paul's command to walk or live by the Spirit continually means yielding ourselves consistently to the desires of the Spirit, whose leading always opposes the desires of our sinful flesh (our old self). We yield to the Spirit's leading through an act of the will, choosing the morally correct conduct to which He prompts us, conduct spelled out in the Scriptures, which He has inspired. We must make that choice daily

---

4 Richard N. Longenecker, *Galatians*, Word Biblical Commentary, vol. 41 (Nashville, TN: Thomas Nelson Publishers, 1990), 247.

by continually saying "yes" to the indwelling Spirit's leading and "no" to the desires of the flesh. This is what Paul means by being led by the Spirit.

To reiterate, saying "yes" to the Spirit's leading requires not only yielding our will to His will, but making this complete by taking concrete action in the form of obedience. Or to put it slightly differently, surrendering and yielding to the Spirit does not mean passively waiting for Him to act, but promptly acting upon the Spirit's leading, especially as it comes to us through Scripture, prayer, fellowship, and worship. As Paul expressed in Romans, "So then, brothers, we are debtors, not to the flesh, to live according to the flesh. For if you live according to the flesh you will die, but *if by the Spirit you put to death the deeds of the body*, you will live" (8:12–14; my emphasis).

As we allow the Spirit to influence, direct, and empower us, and, out of love for God, we respond in obedience, we *can* overcome the flesh. Have no doubt about this, for uncertainty leads to self-defeat.

A Few Examples

Some concrete examples can help us better understand the struggle between the Spirit and the flesh and where surrender to each leads us.

Starting with the flesh, we turn to Galatians 5:19–21, where Paul says, "Now the works of the flesh are evident," and then he lists various works of the flesh common in his day and apparently present to some extent even in the church. The list gives a representative sample only; by no means is it exhaustive. Let's pause and consider the list Paul gives us in more depth. For clarity, I have given a very brief, basic explanation of each word, drawing from the work of F. F. Bruce and Richard Longenecker, two highly acclaimed New Testament scholars.[5]

5 The following discussion is paraphrased and summarized from Longenecker, *Galatians*, 252–264; Bruce, *Epistle to the Galatians*, 246–248; see also William Barclay, *Daily Study Bible*, rev. ed. (Philadelphia: The Westminster Press, 1976), 46–52.

Sexual immorality has troubled human societies since the fall, rooted as it is in one of our strongest drives. The Greek word used here, *porneia* (from which we get the word "pornography"), encompasses a variety of sexual sins, including (but not limited to) hiring prostitutes, committing adultery, engaging in premarital sex, homosexual acts, and incest.

Impurity, an even broader term, covers any inappropriate sexual activity that makes a person unclean and unfit for approaching God. Looking at pornography (which is not just a recent concern but has a long history predating Greco-Roman culture) is one such example.

Sensuality refers to throwing restraint to the wind and indulging oneself without regard for normal moral standards. The pursuit of sexual pleasure so consumes a person that public opinion no longer matters. Our modern era calls this "wild living."

Idolatry, the worship of idols, plagued Israel in the Old Testament and was also common in the Greco-Roman culture of Paul's day. Idolatry includes but goes beyond the worship of material objects made of wood or stone (Deut. 4:28). When Paul describes covetousness (greed) as idolatry (Eph. 5:5; Col. 3:5), he shows that idolatry can take nonmaterial forms such as devotion to money, possessions, career, reputation, ambition, or even to other people. As John Calvin observed, "Man's nature, so to speak, is a perpetual factory of idols."[6] Idolatry is simply giving anything or anyone other than God first place in our life.

Sorcery, the English translation of the Greek word *pharmaka* (from which we get the words "pharmacy" and "pharmaceutical"), refers to "using drugs." In Paul's day, the term was applied (ominously) to drugs used in witchcraft and for poisoning people. Today sorcery would include using drugs for mind-altering purposes. Other occult practices such as astrology and fortune telling also fit here.

---

6 John Calvin, *Institutes of the Christian Religion*, vol. 1, ed. John T. McNeill, trans. Ford Lewis Battles (Philadelphia: The Westminster Press, 1969), 108.

Enmity includes negative attitudes and feelings as well as hostile actions toward others, whether individuals or groups. Examples might include refusing to forgive, actively holding grudges, or working mischief against someone. Enmity also includes prejudice toward people of other races and religions, as well as intense dislike or hatred of political figures and parties.

Strife refers to the relational discord and animosity resulting from a quarrelsome, argumentative attitude from one who takes pleasure in self-assertion and confrontation.

Jealousy refers to the selfish resentment of another's success or achievement.

Fits of anger, which we might call "temper tantrums" today, refers to explosive, uncontrolled outbursts of anger against others.

Rivalries denotes selfish ambition and putting oneself and one's interests above those of others.

Dissensions refers to unbiblical, divisive teaching that disrupts church unity.

Divisions describes a partisan spirit or developing cliques around particular people or teachings.

Envy means not merely begrudging the good fortune of others, but also maliciously resenting it and wanting to spoil it or deprive them of it.

Drunkenness speaks of revelry fueled by alcohol, which impairs moral judgment and inhibitions and often leads to immoral actions.

Orgies, closely connected to drunkenness, denotes wild, partying behavior.

"And things like these" (v. 21) indicates that Paul's list gives only a sampling of the attitudes and behaviors that displease and dishonor God. These sins and more, common in pagan society, no doubt characterized some of the people in the Galatian church before they professed faith in Christ. True, saving faith in Christ involves repentance—a turning away from such sins, followed by a daily battle to root them out in the power of the Holy Spirit. Some in the church, apparently, had continued in these sins and did not seek to forsake them. Whether from ignorance of biblical teaching, backsliding, or lack of true conversion, this persistent sin became a serious issue. At the end of his list, therefore, Paul delivered a sobering comment on such behavior: "I warn you, as I warned you before, that those who do such things will not inherit the kingdom of God" (v. 21).

Obviously, this warning applies just as much now as it did then. Therefore, we must give serious attention to what the writer to the Hebrews said: "Strive for peace with everyone, and for the holiness without which no one will see the Lord" (Heb. 12:14). As we saw earlier, this involves giving ourselves body and soul to God and therefore, by the Spirit's power, ceasing to be conformed to the fallen world and its values, attitudes, and behavior and being transformed by the renewal of our mind (Rom. 12:1–2). This produces the fruit of the Holy Spirit in our lives, so to that topic we will now turn.

Happier Thoughts

Paul shifts to happier thoughts in Galatians 5:22–23, where he writes, "But the fruit of the Spirit is …" He then lists nine characteristics of the Holy Spirit's work in the life of a born-again believer.

Unlike the plural word "works" (of the flesh), the "fruit" of the Spirit is singular in Greek, indicating that the nine characteristics make up part of a unified whole. A believer doesn't have some kinds of fruit and not others, though the relative strength of each may vary. We should note that each aspect of the Spirit's fruit is also a behavior or attitude that Scripture commands us to develop. A brief description of each can help us better understand what God desires our life to become, in contrast to the list of sins we reviewed above.

Love (Greek *agape*) heads the list and refers to the love of God poured into our hearts by the Holy Spirit (Rom. 5:5). The word *agape* describes a reciprocating love for God that evokes a desire to please Him. Worship—giving ourselves wholeheartedly to God—and obedience lie at the heart of pleasing Him, but it doesn't stop there. God's love also produces in us a love for our neighbor, a service-oriented love rooted primarily in our will, not our emotions. It acts for our neighbor's best interest and highest good, independently of what he or she may deserve. As Paul says in Galatians 5:6, the only thing that matters in the Christian life is "faith working through love." And so he writes in Galatians 5:13, "through love serve one another." This humble, servant love characterized Jesus' life and should also typify that of His followers. In a very real sense, the other eight characteristics of the Spirit express and highlight various aspects of this *agape* love.

Joy flows out of the awareness of God's gracious favor to us and the hope of living with Him, His Son, and all His children in the world to come. Hope for the life to come fuels joy and gives it a heavenly anchor. It keeps us from getting blown to and fro by the varied circumstances of life and the hard times that sometimes overtake us. Unlike happiness, joy does not depend on having favorable circumstances.

Peace refers not merely to the absence of conflict, but to the presence of the deep and abiding peace of God, the sovereign and almighty King of creation. Grounded in the assurance of God's rich mercy and personal love for us, true peace reveals itself supremely in His saving us by grace alone, through faith alone, in the finished work of Christ alone, and not by our works. This kind of peace produces a tranquil heart at rest in God. It compels and enables us to be peacemakers—to pursue peace with others, including those in our family, community, church, and across all ethnic, racial, political, and other barriers that often separate and divide people.

Patience, also translated "long-suffering," describes exercising forbearance with other people and not allowing ourselves to get easily offended. It particularly includes people who displease, irritate, provoke, or mistreat us, as well as those who persecute us. It suggests the idea of steadfast endurance with difficult people and circumstances. Is it easy? No, but the Spirit can enable us to manifest it. Such patience illustrates the long-suffering of God with those who provoke Him. It provides a powerful public witness to God's enduring love and strength.

Kindness describes an attitude of graciousness and goodwill toward others, especially those who do not deserve it. Kindness expresses a love that goes above and beyond. It resists all harshness and coldness toward others.

Goodness refers to love and kindness in action together, an expression of moral excellence. It gives generously and spends itself to help others without any expectation of return.

Faithfulness means being trustworthy and reliable to God and to others, being dependable and true to one's word and commitments. Others can have confidence in a faithful person, and our faithfulness strengthens our witness with them.

Gentleness means strength under control, rooted in humility. Although Jesus was gentle, He expressed righteous indignation when appropriate. Gentleness is not mere passivity, and it is never arrogant. It doesn't bully or force others but exercises mildness and consideration in dealing with them.

Self-control engages both mind and body in the business of properly regulating all of one's life. The scope of self-control ranges from such mundane matters as food and drink to material possessions, thought life, speech, the expression of emotions, and much more. Self-control entails the mastery of our passions, especially with respect to sexual matters.

Again, the list Paul provides is not exhaustive. But these nine traits form a beautiful portrait of Jesus as we see Him in the Gospels. In their Christ-centered selflessness, they stand in stark contrast to the self-centered life of the flesh. They come from the Spirit and lie beyond mere human attainment, though we have an essential role in their blossoming.

These traits do not appear piecemeal but all together. Nor do they appear immediately in full bloom; rather, they mature over time as we continue to walk in the Spirit and put sin to death. They have not only a personal dimension but also communal aspects, such as blessing and edifying others and strengthening the unity of the church. And most importantly, they glorify God!

What part do we play in the blossoming of the Spirit's fruit in our lives? After listing the fruit of the Spirit, Paul reminds the believers that they "have crucified the flesh with its passions and desires" (Gal. 5:24)—his way of describing their original turning to Christ from their sin. As he said in Romans, "We know that our old self was crucified with [Christ] in order that the body of sin might be brought to nothing, so that we would no longer be enslaved to sin" (Rom. 6:6).

The image of "crucifixion" in Galatians 5:24 depicts our turning from sin in repentance and to Christ in faith—dying to the old life and coming alive to the new, thus breaking the enslavement of our will to sin. Now liberated, we are able to say "no" to sin. This does not mean that we never sin, but that we have been set free to obey God. We must choose, however, to yield ourselves to Him, body and soul (Rom. 6:12–14; 12:1–2), and must act on that choice moment by moment. If we don't, we will remain mired in sin, or, as we drift off and on the path of obedience, our life and witness will be like a flickering light at best.

Keep in Step with the Spirit

Paul goes on to reiterate to the Galatians, using slightly different phrasing: "If we live by the Spirit, let us also keep in step with the Spirit" (5:25). This phrase "keep in step" is slightly different from Paul's earlier command to "walk" and puts more focus on active engagement with the Spirit and on staying in line with His direction in our lives. The Spirit leads and empowers us to walk in obedience to God; our part is to pay attention and intentionally march in line with him. Pastoral theologian John Stott says it very well:

> In Galatians 5:25 this "rule" or "line" is the Holy Spirit Himself and His will. So to "walk by the Spirit" is deliberately to walk along the path or according to the line which the Holy Spirit lays down. The Spirit "leads" us; but we are to "walk by" Him or according to His rule. … This will be seen in our whole way of life—in the leisure occupations we pursue, the books we read and the friendships we make. Above all in what older authors called "a diligent use of the means of grace," that is, in a disciplined practice of prayer and Scripture meditation, in fellowship with believers who provoke us to love and good works, in keeping the Lord's day as the Lord's day, and in attending public worship and the Lord's Supper. In all these ways we occupy ourselves in spiritual things. It is not enough to yield passively to the Spirit's control; we must also walk actively in the Spirit's way. Only so will the fruit of the Spirit appear.[7]

Summing It Up

As we have seen, being led by the Spirit, walking by the Spirit, and keeping in step with the Spirit all depend on our having given ourselves wholeheartedly to God in response to His grace, as an act of our will.

---

7 John R. W. Stott, *The Message of Galatians: Only One Way*, The Bible Speaks Today (Downers Grove, IL: InterVarsity Press, 1986), 153–154.

We make this choice, repeatedly, every day. We say "yes" to God and to the Spirit's leading and "no" to the desires of the flesh.

God knows our weakness; He knows it far better than we do. When the disciples fell asleep in the Garden of Gethsemane after Jesus had asked them to pray for Him just before His arrest, He declared, "The spirit indeed is willing, but the flesh is weak" (Matt. 26:41). Long before that, the psalmist declared that God "knows our frame; he remembers that we are dust" (Ps. 103:14). And the Lord has made provision for our weakness and frailty—in fact, this is precisely the reason He gave us the Holy Spirit!

The Spirit is ready, willing, and eager to reign in us as we yield to Him.

In ways that amaze and delight us, the Holy Spirit actively carries forward the process of transforming us through the renewing of our mind. The process works from the inside out—not simply changing external behaviors, but changing their source. Renewed minds produce renewed thinking, values, attitudes, desires, motives, and behaviors.

At the deepest level, we will begin to identify with what Scottish minister Thomas Chalmers called "the expulsive power of a new affection."[8] Our heart will increasingly appreciate God's grace to us, and our mind will increasingly desire God and His will more than our sin and its pleasure, thus weakening its influence over us.

By immersing ourselves in the Scriptures, prayer, and worship, and when we consistently walk in the Spirit, ask God to reveal the glory of Christ to us, and obediently follow as He leads, we will see the fruit of the Spirit maturing in our life. We will find ourselves being transformed from one level of glory to another by the Spirit, transformed into the image of Jesus Himself (2 Cor. 3:18). And we will be a light in the darkness of this fallen world and Christ's instrument to reach the lost.

---

8 See Thomas Chalmers, *The Expulsive Power of a New Affection* (Wheaton, IL: Crossway, 2020).

No, this transformation isn't easy. It involves challenge and discipline. It may lead to hardship or persecution. And it takes a lifetime. But the rewards are infinitely greater than anything this world can offer.

Questions to Ponder

1. What does Paul mean by his exhortation to be "led by the Spirit" (Rom. 8:13–14)?
2. Which "works of the flesh" mentioned in Galatians 5:19–21 are most prevalent in the culture in which you live? In the church? Which "works of the flesh" most tempt you in your current season of life?
3. What is the significance of the fact that the alternative to "works of the flesh" is the "fruit of the Spirit" (Gal. 5:22–23)?
4. Read over Paul's sample list of works of the flesh and ask God to convict, forgive, and deliver you of any that may be present in your life.
5. Memorize the fruit of the Spirit and regularly ask God to help you mature and abound in each one.

18

Manifesting the Spirit's Gifts

To each is given the manifestation of the Spirit
for the common good.
1 Corinthians 12:7

Charles Spurgeon, arguably the greatest preacher in all of Victorian England, was an English Baptist. Christians from various denominations still highly respect him and read his sermons. In his autobiography, Spurgeon, who was a cessationist,[1] relates an interesting story:

> While preaching in the hall on one occasion, I deliberately pointed to a man in the midst of the crowd and said, "There is a man sitting there who is a shoemaker; he keeps his shop open on Sundays, it was last Sabbath morning, he took nine pence, and there was four pence profit out of it; his soul is sold to Satan for four pence.[2]

Sometime later, this man described the event and its impact on him:

---

1 Cessationists believe that gifts of the Spirit such as speaking in tongues, prophecy, and miraculous healing, sometimes called "sign gifts," were special provisions from God during the early formation of the church but ceased after the death of the apostles.

2 Charles Spurgeon, *C. H. Spurgeon Autobiography, Volume 2: The Full Harvest 1860–1892*, ed. Susannah Spurgeon and Joseph Harrald, rev. ed. (Carlisle, PA: The Banner of Truth Trust, 1973), 531.

> I went to the music hall and took a seat in the middle of the place. Mr. Spurgeon looked at me as if he knew me, and in his sermon pointed to me and told the congregation that I was a shoemaker, and that I kept my shop open on Sundays; and I did, sir. I should not have minded that; but he also said that I took nine pence the Sunday before, and that there was a four pence profit; but how he should know that I could not tell. Then it struck me that it was God who had spoken to my soul through him, so I shut up my shop until the next Sunday. At first, I was afraid to go again to hear him; but afterwards I went, and the Lord met with me, and saved my soul.[3]

Spurgeon added:

> I could tell as many as a dozen similar cases in which I pointed at somebody in the hall without having the slightest knowledge of the person, or any idea that what I said was right, except that I believed I was moved by the Spirit to say it; and so strikingly has been my description, that the persons have gone away and said to their friends, "Come see a man who told me all things that ever I did; beyond a doubt, he must have been sent by God to my soul or else he could not have described me so exactly."[4]

A story like this raises a number of questions about the gifts of the Holy Spirit, questions many believers wonder about. What is a spiritual gift? What are some examples of spiritual gifts? What purpose do spiritual gifts serve? How many spiritual gifts are there? Can I choose the spiritual gift(s) I want? How can I discover my spiritual gift(s)? How do I use my spiritual gift(s)? Can I ask God for additional gifts? Do one's spiritual gifts indicate one's spiritual maturity? What do spiritual gifts look like in action? Where are the gifts of the Spirit listed in

3 Spurgeon, *Spurgeon Autobiography, Volume 2*, 531.

4 Spurgeon, *Spurgeon Autobiography, Volume 2*, 532.

the New Testament? Are all the gifts mentioned in the New Testament still available today, or only some?

This chapter will look at what Scripture says about these questions. It will conclude with some perspectives on spiritual gifts and give time-tested suggestions for discovering your own spiritual gifts.

What Is a Spiritual Gift?

A spiritual gift is a special manifestation or enablement given by the Holy Spirit to each believer to perform a particular function in the body of Christ, typically in the form of words, actions, or abilities. A spiritual gift is not a natural ability, like being intelligent or athletic or artistically gifted, though God can take a natural ability and use it for spiritual purposes.

In the New Testament, spiritual gifts range from relatively unspectacular ones such as serving, teaching, exhorting, giving, leading, and mercy (Rom. 12:7–8) to the more striking and dramatic gifts such as prophecy, healing, working of miracles, and speaking in tongues (1 Cor. 12:9–10). The Bible also describes *people* as gifts of God's grace to the church: "And he gave the apostles, the prophets, the evangelists, the shepherds and teachers, to equip the saints for the work of ministry, for building up the body of Christ" (Eph. 4:11–12).

What Is the Purpose of Spiritual Gifts?

In his first letter to the Corinthians, Paul says, "To each is given the manifestation of the Spirit for the common good" (1 Cor. 12:7). In other words, the Holy Spirit manifests Himself through each believer in a specific way (a gift) to benefit others and to glorify Christ. His gracious gifts enable us to serve others through love (Gal. 5:13) and help build up the congregation. In some instances, spiritual gifts can also be used to bless nonbelievers.

How Many Spiritual Gifts Are There?

Overlapping lists in the New Testament mention at least eighteen spiritual gifts,[5] but we have no indication that these lists are exhaustive. There may be other spiritual gifts not listed in the Bible. Below we will review some of the key passages that give lists of gifts.

Are All the Gifts Available Today?

Christians in the evangelical world agree that most spiritual gifts named in Scripture are available today. However, opinions differ about what some believers call the so-called "sign gifts"—tongues, prophecy, miracles, and healing. Four main groups of opinions have emerged concerning these gifts that typically confirmed either an apostle's authenticity or the truth of his message.

Traditional cessationists believe that the so-called "sign gifts" were necessary to establish the church in a hostile culture but faded out after the death of the apostles and the establishment of the canon of Scripture. They hold that history did not see such gifts after the apostles except in unorthodox groups, and that Christians today should not desire or expect these gifts. While cessationists do not believe individual believers receive sign gifts today, they do believe that in His sovereign will, God may do miracles and grant healing today.

Soft cessationists, whose views are often influenced by reports from the mission field today, believe that God may indeed sometimes grant the sign gifts in hostile cultures where the gospel is preached amid intense opposition or when it is being preached for the first time. Essentially, they hold a similar view to traditional cessationists, but they believe that God sometimes chooses to bestow the sign gifts in a limited range of circumstances.

Continuationists differ from cessationists in that they believe all of the gifts in the New Testament remain available today and are needed

5 Rom. 12:6–8; 1 Cor. 12:7–11; 1 Pet. 4:10–11.

and available until Jesus returns. They point out that the Scripture nowhere suggests that any of the gifts will be withdrawn, and that Paul specifically encourages the gift of prophecy and says, "Do not forbid speaking in tongues" (1 Cor. 14:39; see 14:1). They also note that in 1 Corinthians 14:18, Paul says he practices tongues more than any of the Corinthians. Continuationists also point out that examples of the so-called sign gifts have been identified at various points in church history and thus did not altogether disappear after the apostles died. They attribute the infrequency of such gifts after the time of the apostles to the increasing institutionalization of the church and the rise of heresies such as the Montanist movement, which overemphasized charismatic gifts and brought them into disrepute.

A fourth group, describing themselves as *cautiously open*, has emerged in recent decades. Its adherents say they are "cautiously open" to the continuationist position, meaning that they are open to the idea of apostolic gifts operating today, provided they are exercised with discernment and adherence to biblical guidelines.

Adherents of all of these viewpoints are Bible-believing, earnest seekers after truth, and each side raises significant issues that need to be addressed and resolved in the pursuit of correct biblical understanding. Toward that end, good and godly scholars representing different perspectives on spiritual gifts periodically discuss these matters in an irenic spirit and desire for unity. For brief representative views on both sides, see *Spiritual Gifts: What They Are and Why They Matter* by Thomas Schreiner, which presents a cessationist perspective. For a continuationist view, see *God, Gift and Guide: Knowing the Holy Spirit* by Gregg Allison. Both hold to Reformed theology and are highly respected scholars. As Christian scholars continue to study and to come together in humility and prayerful, friendly dialogue, there is good reason to expect that greater agreement will emerge. May the same be true as ordinary believers study and discuss these matters with one another.

Angry, bitter and acrimonious argument, which has sometimes erupted in discussions about the Holy Spirit and His gifts, delights the devil, dishonors God, and has no place among God's children.[6] We should judge the views of fellow believers with charity and assume that their intentions are good. This means that we judge their positions by their strongest arguments, not their weakest, and their exemplars when they are at their best, not their worst.

Now is a good time to note that a fringe movement known as "the prosperity gospel" has become popular today in some circles. Unbiblical teaching about healing and prosperity characterizes this movement and misleads its adherents, often producing serious spiritual harm. One notable example of harm occurs when people abandon their faith after their prayers for healing, financial prosperity, or other blessings are not answered. This movement is an aberrant outgrowth of the Pentecostal and Charismatic movements. But classical Pentecostals, such as the Assembly of God, and most charismatics, distance themselves from it. We should pray for God to send His light to those involved and to bring them to an understanding of the truth.[7]

Can I Choose the Spiritual Gift I Want?

No. The Holy Spirit knows how He intends to use each believer and sovereignly determines who is given which gifts. This does not mean you can't ask God for additional gifts. In fact, Paul encouraged the Corinthian church to seek additional gifts, especially those that would most help the broader congregation (see 1 Cor. 12:31). We have no guarantee that the Lord will give us the specific gift(s) we desire, but Paul still encourages us to ask. Perhaps the best way forward is to express your preference, but then to ask the Lord to give you which-

---

6 Those desiring more on this subject may wish to read *Are Miraculous Gifts for Today? Four Views*, ed. Wayne Grudem (Grand Rapids, MI: Zondervan, 1996).

7 For more, see David W. Jones, "5 Critical Errors of the Prosperity Gospel," The Center for Faith and Culture, Southeastern Baptist Theological Seminary (cfc.sebts.edu), October 16, 2019.

ever additional gift(s) He wants you to have and to help you use them effectively to serve others.

How Can I Discover My Spiritual Gift(s)?

Many believers today use a spiritual gift survey to identify their gifting. This can be instructive, but it is not necessary. Since the days of the early church, believers have discovered their gifts simply by serving in the congregation and noticing which of their efforts the Holy Spirit blessed.

Fruitfulness in a particular area likely indicates giftedness. Members of the congregation will recognize this fruitfulness and can confirm the gift. Thus, the person who finds pleasure and special satisfaction in serving others (who report being blessed by their efforts) would appear to have a gift of serving. Or the person who reads and studies Scripture and likes to present teaching in the church would seem to have a gift of teaching—again, provided that people learn and are edified by their efforts. And so on, with other gifts.

Ideally, spiritually alert people in the church will recognize a member's gift and bring it to that person's attention, but there are certainly cases where this doesn't happen. Once you become aware of a possible gift, ask some Christian friends who know you well what they think about your idea and whether they can confidently confirm it. If they do, look for opportunities to exercise it, and see if there is fruit. Or if you are unaware of any potential gift, ask Christian friends to help you see what you might be missing and to pray for the Spirit to help you recognize your gifting. In addition, once you know your gifting, you can assist others in discerning their gifts when you observe and appreciate the Spirit's work through them.

How Do I Use My Spiritual Gift(s)?

Ultimately, using our spiritual gifts is simply a matter of walking in and by the Holy Spirit, who gave them to us. So, using our spiritual gifts doesn't mean trying harder or seeking to achieve something in our own strength. Knowing how to use our spiritual gifts begins with prayer, listening to the Spirit's leading through God's Word, and seeking to serve. An attitude of love—seeking the good of the other person—provides the foundation for properly exercising a spiritual gift. Paul makes this clear when he says:

> If I speak in the tongues of men and of angels, but have not love, I am a noisy gong or a clanging cymbal. And if I have prophetic powers, and understand all mysteries and all knowledge, and if I have all faith, so as to remove mountains, but have not love, I am nothing. If I give away all I have, and if I deliver up my body to be burned, but have not love, I gain nothing. (1 Cor. 13:1–3)

The love Paul speaks of here reveals itself through humble servanthood (vv. 4–7). This is how God uses spiritual gifts to build up the church, the body of Christ.

Do Spiritual Gifts Indicate Spiritual Maturity?

The answer is obviously no. The Corinthians were "not lacking in any gift" (1 Cor. 1:7), but they were hardly mature. The church suffered from a partisan spirit and internal divisions (3:1–9), shocking sexual immorality (5:1–2), pride (8:1–3), lawsuits against one another (6:1–8), and drunkenness and other abuses at the Lord's Supper (11:17–34), along with misuse of their spiritual gifts (14:1–25).

Paul inserted his comments on love in the middle of his discussion of spiritual gifts precisely to challenge the fleshly, immature Corinthians to grow up spiritually. And he was concerned that, if they did not mature, he "may have to mourn over many of those who sinned earlier and have not repented of the impurity, sexual immorality, and sensuality that they have practiced" (2 Cor. 12:1).

Where Does the New Testament Discuss Spiritual Gifts?

In addition to writing about spiritual gifts in 1 Corinthians 12–14 and Ephesians 4:11, Paul says in Romans:

> For as in one body we have many members, and the members do not all have the same function, so we, though many, are one body in Christ, and individually members one of another. Having gifts that differ according to the grace given to us, let us use them: if prophecy, in proportion to our faith; if service, in our serving; the one who teaches, in his teaching; the one who exhorts, in his exhortation; the one who contributes, in generosity; the one who leads, with zeal; the one who does acts of mercy, with cheerfulness. (12:4–8)

The apostle Peter also speaks about spiritual gifts:

> As each has received a gift, use it to serve one another, as good stewards of God's varied grace: whoever speaks, as one who speaks oracles of God; whoever serves, as one who serves by the strength that God supplies—in order that in everything God may be glorified through Jesus Christ. To him belong glory and dominion forever and ever. Amen. (1 Pet. 4:10–11)

Peter echoes Paul: both connect spiritual gifts with serving others for God's glory. Rather than listing individual gifts, Peter divides the gifts into two broad categories: speaking and serving.

What Do Various Spiritual Gifts Look Like in Action?

Many gifts are fairly straightforward, such as serving, teaching, exhorting, giving, leading, helping, and mercy (Rom. 12:4–8). Others, however, seem less clear about what is expected. Since we have limited evidence, and the Bible doesn't specify, we cannot be sure exactly what several of the gifts looked like in the early church.

A brief sampling shows how challenging a definition can be in some cases. First Corinthians 12:8 names "the utterance of wisdom" as a spiritual gift. Is this "utterance" (or "word") an instance of spontaneous supernatural wisdom given to address a particular problem or issue, as continuationists believe? Or is it the result of studying God's Word and seeing its application in a given situation, as cessationists believe? Is the slightly different "utterance of knowledge" (also mentioned in verse 8) a spontaneous supernatural insight into a person or situation (continuationists), or is it the knowledge gained from study and meditation on God's Word (cessationists)?

What about the gift of faith (v. 9)? Is saving faith in view? Or is this possibly the faith to "move mountains" (1 Cor. 13:2; see Matt. 17:20)? Many commentators think the reference is not to saving faith but to a surge of confidence from God to trust Him for a specific outcome in a particular situation. One writer described it as an "indomitable assurance that God can overcome any difficulties and meet any emergencies."[8] Such experiences have been reported by missionaries past and present. But they can also occur in the lives of ordinary believers who are not involved in full-time ministry.

Supernatural healings were common in the early church. But are "gifts of healing" (1 Cor. 12:9) instances of supernatural healing that the gifted person can impart at will and see people healed? Or do they come to the recipient only at God's sovereign pleasure in specific situations? And does the plural "gifts" indicate that "each occurrence is a gift in its own right"?[9]

---

8 James Moffatt, as quoted in Alan F. Johnson, *1 Corinthians*, The IVP New Testament Commentary Series, vol. 7 (Westmont, IL: IVP Academic, 2004), 221.

9 Gordon Fee, *God's Empowering Presence: The Holy Spirit in the Letters of Paul* (Peabody, MA: Hendrickson Publishers, 1994), 169.

Many mainstream Bible translations use the phrase "working of miracles" in 1 Corinthians 12:10, but the Greek word for "working" is plural. What form did these powerful supernatural works take? We don't know for sure. Probably a range of supernatural acts in addition to healings are in view.

What about "prophecy" (v. 10)? Is it revelation from God like we find in the prophetic literature of the Old Testament, or is it a message inspired by God and spoken by someone in the church to address the needs of a person or a situation in the congregation—a message that needs to be weighed, as 1 Corinthians 14:29 suggests? Were the messages that Charles Spurgeon gave to various people in his church, reported at the beginning of this chapter, instances of such prophecy? Most evangelical, Pentecostal, and charismatic Christians would deny that this kind of prophecy is revelation on par with Old Testament prophecy or has the same authority as Scripture. But there is no clear agreement on exactly how to understand it or what role it plays in the life of a disciple of Christ.

The ability to "distinguish between spirits" (1 Cor. 12:10) seems a bit clearer in scope. Broadly, it likely refers to the ability to recognize whether an activity, prophecy, or other utterance comes from the Spirit of God, from the human spirit, or from a demonic spirit.

Is speaking in "tongues" (v. 10) giving a message in an unlearned human language, as we see in Acts 2? Or could it be speaking the language of angels (1 Cor. 13:1)? Or ecstatic speech (1 Cor. 14:2)? Opinions are mixed. The "interpretation of tongues" mentioned in 1 Corinthians 12:10 seems clear enough: the translation of a message given in tongues so that the congregation can understand it.

Because even leading Bible-believing scholars have different opinions on some of these questions, it is wise to tread cautiously, humbly, and prayerfully as we seek to discern truth and to be open to whatever gift(s) the Holy Spirit wants to give and manifest through us. As we do, we can be confident that He will give us whatever He wants us to have, regardless of whether we understand it or not, as the case of Charles Spurgeon illustrates. Professor Millard Erickson puts it well: "Each of us is to aspire to giving the Holy Spirit full control of his or her life. When that happens, our lives will manifest whatever gifts God intends for us to have, along with the fruit and acts of empowering that he wishes to display through us."[10]

A Few Cautionary Notes

Spiritual gifts are vital for a healthy church, and, in humility, we should be open to and desire whatever gifts the Spirit wishes to give us. But as we see in the church at Corinth, believers can become preoccupied with spiritual gifts, and this can subtly devolve into a preoccupation with "self," particularly when it comes to gifts of a more spectacular sort. While spiritual gifts have an important place in the church, we must beware of churches like Corinth that focus too much on gifts and too little on character, reveling in a climate of fleshly excitement and sensationalism. When gifts, especially the more extraordinary ones, become the focus in a church or in our lives, the concern for sound teaching of the Word and for holiness of life easily can, and often does, retreat to the margins of consciousness. Attention shifts to anticipating the next exciting manifestation of the Spirit. And church leaders can easily fall into the trap of trying to produce such things in the flesh. If our focus is more on the gifts than the Giver, we know we are on the wrong path.

Early in my Christian life, I was often invited to share my testimony in churches of various denominations. Once I spoke in a Pentecostal church and heard the pastor say something that put the manifestation of spiritual gifts in proper perspective for me. He said, "It's not how high you jump that matters most, but how straight you walk when you hit the ground."

---

10 Millard Erickson, *Christian Theology*, 3rd ed. (Grand Rapids, MI: Baker Academic, 2013), 802.

The Holy Spirit, who is sometimes called the "shy" member of the Trinity because He seems to act in the background, neither glorifies nor calls attention to Himself. Nor does He seek to entertain people or stir up excitement. Rather, He glorifies Christ by filling Jesus' followers, helping them become holy and empowering them for gospel ministry. He convicts unbelievers of their sins and draws them to Christ. He distributes spiritual gifts to enable believers to glorify Christ through serving others in love.

We must strive to keep the main focus in the church on worshiping God "in spirit and truth" (John 4:24). This requires prayerful, Spirit-anointed preaching and teaching of God's Word, with a primary and balanced focus on God the Father, Jesus Christ, and the Holy Spirit. This ministry of the Word should include practical application for Christ-centered, Spirit-empowered living in daily life. At the same time, Jesus' disciples must also exercise whatever spiritual gifts they have been given in humble service to one another. This "makes the body grow so that it builds itself up in love" (Eph. 4:16).

The noted British pastor and scholar David Watson said it well: "All word and no Spirit, we dry up; all Spirit and no word, we blow up; both word and Spirit, and we grow up."[11]

---

11 David Watson, *I Believe in the Church* (Grand Rapids, MI: Eerdmans, 1979), 157.

Questions to Ponder

1. When Christians talk about "spiritual gifts," what do they mean? How are spiritual gifts different from natural gifts?
2. After reading this chapter, what would you say is the purpose of spiritual gifts?
3. How can you best discover your spiritual gift(s)?
4. Ask the Holy Spirit to help you recognized the gift(s) He has given you and how to use them for the good of others and for God's glory.
5. How does Paul's teaching on love in 1 Corinthians 13 relate to the use of spiritual gifts?
6. Name some dangers of ignoring the Bible's instructions on the use of spiritual gifts.

19

Being Guided by the Word and the Spirit

Your word is a lamp to my feet and a light to my path.
Psalm 119:105

As a loving Father, God communicates with His children and guides them by His Word and His Spirit to fulfill His purposes for His glory. We have only to look at the people and events in the Bible and the world around us to see God as the greatest-ever strategic master planner. He works to bring to fruition His good plans for each of His children, giving them specific instructions and guidance in certain important areas of life while allowing them liberty to choose what they prefer in others. For instance, God does not typically give guidance about any number of inconsequential matters in life, such as which brand of toothpaste we use or whether we should wear solids or plaids.

The apostle Paul tells us that God has created each of us as a unique work of art in Christ Jesus to do good works, which He planned for us long ago (Eph. 2:10). As He works daily to make us more like Jesus, He has specific things for us to do to glorify Him and spread His kingdom. These go far beyond giving pocket change to a homeless person or helping a vulnerable person to safely cross a busy street. Discovering and fulfilling God's plans for us should be among our highest priorities. Only by following His guidance and direction will this happen, and when it does, we will find our deepest satisfaction and fulfillment in life.

We should regularly ask God to transform us, guide us, and fulfill His plans for our lives. Although some people may find it hard to believe God can use them, the Bible shows us that God can use *anyone*. One anonymous believer said, "He can use any pipe that is open on both ends."

How Does God Guide?

How and when does God guide us? As the sovereign Lord over all creation, God can guide us in any way He chooses and at any time He chooses. The psalmist says, "Good and upright is the Lord; therefore he instructs sinners in the way. He leads the humble in what is right, and teaches the humble his way. All the paths of the Lord are steadfast love and faithfulness, for those who keep his covenant and his testimonies" (Ps. 25:8–10). In another psalm, we read, "I will instruct you and teach you in the way you should go; I will counsel you with my eye upon you" (Ps. 32:8). The Scriptures reveal a variety of ways in which He has done this with people in the past.

For the sake of simplicity, we can put these examples into two categories: *ordinary* and *extraordinary*. God's *ordinary* guidance covers the vast majority of what we need to know for daily life. His *extraordinary* guidance covers a much smaller number of situations.

God's ordinary guidance

God ordinarily guides us by instructing us through His Word: "Your word is a lamp to my feet and a light to my path" (Ps. 119:105). The vast majority of what we need to know about God and how He wants us to live in this world can be found in His inspired Word, the Bible. The Old and New Testaments comprise His Word and are fully trustworthy; both overflow with important precepts and examples that can help guide our daily lives.

We should note, however, that as far back as the heretic Marcion (who lived from around AD 85 to 160), some people have rejected the Old Testament. Even those who do not explicitly deny it may minimize or neglect it in their study. But Jesus and Paul referred to it constantly, and Paul commended it strongly when he said, "For whatever was written in former days was written for our instruction, that through endurance and through the encouragement of the Scriptures we might have hope" (Rom. 15:4).

What are some reasons we should seek to deepen our knowledge of God's revelation in the Old Testament? A quick sample might include:

- the basic foundations of the Christian worldview, including the nature of God, His creation of the world, the fall of humankind, God's plan for redemption, and the coming consummation of all things
- the Ten Commandments, which give us God's enduring moral guidance for life in this fallen world
- the prophets and historical books, which contain accounts of God's works, past and future, and many stories rich with moral and practical guidance
- Proverbs, which provides timeless wisdom to guide us
- Psalms, which teaches us how to pray and shows us how to walk with God through the ups and downs of life (see 1 Cor. 10:11)
- The history of redemption up to the time of Jesus and many Scriptures that speak of His coming and His kingdom.

The Old Testament is a crucial part of God's revelation to us. And in the New Testament, especially the life and teaching of Jesus, the Son, God has given us the rest of what He wants us to know (see Heb. 1:2). The Gospels are a gold mine indeed, showing us Jesus' life, ministry, atoning death, resurrection and ascension (Luke 24:51). The Sermon on the Mount and many other passages in the Gospels give key precepts to guide us in following Jesus and in living in God's kingdom, as well as a lens through which to look back and properly understand the Old Testament. The book of Acts reiterates Jesus' ascension (1:6–11) and shows the birth of the church and the Great Commission in action as the growing community of Jesus' disciples spreads the gospel throughout the world. The Epistles give a picture of various issues that arose in the early church, many of which still occur today. And they provide amplification and clarification of the actions and teachings of Jesus and how they apply to life in the church and the fallen world.

God's ongoing transformation of our lives includes the vital component of guiding us by His Word. The more we prayerfully listen to, read, study, memorize, meditate on, internalize, and obey His Word, the more His transforming light will shine into our hearts and minds. That is why Paul urged the Colossians to "let the word of Christ dwell in you *richly*" (Col. 3:16; my emphasis). That is, he charged them to saturate themselves with the words of Jesus. And as we also do so, we will increasingly develop the mind of Christ (1 Cor. 2:16; Phil. 2:5), enabling us to know Him better, love Him more, become increasingly like Him, enter more fully into His ongoing ministry in the world, and more readily recognize how He wants us to respond in any circumstance that we encounter.

Prayerfully looking at our circumstances through the lens of Scripture and the eyes of Christ gives us the most basic form of God's guidance. As we do so, the Holy Spirit will prompt and empower us to obey Him and reject the desires of the flesh (Gal. 5:16–18). In this way, the Spirit transforms us increasingly into the image of Jesus and glorifies God through us (see Rom. 8:29; 2 Cor. 3:18).

Unfortunately, however, the low level of biblical literacy among believers today presents real challenges for experiencing such basic guidance and underscores our urgent need to regularly read and study Scripture. If we do not seek God's guidance in this most basic way, why should we expect Him to provide it through extraordinary means?

God's extraordinary guidance

God's extraordinary guidance is a supplement to His ordinary ways of leading us, and the two will never conflict. I say "supplement" because only a small fraction of life's issues call for extraordinary guidance. But it is an important fraction. As with God's ordinary ways, they also fulfill His purposes for His glory. In many instances, they involve aspects of ministry and mission requiring direction that biblical texts cannot give: situations that need real-time, on-the-ground navigational direction.

We find some instances of this kind of guidance in the book of Acts, especially where the Lord guided preachers of the gospel who sought to spread God's kingdom. For example, Jesus *spoke directly* to Paul on two occasions (Acts 9:4–6; 23:11), through a *vision* twice (16:9; 18:9–10), a *trance* once (22:17–18, 21), and *prophetic messages* four times (11:27–30; 20:22–23; 21:4; 21:10–11). Jesus also spoke once in a *vision* to Ananias (9:10–16). An *angel* spoke once to Cornelius (10:1–6), twice to Peter (5:19–20; 12:7–8), and once to Paul (27:21–26). And the Holy Spirit spoke a direct message to Philip (8:29), to Peter (10:19–20), and to Paul (13:1–3; 16:6–7). These experiences came not only to apostles but also to ordinary believers who were filled with the Holy Spirit, and they had a divine quality, immediacy, and force that were self-authenticating.

It would be easy to assume that such exciting, extraordinary occurrences took place frequently in the early church, but that would be incorrect. We have no indication that either Peter or Paul (or any other New Testament leader) experienced a steady stream of such special guidance. Remember that the book of Acts covers a period of about thirty years and that the instances of guidance recorded there spread out over that period. Luke does not present them as common, everyday experiences but rather shows that they came unsought to people actively serving God. Most often they seem intended to help advance the work of God's kingdom in some way. Moreover, they focused on important issues that the recipients would not otherwise have known about or even considered. And significantly, they demonstrated that through the Spirit, Jesus remained with His followers, as He had promised (Matt. 28:20). Through them, He continued to do the work of making disciples that He began while on earth.

Does God Still Guide Today?

God's kingdom has continued to spread to the present day, and we may well ask: Does God still guide people in such special ways? Anyone who has been a believer very long will know of people who *thought* God was guiding them, only to discover they were wrong. That can prompt some to adopt a skeptical attitude about extraordinary guidance. While we do need to be discerning, we must not throw out the proverbial baby with the bathwater. Consider the following examples of two godly, Spirit-filled men.

Dr. R. A. Torrey, a close friend and colleague of D. L. Moody, who led the school now known as Moody Bible Institute at the turn of the twentieth century (1889–1904), was educated at Yale University and Yale Divinity School. He then did further theological studies at the universities of Leipzig and Erlangen in Germany. Torrey was not prone to give himself to frivolous, impulsive ideas. He recounts how one day as he walked down a busy street in Chicago, he received a direct word from the Holy Spirit:

> Suddenly I met a man, a perfect stranger, and it seemed to me as if the Spirit of God said to me, "Speak to that man." I caught up to him … laid my hand on his shoulder … and said to him, "Are you a Christian?" … He stopped and hung his head. He said, "This is very strange. I am a graduate of Amherst College, but I am a perfect wreck through drink here in Chicago, and only yesterday my cousin, who is a minister in this city, was speaking to me about my soul, and for you, a perfect stranger, to put this question to me here on this busy street…" I did not

> succeed in bringing the man to a decision there on the street, but shortly afterward he was led to a definite acceptance of Christ.[1]

As another example, consider the following account of extraordinary guidance:

> In 1873, before the days of radio, the ship *Ville de Harve* sailed from New York, collided with the ship *Loch Erne*, and sank in eight minutes. Some survivors were saved by the *Loch Erne* and some by the ship *Trimountain*, which soon sailed away.
>
> The next day, the *Loch Erne* began to sink. It lost its ability to steer and a strong wind blew the ship far out of the normal lane where Atlantic vessels traveled. Each day the ship settled lower in the water, and finally the captain announced that the ship would sink within a day.
>
> On board was a godly minister by the name of Cook. After long hours of prayer, he announced that God had assured him all would be saved. By morning, the passengers stood knee-deep in water and expected the ship to take the final plunge to the bottom at any moment. Suddenly, the *British Queen* hove into sight, rescuing all on board.
>
> What had happened?
>
> The night before, the captain of the *British Quee*n, a Christian, felt impressed that God had a special work for him to do, someone to save. He felt led to turn the ship in a more northerly direction. Then he heard the inner voice say, "Steer north." He turned the ship still further north and ordered that the ship

1 R. A. Torrey, "How God Guides," sermon, Sermon Index (sermonindex.net); see also Chapter 6 of Torrey's book *How God Guides.*

sail at top speed all night. At the crack of dawn, the lookout called "Ship ahead!" There lay the *Loch Erne.*

God had a Christian who discerned the voice of the Spirit, and through him the Lord saved the lives of everyone on board the *Loch Erne.*[2]

These two stories are examples of how God has guided people in extraordinary kingdom-oriented situations in more modern times. Over the centuries and up to the present day, believers have reported instances of such guidance which, when acted upon, later were confirmed to have come from the Holy Spirit. Are they everyday occurrences for all believers? No. But they do still happen, perhaps more frequently than we realize.

Here's an extraordinary but much less dramatic experience from my own life—something that most people can relate to. One day in 2012, my car, which had about 143,000 miles on it, began to overheat. Instead of pulling over and turning off the engine, I decided to continue the mile or so to my home. That was all it took to destroy the engine. The dealership recommended installing a used engine. While they were searching for one, a friend from the other side of the country who knew nothing of this problem called me and said right away, "The Lord told me you need money. What's going on?"

I told her what had happened, and she said that she and her husband would ask the Lord what to do. Meanwhile, the dealer found an engine and gave a total installed price of $4,957. A day or two later, a check arrived in my mailbox for $5,000. I was stunned! With no knowledge whatsoever of the amount I would need, they were led to send $5,000—covering the entire cost of replacement plus a little extra for a full tank of gas. This was obviously a great help financially, but even more importantly, it was a great encouragement to my soul for the

---

2 Wesley Duewel, *Let God Guide You Daily* (Grand Rapids, MI: Zondervan/Francis Asbury Press, 1988), 113.

Father to give me such an unmistakable assurance of His love and care. It was an example of God's extraordinary guidance to my friend, who heard the Lord and responded. I could tell other stories like this, and so could people from a range of backgrounds, including what we call fundamentalist, evangelical, charismatic, and Pentecostal.

God has no problem guiding us whenever He wants to. He has many options to direct us, and He will always use the method best suited to the situation.

What Does God's Ordinary Guidance Look Like?

Do these stories of God's extraordinary guidance in mission and ministry situations mean that we should expect Him to guide us similarly in the affairs of our daily lives? And if so, when, and how often? Should we expect direct guidance from God for questions such as the following: What career shall I pursue? Where shall I attend university? Which job shall I take? Where shall I live? What church shall I join? Shall I get married, and if so, to whom? These questions and others like them are vitally important, and we can be sure that God wants to guide us . . . but how?

Relying on God's ordinary guidance through his Word may seem incomplete in these situations because no verses in the Bible tell us to pursue a specific career, attend a certain university or church, work for a particular company, or marry a certain person. Prayerfully considering relevant biblical principles, our abilities, interests, desires, opportunities, and circumstances will all play an important part in our discerning of God's direction, but they cannot give us a definitive answer. Thus, in addition to pondering all the factors listed above, some people will seek extraordinary guidance, such as a sign or special word from God.

While we should definitely expect the Good Shepherd to guide us when and where needed to fulfill His plans and purposes for us (Ps. 23:2–3; 32:8–9), nowhere does Scripture tell us to seek or expect Him to do so by special, extraordinary means. He can certainly do so if He chooses, and sometimes He does. But in most cases, He wants us to use our minds to think and pray through the possibilities in light of the moral precepts, wisdom, stories, and examples (positive and negative) we discover by searching Scripture and seeking the wise counsel of mature believers. Why does He desire this? Because doing so helps us develop a deeper knowledge of His Word, His ways, and, ultimately, Himself.

Let's take a brief look at two common examples in American culture for the sake of illustration: considering whom to date and marry, and determining what kind of work to do.

Guidance for Dating and Marriage

Scripture tells us that anyone who wants to marry is free to do so, provided they marry another believer (1 Cor. 7:39). Based on that teaching alone, we might close our Bibles and consider the matter settled. Any believer to whom I feel deeply attracted is an option for me, right?

Well, yes. But is every believer a *wise* option for you?

Scripture calls us to use wisdom in making important decisions. It will shock many to discover that romantic attraction, while exciting and desirable, is not the only or even the most important consideration in choosing a spouse. Nor is it the wisest, because not all potential candidates are equally suitable partners for marriage. Thus, we should go further and seek biblically derived wisdom to answer significant questions such as these:

- What basic characteristics does a good husband or wife possess?
- How committed is the potential spouse to Christ and spiritual maturity?
- Will this person join, support, and encourage me as I seek to faithfully follow Christ?
- Could I do the same for him or her?

- Do we have compatible higher-level priorities and life goals and enough in common to sustain a healthy marriage?
- How compatible as a couple would we be in other ways?
- Is this person emotionally healthy enough to be a lifelong partner? Am I?
- What is the place for discernment and advice from parents, godly spiritual leaders, and friends?

For example, "Tim" and "Susan" both worked on Capitol Hill, though for different congressmen. Tim felt the time had come for him to get married and start a family. He felt attracted to Susan and prayed about whether he should begin dating her. He saw in her some of the qualities listed above. The better he got to know her, he saw even more, and the attraction grew.

Tim approached a man who had mentored him (who also knew Susan) and asked him for counsel. As the two discussed whether he should consider her as a marriage partner, it looked like a very good choice. The longer the pair dated, Susan concluded the same about Tim, also through prayer and godly counsel. Though romance blossomed, they did not have a relationship of mere emotional infatuation but one that also included sober, sensible consideration of whether the two of them would make a good couple and good parents, and whether they would have a fruitful ministry together.

This couple has now been happily married for more than twenty-five years and has three children, all of whom walk with the Lord. And they have had a fruitful ministry of evangelism over the years.

Guidance for Work

Or consider work. We may freely choose any type of work that is not illegal, immoral, or ungodly. But here as well, not all options are equally wise or God-glorifying. What does the Bible teach about our work?[3]

A very basic principle, derived from Genesis 1 and 2, holds that God has called human beings to work and that He has endowed each of His children with the gifts and abilities necessary to fulfill His plans for their work lives. Thus, we can start by taking into account our God-given gifts, abilities, and motivations. If you did poorly in math and science while in school, God probably has not destined you to become an engineer or astronaut! Once our gifts become reasonably clear, we might ask questions such as these:

- Is a given job a good fit for my gifts and abilities, strengths and weaknesses, personality and temperament?
- Does it appeal to me?
- Will my gifts enable me to glorify God in this position?
- Is there a realistic possibility of being salt and light (see Matt. 5:13–16) to those among whom I labor?

Prayer, sometimes with fasting, can aid us in achieving an accurate self-understanding. Godly counsel also can help, along with the Spirit's guidance and self-surrender. Many modern believers will need to repeat this process a number of times over the course of their working lives. Such transition periods, though sometimes difficult, can play a crucial role in discerning and fulfilling God's plans for them.

"Rich" was a senior leader in an organization. He met periodically with a mentor over several years. Though Rich was quite successful and satisfied in his career, it became clear to his mentor that Rich had undeveloped potential. The two talked about whether he might want

3 An excellent book on calling is Os Guinness' *The Call: Finding and Fulfilling God's Purpose for Your Life* (Thomas Nelson, 1998, 2018). Also available is a six-part study guide from the C. S. Lewis Institute featuring interviews with the author (https://www.cslewisinstitute.org/the-call-study-guide/).

to pursue some new opportunities for growth and service. He took several months to consider the idea, pray, and consult with his wife. As he pondered these questions, he concluded that he did have such a desire, which led to him getting additional education that built on his existing strengths, experiences, and interests. It also equipped him to work in a different field that has given him great satisfaction and fruitfulness.

If God wants to give us extraordinary guidance in such situations, He can certainly do so. But the voice of God is normally heard through a combination of prayer, Bible reading and meditation, discernment of circumstantial factors, godly counsel, and sometimes the promptings of the Holy Spirit. Though this path typically takes longer, feels less exciting, and may involve more difficulties, it has the great benefit of helping us grow into greater maturity and Christlikeness—God's first priority in our lives.

In instances when God does grant special guidance, we can be sure that such guidance will never conflict with the morality and wisdom we find in Scripture. Any supposed special guidance that conflicts with the plain teaching of the Bible is not from God. It really is just that simple. We can be sure, for example, that God will *never* tell us that in our "unique" circumstances, it is okay to lie to or steal from our employer, or cheat on our taxes or on our spouse, or move in with our girlfriend or boyfriend. Any guidance God gives us about specific circumstances will always accord with the guidance He gives us in His Word.

What about Inner Impressions?

This brings us to a consideration of what some refer to as a prompting, inner impression, or nudge from the Holy Spirit. What are we to think about such things? Frankly, clear biblical examples here are not easy to find. Anecdotal evidence from the faithful seems to be the best we can do.

Are impressions and promptings a form of extraordinary guidance? Opinions differ. The passages sometimes cited in support of it, such as John 10:3–4 and 10:27, when read in context, do not deal with inner guidance. In John 10, Jesus is speaking about bad versus good shepherds, salvation, and the abundant life. When He says that His sheep hear His voice, He seems to be referring to His audible voice in preaching and teaching, not an inner impression.

And the examples of God speaking to the boy Samuel (1 Sam. 3:1–18) and His "still small voice" speaking to Elijah (1 Kings 19:12 KJV) both featured audible words, not inner impressions. Nor was Philip given an inner impression to encounter the Ethiopian eunuch; rather, an angel gave him a specific, detailed command, and then the Holy Spirit gave him additional instructions (Acts 8:26, 29).

Did God speak audibly to kings (especially David) and the Old Testament prophets? We don't know. In any case, the Bible never suggests that we should seek guidance in this way. The Old Testament passages cited above do show, however, what we see in the New Testament: God has sometimes spoken audibly to people.

This doesn't prove that He also speaks inaudibly, but does it leave open the possibility that He may also sometimes speak inaudibly through inner impressions and nudges? This seems plausible in light of the fact that the Holy Spirit is a Person who dwells in us, and that Scripture describes Him as the Spirit of truth and as our Teacher and Helper.

It also seems plausible when we consider that Jesus said "this is eternal life, that they know you, the only true God, and Jesus Christ whom you have sent" (John 17:3). In this context, the verb translated "know" (Greek *ginosko*) means personal knowledge. As New Testament scholar Andreas Köstenberger explains, "In biblical parlance, 'to know' God does not refer merely to cognitive knowledge (the Greek conception); it means living in fellowship with God." He goes on to quote D. A. Carson, who says "knowledge of God and of Jesus Christ entails fellowship, trust, personal relationship, faith."[4] All of these things are mediated by the Holy Spirit.

What can we learn from anecdotal reports? Over the centuries, believers have testified to having "promptings" that later proved to have come from the Lord.

Such experiences do not happen every day, nor do they happen to every believer; but believers from all walks of life do continue to report them, and they are probably more common than we know. They also seem to be reported more often by those who walk humbly with God and who seek to be led by His Spirit.

What should we conclude about impressions and nudges? The possibility of self-deception is a legitimate concern, but "an abuse does not nullify proper use."[5]

What should we do if we believe we've received a nudge from the Spirit? Acting on promptings to do good—to help someone in a practical way or to share the gospel—offers an opportunity for God to use us, as well as for us to discover whether the prompting really is from Him and to experience the thrill of His using us when it is. Assuming the nudge presents no conflict with biblical teaching or wisdom, proceeding with a gentle, humble approach seems appropriate.

I had such a nudge several years ago, when a Christian professor from an Eastern European country who had come to Washington for an academic conference called the C. S. Lewis Institute office to inquire about dropping by for a visit to learn more about our work. She asked whether I could meet with her the following day. Before I left home to go to work that day, I had an impression or nudge that I should give her some money, even though I knew nothing about this perfect

---

4 Andreas J. Köstenberger, *John*, Baker Exegetical Commentary on the New Testament (Grand Rapids, MI: Baker Academic, 2004), 488.

5 This general theological principle (Latin: *abusus non tollit usum*) has sometimes been attributed to Thomas Aquinas and does encapsulate his perspective, although the exact phrase does not appear in his writings.

stranger. We had a cordial conversation about her efforts to introduce the thought of C. S. Lewis into her mostly atheistic university, and I gave her some of our material to help her efforts.

At the end of our conversation, I reached into my pocket and pulled out $100. "I think I am to give this to you," I said. The gift surprised her, and she expressed deep gratitude for it, because as she later confided, she had no money for taxi fare back to her hotel. She had stepped out in faith, trusting God to somehow provide her for need … and He did.

Or consider another, more recent example. A British young lady whom I have known since her childhood recently graduated from Edinburgh University with a degree in philosophy and theology (to aid her in evangelizing secular Europeans). She is very smart, shy, and humble. After graduation, she took an unpaid position as a church missions worker in the south of England, trusting God to provide for her needs.

One day she had a strong impression to walk to an IKEA store about a mile away, and that, if she did so, there she would see a blue couch on display and a woman sitting on it with whom she was to speak about Christ. Without delay, she walked to the IKEA store and saw a blue couch with a woman sitting on it. She gently engaged her in conversation about Christ and found her open to meeting for Bible study.

In situations like these, we may not have time for a discernment process. And in any case, the consequences of a mistake usually involve little more than embarrassment.

But in matters of greater significance, J. I. Packer urges discernment by the community of faith, "lest impressions that are rooted in egoism, pride, headstrong unrealism, a fancy that irrationality glorifies God, a sense that some human being is infallible, or any similar unhealthiness of soul, be allowed to masquerade as Spirit-given."[6]

---

6 Packer, *God's Plans for You*, 105–106.

The church has a long history of believers who have made claims of promptings and impressions from God, only to see them later proven false. We see the same thing today. It has become especially problematic in contemporary Western culture, which is so oriented to feelings, sentiment, and the subjective aspects of life. We can easily mistake our random thoughts, desires, intuitions, or internal self-talk for a word from God, especially when we have a strong preference about a matter.

The great eighteenth-century evangelist George Whitefield is a classic example. He named his newborn son "John" because he believed God had shown him that the child would be a mighty preacher like John the Baptist. But when his little son died four months later, Whitefield realized that the Spirit had not spoken to him and that he had "misapplied" the Scripture. He had deceived himself, undermined his own credibility, and brought public reproach upon God's name. His error had significant consequences.[7]

What would cause a strong, mature believer like Whitefield to make such a great mistake? In one word: self-deception. Any of us can tell ourselves what we want to hear and assume that it is God speaking to us, especially when we deeply desire it. Self-deception can afflict all believers, including leaders.

John Wesley saw this during his long ministry and advised (quoting 1 John 4:1), "Do not hastily ascribe things to God. Do not easily suppose dreams, voices, impressions, or revelations to be from God. They may be from him. They may be from nature. They may be from the devil. Therefore, believe not every spirit, but 'try the spirits whether they be from God.'"[8]

Wesley's advice is rooted in Scripture and highlights the importance of testing, wherever possible, any impressions or messages we think might have come from the Holy Spirit, as well as any dreams,

---

7 Arnold Dallimore, *George Whitefield*, vol. 2 (London: Banner of Truth, 1980), Letter DXLVII.

8 John Wesley, *Farther Thoughts on Christian Perfection*, section 25, question 33.

visions, or prophetic words. In addition to our own assessments via prayer and study of God's Word, it is wise to discuss these with a trusted spiritual advisor who can help us discern the validity of these perceptions, whether they align with Scripture, and whether we are deceiving ourselves.

What about Prophetic Utterances?

On the question of prophetic utterances, the apostle Paul knew very well of the critical need to discern the source of such things. "Do not quench the Spirit," he told the Thessalonians. "Do not despise prophecies, but test everything; hold fast what is good" (1 Thess. 5:19–21). The apostle John likewise said, "Dear friends, do not believe every spirit, but test the spirits to see whether they are from God" (1 John 4:1).

The testing that Paul commands relates specifically to a prophetic word given by one believer to another or to a whole congregation (a practice that is more common these days in some circles than in others). Paul himself had received such a message from the prophet Agabus (Acts 21:10–11). He strongly encouraged the gift of prophecy because he knew from experience that "the one who prophesies speaks to people for their upbuilding and encouragement and consolation" (1 Cor. 14:3). This type of prophetic utterance was valued but was not considered on par with inspired Scripture.

How, then, do we understand such prophetic utterances? That question provokes much discussion and debate among scholars and is too complicated to address fully here. What we can say with certainty is that Paul required that prophetic words be "weighed" to assess their validity (1 Cor. 14:29). And we can also say with certainty that such words would never conflict with Scripture.

Leaders in congregations that experience public prophetic words have a special responsibility as shepherds of the sheep to carefully and prayerfully test the supposed prophecy, especially in light of the growing number of false and erroneous public prophecies that have spectacularly failed in recent years. Christians should publicly identify failed or erroneous prophecies and not sweep them under the rug, which is all too common.

Paul provides sound guidance on this matter. For him, testing meant evaluating a prophecy or other special guidance against the teaching of Scripture. He would have strongly insisted that no God-given prophetic word, dream, vision, nudge, or prompting from the Holy Spirit will ever conflict with the Holy Scriptures, which the Spirit inspired. Likewise, he would insist that God does not contradict Himself and His words never fail to come true. Nor does God put bizarre or outlandish or immoral ideas into our minds—although on occasion He may guide people to do things that may not make sense at the time, as with Philip (Acts 8:26) or Peter (Acts 10:9–48).

Godly, wise, and mature pastors and elders with a solid grounding in the Scriptures and in the spiritual life should do the testing Paul commands. In the case of a prophetic message, they should consider not only the content, but the life of the one who delivers it. Does orthodox belief, holiness, humility, and a servant heart characterize the person (as with Charles Spurgeon)? If they don't know the answer, can they find someone who can verify the individual's character and the genuineness of their gift? Leaders must reject any message from a person who embraces heretical beliefs. And they must be cautious of utterances from anyone who displays pride, haughtiness, attention seeking, narcissism, or other fleshly religiosity. Also, they should ask: Does the message edify? As mentioned above, Paul says, "The one who prophesies speaks to people for their upbuilding and encouragement and consolation" (1 Cor. 14:3).

Some Final Counsel

God loves us and has specific purposes and plans for each of our lives. You have a destiny, a significant role in God's kingdom, and He wants to guide you in fulfilling it (Ps. 139:1–16). While this plan is for your good, it's even more for His glory. What a tragedy it would be if, when we stand before the judgment seat of Christ, we were to discover that we had spent our entire life fulfilling our own plans and not His!

To wrap up this chapter, let's review some of the most important principles of guidance:

Make prayer the starting point for seeking guidance.

Not casual prayer, but earnest, concentrated prayer. This begins with self-examination and a request for God to search our heart (Ps. 139:23–24). It involves repentance and confession of any known sin and asking forgiveness from anyone we have offended (Matt. 5:23–24). Humble yourself, for "he leads the humble in what is right, and teaches the humble his way" (Ps. 25:9).

Search God's Word.

Once you have begun to pray, you should start searching for insights and wisdom in Scripture that apply to your situation, for God ordinarily guides us through His Word. This may come directly or indirectly, through precepts, principles, examples, stories, and more. In some cases, you may find yourself addressed by the Holy Spirit through a particular verse or passage that you know specifically applies to you in this circumstance.

Also, take note of ideas that keep coming back and explore them. God sometimes uses them to get our attention. And remember that when God does give us guidance, He usually gives just enough light to take the next step of faith and obedience, not a comprehensive master plan. If you lack a thorough grounding in the Scripture, seek counsel from someone who has it (see #5 below).

Be patient.

Wait on the Lord. Do not rush ahead and do what you desire if guidance doesn't come when you want it. His timing is an extremely important factor. Knowing what God wants us to do is only part of the equation. Knowing when to do it is also crucial, and disregarding God's timing can create big problems. *While praying, searching the Scriptures, and waiting on God, think through your circumstances.*

God has made us rational creatures and expects us to use our minds as we seek to know and do His will. Circumstances are part of the way He guides us. Make a careful, realistic assessment of your circumstances and possible options, including the likely outcomes of different courses of action. Then live with each one for a couple of days. Sometimes God's will becomes clear as we consider His providential ordering of the circumstances in our life. But we should do our thinking and pondering from a posture of faith, with our mind submitted to His wisdom and will. "Trust in the Lord with all your heart, and do not lean on your own understanding" (Prov. 3:5).

Surrender yourself fully to God (Rom. 12:1).

This means committing yourself to doing His will, whatever it may be, and opens the door to being filled with the Holy Spirit, whom God uses to illuminate our understanding of the Scriptures and to guide, empower, and transform us.

Some may struggle to make this surrender, but they have no way forward in the Christian life (or in discerning God's will) until they do. If you refuse to do God's will or have disregarded His previous guidance, is He likely to give you more? Obedience is crucial. To receive more light, we must walk in the light He has already given. To be guided, we must come to a point where we desire His will more than our own, even if it conflicts with our wishes and desires (John 7:17).

Otherwise, our desires will influence our thinking like a magnet does a compass, pulling it away from the true north.

George Müller said, "Nine-tenths of the trouble with people … are overcome when our hearts are ready to do the Lord's will, whatever it may be. When one is truly in this state, it is usually but a little way to the knowledge of what his will is."[9] This reality prompted one wise saint to comment, "There are few crises of guidance, but there are many crises of obedience."[10]

Seek counsel as needed.

The experience of wise, godly, mature believers who have walked with God for years and who know Scripture well can often greatly help us as we ponder the way forward. Depend upon a community of honest believers who will speak the truth, not necessarily what you want to hear (see Acts 15). In cases where you are seeking confirmation of guidance you believe you have received, say, "I think the Lord is telling me" (rather than "God told me…," which shuts down further discussion). This requires humility of heart, which God promises to bless, for He "leads the humble in what is right, and teaches the humble His way" (Ps. 25:9).

While you wait for God's guidance, do the duty that lies nearest at hand.

As Elisabeth Elliot, wife of missionary martyr Jim Elliot advised, "Just do the next right thing." That is, do the next right thing in life, considering how Scripture says we should live and conduct ourselves, even if you cannot yet see how it fits into the big picture or where each step is leading.

---

9 Basil Miller, *George Müller: Man of Faith* (Minneapolis, MN: Bethany House, 1972), 43. See also Roger Steer, *The Spiritual Secrets of George Müller* (Robesonia, PA: OMF Books, 1987), 40, 42.

10 Campbell McAlpine, related by his son, Rev. Stuart McAlpine, in personal conversation with the author.

For difficult situations in which you cannot clearly see the way forward, consider the wisdom of Andrew Murray.

Missionary Amy Carmichael records witnessing how Andrew Murray responded to a particularly painful situation in his life:

> He was quiet for a while with his Lord, then he wrote these words: "First, He brought me here, it is by his will I am in this straight place; in that fact I will rest. Next, He will keep me here in his love, and give me grace to behave as His child. Then, He will make the trial a blessing, teaching me the lessons He intends me to learn, and working in me the grace He means to bestow. Last, in His good time He can bring me out again—how and when He knows. Let then me say I am here, (1) By God's appointment, (2) In His keeping, (3) Under His Training, (4) For His time."[11]

Give yourself wholeheartedly to God and ask Him to fulfill His plans for your life, calling upon the Holy Spirit to give you whatever guidance and direction you need through His Word or through any other way He desires.

---

11 Amy Carmichael, *Though the Mountains Shake* (New York: Loizeaux Brothers, 1946), 12.

Questions to Ponder

1. How would you describe the focus of the Bible's teaching on divine guidance?
2. In what ways have you experienced God's guidance, both ordinary and extraordinary?
3. What do you think about the idea of "inner prompting" in the life of a disciple of Jesus?
4. How can we avoid self-deception in guidance?
5. When considering God's direction for our lives, what are some actions we should take?

20

Being Assured of Salvation

I write these things to you who believe in the name of the Son of God, that you may know that you have eternal life.
1 John 5:13

In this concluding chapter, we look at a question that troubles many (but not all) followers of Jesus at some point in their Christian life: Can I be sure that I am saved and will go to heaven when I die? This question is of vital importance for everyone who professes to be a Christian and can arise at any time in a person's life. When it does, it can cause anguish and anxiety.

Despite differences of opinion among believers,[1] if we look to Scripture as our guide,[2] the answer must be yes, we *can* be sure of our salvation. True believers can indeed have assurance of their salvation, and this assurance gives them great encouragement, comfort, and hope in life and in the hour of death. Some believers enjoy this assurance throughout their lives and never doubt; others question, struggle, and experience it only after earnest seeking. Still others, who give good evidence of being truly saved, never find full assurance, for assurance is not of the essence of saving faith.[3]

1 The Roman Catholic Church holds that Christians cannot be assured of final salvation except in special cases.

2 Read the following verses: Job 19:25–26; Rom. 8:38–39; 1 Cor. 1:8; 2 Cor. 5:1, 6; 2 Tim. 1:12; 4:6–8; 1 Pet. 1:3–5; 2 Pet. 1:10; 1 John 3:14; 5:13, 19.

3 *Westminster Confession of Faith* 18.3.

There is also such a thing as false assurance of salvation, and that is where we will begin. Scripture gives a number of examples of people who believed themselves to be saved but were not. Judas Iscariot, for example (John 6:70–71). Or the "many" on Judgment Day, spoken of by Jesus:

> Not everyone who says to me, "Lord, Lord," will enter the kingdom of heaven, but the one who does the will of my Father who is in heaven. On that day many will say to me, "Lord, Lord, did we not prophesy in your name, and cast out demons in your name, and do many mighty works in your name?" And then will I declare to them, "I never knew you; depart from me, you workers of lawlessness." (Matt. 7:21–23)

In this sobering passage, we see people who feel confident of their salvation and cite impressive examples of supernatural ministry in Jesus' name: prophesying, casting out demons, doing mighty works. Jesus did not dispute their claims of activity in His name (for His name is indeed powerful), but He did dispute their claim to salvation. Tragically, they had deceived themselves; they had false assurance. Their profession of faith was orthodox ("Lord, Lord"), and their ministry was striking, but the fruit of their lives revealed an unconverted heart. Notably, Jesus declares they are "many" in number, not few.

In light of the possibility of false assurance and the blessing of true assurance, how can we be sure that our salvation is genuine? Jesus, John, and Paul give us helpful guidance, and we will look at each in turn.

What Does Jesus Say?

As we just read, Jesus says that those who enter God's eternal kingdom are not people who merely say "Lord, Lord," but those who actually do "the will of my Father who is in heaven." *Profession* of true faith does not guarantee *possession* of true faith, which is manifested not only in one's words but also in one's deeds. John Stott explains, "The reason for their rejection by him is that their profession was verbal, not moral. It concerned their lips only, and not their life. They called Jesus 'Lord, Lord', but never submitted to his lordship or obeyed the will of his heavenly Father."[4] Jesus said, "The Father loves the Son and has given all things into his hand. Whoever believes in the Son has eternal life; whoever does not obey the Son shall not see life, but the wrath of God remains on him" (John 3:35–36).

Jesus called attention to this fact when He described these individuals as "workers of lawlessness." They were not ordinary believers who experienced occasional lapses into sin (which is normal), but people who habitually disobeyed God's will and Word (they were "workers of lawlessness" in an ongoing manner). By contrast, true disciples of Jesus rejoice in God's grace and delight to do His will as taught by Jesus, even though they sometimes sin. Clearly, those whom Jesus "never knew" had an imaginary Christ—that is, a Christ of their own making. And as John Owen commented long ago, those who have an imaginary Christ will one day discover that they have an imaginary salvation.[5]

This puts a sharp point on questions such as "Am I truly converted?" or "Have I opened my heart to the good news of God's kingdom and heeded Jesus' call to 'repent and believe in the gospel'?" (Mark 1:15). As we saw in Chapter 3, repentance involves an awakening to and turning from our sins, while faith involves both believing that Jesus is indeed God's Son, the Messiah, *and* trusting Him and His atoning sacrifice to pay for our sins. Like different sides of the same coin, repentance and faith are inseparable. Repentant faith is the door through which we enter God's kingdom as well as the path on which we walk

---

4 John Stott, *Christian Counter-Culture: The Message of the Sermon on the Mount* (Downers Grove, IL: InterVarsity Press, 1979), 207.

5 In *Meditations and Discourses on the Glory of Christ* IV.5, John Owen said, "The ancient Christians told … the truth—namely, that 'as they had feigned unto themselves an imaginary Christ, so they should have an imaginary salvation only'" (London: Bible-and-Crown, 1764), 83.

thereafter. Faith and repentance are not simply one-time events at the moment of conversion but are ongoing realities in our lives.

The experience of coming to genuine faith and repentance can be sudden or gradual, dramatic or quiet, but it is always the work of the Holy Spirit—and Jesus says it contains an element of mystery. Like the wind, it is invisible, but we can see its effects (John 3:8). Some believers know the exact time of their conversion, while others (often those raised in Christian families) do not. In all cases, however, new birth brings new life and with it a Godward change of direction in one's life. That change begins in the heart and moves outward to attitudes and behavior. We usually experience some degree of change right away, but sometimes change emerges more slowly. The degree of observable change will vary depending on a person's lifestyle prior to conversion. For example, someone who was living a generally honest and morally upright life before meeting Christ may not have as much external behavior to change as a person who was living a wild, immoral lifestyle.

Jesus said, "I am the way, and the truth, and the life. No one comes to the Father except through me" (John 14:6), and "This is the will of my Father, that everyone who looks on the Son and believes in him should have eternal life" (John 6:40). Do you believe these words? Have you been drawn to believe in and trust Jesus as your Savior and Lord? Do you see signs of this new life in the Spirit? Take time to consider these fundamental questions. If you have truly come to Jesus, you can rest in the assurance of Jesus' powerful words: "All that the Father gives me will come to me, and whoever comes to me I will never cast out" (John 6:37).

What Does the Apostle John Say?

John wrote his first epistle "to you who believe in the name of the Son of God, that you may know that you have eternal life" (1 John 5:13). He devoted 1 John to providing that assurance to God's children.

This epistle gives us a front row seat from which to observe how John advised people about this vital subject and reminds us that it has always been an important question for believers. John gives practical, objective ways to assess our lives, and they are just as applicable today as they were when he first wrote. Ask yourself the following questions and prayerfully reflect on the scriptures that follow:

Do I "believe in the name of the Son of God"?

As we saw earlier (in Chapter 3), when John uses the word "believe," referring to Jesus and salvation, he doesn't mean giving bare intellectual assent to the fact that Jesus was God's Son. Remember that in the Gospels, even demons recognized Jesus as the Son of God, and James 2:19 likewise says that "even the demons believe—and shudder." Rather than simply believing that certain facts about Jesus are true, John has in mind both a belief that Jesus is truly God's Son and Messiah *and* a personal trust and commitment to Him as Savior and Lord. You cannot have salvation without this kind of belief and trust in Jesus.

You must embrace it personally as well as accept it doctrinally, for this kind of trust grasps God's pardoning love in Christ and inspires an answering love in your heart. Does such belief and trust in Jesus characterize you? Does your heart have a responsive, grateful love for God and His Son? Answering this question isn't just about how we feel in the moment, for it is not unusual to go through dry spells where our depth of feeling wanes. When considering these questions, step back and look at your life with God over time. Do you trust God with your life?

Am I seeking to obey the commandments of Jesus and live as He lived?

John says genuine belief reveals itself in a changed life, one characterized by obedience to God rooted in love:

> And by this we know that we have come to know him, if we keep his commandments. Whoever says "I know him" but does not keep his commandments is a liar, and the truth is not in him, but whoever keeps his word, in him truly the love of God is perfected. By this we may know that we are in him: whoever says he abides in him ought to walk in the same way in which he walked. (1 John 2:3–6)

Ask yourself, "Do I desire to walk as Jesus walked—to consciously obey God in my daily life?" The question is not whether you do so perfectly (no one does) but whether you are making a serious effort to do so out of love for God and a desire to please Him.

What about remaining sin in my life?

No Christian attains sinless perfection in this life. Sin still tempts all believers, and sometimes they give in. Some also struggle with what is called a besetting sin—one especially hard to overcome. But if they confess, repent, and return to the Lord, He forgives and restores them, and they can focus on rooting it out of their lives. This differs from a lifestyle of disobedience to God, which raises serious questions about the presence of genuine belief, the indwelling of the Holy Spirit, and thus eternal life. John says, "No one who abides in him keeps on sinning; no one who keeps on sinning has either seen him or known him" (1 John 3:6). A few sentences later, he adds: "By this it is evident who are the children of God, and who are the children of the devil: whoever does not practice righteousness is not of God, nor is the one who does not love his brother" (v. 10). These verses do not refer to occasional sins by a believer who otherwise seeks to obey God and follow Jesus, for John recognizes that believers do sometimes sin and says that "if we say we have no sin, we deceive ourselves … . If we confess our sins, he is faithful and just to forgive our sins and to cleanse us from all unrighteousness" (1 John 1:8–9). Rather, as the Greek verb tense indicates, they refer to a pattern of continual, habitual sin by someone who has no interest in living a righteous life but who lives in persistent sin. Is that true of you? Do you live in persistent sin and have no interest in living a righteous life? Or do you seek to live a life that pleases God even though you sometimes fail Him?

Do I love fellow believers?

Next, John says, "We know that we have passed out of death into life, because we love the brothers. Whoever does not love abides in death" (1 John 3:14). Obedience to the command to love fellow believers indicates the presence of eternal life. This love is not simply a positive sentiment or emotion but is a disposition expressed in acts of the will in which we seek the good of our fellow believers in practical ways. John gives us an example, "By this we know love, that he laid down his life for us, and we ought to lay down our lives for the brothers. But if anyone has the world's goods and sees his brother in need, yet closes his heart against him, how does God's love abide in him? Little children, let us not love in word or talk but in deed and in truth" (vv. 16–18). We are also to seek the good of our neighbor, which includes those who are not believers (Matt. 22:39; Gal. 6:10).

Loving other believers is so important that John repeats his point. In the next chapter, he exhorts: "Beloved, let us love one another, for love is from God, and whoever loves has been born of God and knows God. Anyone who does not love does not know God, because God is love" (1 John 4:7–8). Loving fellow believers "in deed and truth" (3:18) is another sign that we have eternal life. Conversely, a lifestyle that ignores the needs of others is a sign that we do not. Do you love fellow believers and seek their good in practical ways such as prayer, service, encouragement, finances, and more?

Does the Holy Spirit abide in me?

The power to believe, to love God and neighbor, and to obey Jesus' commandments comes from the Holy Spirit, who dwells in everyone who has eternal life. "By this we know that we abide in him and he in us, because he has given us of his Spirit" (1 John 4:13). Do you see evidence of the Spirit living in you, prompting and empowering you to love God and others and to walk in obedience to the teaching of God and Jesus?

We can sum up John's comments in this New Testament letter by saying that those who have eternal life believe that Jesus is God's Son and Messiah and trust Him for salvation, have evidence that the Holy Spirit indwells them, have a desire to obey His commands and to love fellow believers, do not live in persistent sin, and seek to walk as Jesus walked.

What Does the Apostle Peter Say?

Peter gives us encouraging, practical guidance as we seek assurance. Because God's "divine power has granted to us all things that pertain to life and godliness" (2 Pet. 1:3), Peter exhorts believers to "be all the more diligent to confirm your calling and election" and assures us that by doing so, "you will never fall" (v. 10). He is saying that earnest pursuit of Christ and growth in grace will confirm our calling and election. To this end, he lists a series of important moral qualities that supplement one's faith (vv. 5–7). These require active engagement and will "keep you from being ineffective or unfruitful in the knowledge of our Lord Jesus Christ" (v. 8). Memorizing and meditating on this passage and applying it to daily life will encourage the soul and give hope!

What Does the Apostle Paul Say?

Although John spoke only briefly about the indwelling Holy Spirit as a sign of eternal life, and Peter said even less, the apostle Paul explains the role of the Spirit in greater detail. And he also insists that no one has eternal life unless the Holy Spirit dwells in them. Ask yourself the following questions and prayerfully reflect on the Scriptures that follow.

Does the Holy Spirit dwell in you?

In Romans 8, Paul says, "You, however, are not in the flesh but in the Spirit, if in fact the Spirit of God dwells in you. Anyone who does not have the Spirit of Christ does not belong to him" (v. 9). Paul insists that the decisive evidence of whether a person is a true Christian is the presence of the Holy Spirit in his or her life.

How do we know if the Spirit dwells in us? One of the main signs of the Spirit's presence is His convicting of sin and leading and empowering the believer to obey God's Word, resulting in moral transformation: "If by the Spirit you are putting to death the deeds of the body, you will live. For all who are being led by the Spirit of God, these are sons and daughters of God" (Rom. 8:13–14 NASB 2020). Here again the present tense verb ("are putting to death") indicates something that occurs on a continuing basis. It does not indicate an experience of instant transformation.

Do you experience conviction of sin? Is the Spirit leading and empowering you to steadily seek to put to death the sinful deeds of the body? Do you see growing victory over areas of remaining sin in your life? These are signs of true conversion.

Does your life bear the fruit of the Holy Spirit?

A closely related question is whether the fruit of the Spirit is evident in our lives. Putting to death the deeds of the body, like uprooting weeds in a garden, clears the ground for the fruit of the Spirit to emerge.

This process unfolds over time, like the growth of apples on a tree. Just as fruit reveals the nature of the tree, so the fruit of a person's life reveals the nature of his heart. "The fruit of the Spirit is love, joy, peace, patience, kindness, goodness, faithfulness, gentleness, self-control," wrote Paul (Gal. 5:22-23), and those qualities showing up in an individual's life reveal a converted heart. Can you see some measure of the Spirit's fruit in your life? Not perfection, but ongoing growth. More this year than last year or the years before?

By contrast, works of the flesh reveal the unconverted heart. Paul also says to the Galatians, "Now the works of the flesh are evident: sexual immorality, impurity, sensuality, idolatry, sorcery, enmity, strife, jealousy, fits of anger, rivalries, dissensions, divisions, envy, drunkenness, orgies, and things like these. I warn you, as I warned you before, that those who do such things will not inherit the kingdom of God" (5:19–21). He gives similar warnings in 1 Corinthians 6:9–11 and Ephesians 5:5–8. Like John, Paul speaks of a lifestyle of persistent, ongoing sin, not an occasional failure. Do any of the works of the flesh characterize your life? If so, and you are at ease with them and not trying to root them out, take heed to Paul's warning, and seek God's mercy.

Does the Holy Spirit assure you that God is your Father?

Paul had a strong and clear sense that God had adopted him and was his Father. Note that in Romans, he addresses a group of people like himself who have been "called to belong to Jesus Christ … and are loved by God" (Rom. 1:6–7). He goes on to write, "You did not receive the spirit of slavery to fall back into fear, but you have received the Spirit of adoption as sons, by whom we cry, 'Abba! Father!' The Spirit himself bears witness with our spirit that we are children of God" (Rom. 8:15–16). Clearly, these Romans were born-again believers, God's adopted children, and Paul expected that the inner witness of God's Spirit would be a normative part of their experience.

Does the Holy Spirit witness to your spirit that God is your Father and that you are His dearly loved child? This subjective aspect of assurance, this inner knowing, is the birthright of God's children. It is "a direct and immediate sense of God's fatherly love given as kind of an immediate communication, like God saying, 'I love you,' immediately to the soul through His word."[6] Some experience this more intensely than others, and it can manifest itself in various ways at different seasons of life. Some have reported dramatic experiences of being filled with the Spirit that bring a palpable sense of God's love, while others experience a quieter and more gentle form of assurance. But whether strong or weak, this inner witness gives assurance of the Spirit's presence in us and our adoption into God's family. (In cases of serious sin or backsliding, which grieve the Spirit, He may hide His face from us and withdraw the sense of His presence, even though He remains present.)

There have always been believers who, despite earnestly seeking, never experience the inner witness of the Spirit. The cause varies. Lack of good teaching (or any teaching at all) explains some cases. In other instances, unrepented sin, ignoring the indwelling Spirit, distrust of subjective experiences, a deficit of parental love in childhood, depression, or other barriers may be at work. Anyone who lacks the inner witness of God as Father should continue to seek it; and as they do, they should look to, meditate on, and trust the promises of eternal life in God's written Word, especially the invitations and promises of Christ, as well as the more objective aspects of assurance we have just considered. The counsel of a spiritually mature, godly pastor or elder can be of great help in working through these concerns. If emotional issues or a dysfunctional background are involved, a biblically grounded, spiritually mature Christian counselor can be a valuable help.

---

6 J. I. Packer, in Ray Galea, "Assurance," *The Gospel Coalition* (https://www.thegospelcoalition.org/essay/assurance/), accessed December 22, 2025. See also J. I. Packer, "Sanctification and Assurance," YouTube, posted July 18, 2020, by BRMinistries.

Ultimately, we must all rest in that fact that God knows the best way to assure each of us of His fatherly love. And we remember Paul's declaration: "God's firm foundation stands, bearing this seal: 'The Lord knows those who are his'" (2 Tim. 2:19).

Apostolic Confidence and Ours

The apostle Paul moves on from the witness of the Spirit to say:

> We know that for those who love God all things work together for good, for those who are called according to his purpose. For those whom he foreknew he also predestined to be conformed to the image of his Son, in order that he might be the firstborn among many brothers. And those whom he predestined he also called, and those whom he called he also justified, and those whom he justified he also glorified. (Rom. 8:28–30)

Do you love the God who has been so merciful, gracious, patient, and loving as to call you to Himself through Christ? If so, you may take comfort from this passage. This powerful affirmation assures us of a glorious destiny regardless of what may happen in our lives. God's calling *will* be fulfilled; He *will* preserve us unto glorification in His eternal kingdom. Because this is true, Paul can go on to proclaim,

> What then shall we say to these things? If God is for us, who can be against us? He who did not spare his own Son but gave him up for us all, how will he not also with him graciously give us all things? Who shall bring any charge against God's elect? It is God who justifies. Who is to condemn? Christ Jesus is the one who died—more than that, who was raised—who is at the right hand of God, who indeed is interceding for us. Who shall separate us from the love of Christ? Shall tribulation, or distress, or persecution, or famine, or nakedness, or danger, or sword? As it is written,

> "For your sake we are being killed all the day long;
> we are regarded as sheep to be slaughtered."
>
> No, in all these things we are more than conquerors through him who loved us. For I am sure that neither death nor life, nor angels nor rulers, nor things present nor things to come, nor powers, nor height nor depth, nor anything else in all creation, will be able to separate us from the love of God in Christ Jesus our Lord. (Rom. 8:31–39)

Assurance Can Grow Over Time

We conclude with some helpful and encouraging pastoral observations about how we grow in assurance of our salvation from the English pastor, John Newton:

> Assurance grows by repeated conflict; by our repeated experimental proof of the Lord's power and goodness to save; when we have been brought very low and helped, sorely wounded and healed, cast down and raised again, have given up all hope, and been suddenly snatched from danger, and placed in safety; and when these things have been repeated to us and in us a thousand times over, we begin to learn to trust simply to the Word and power of God, beyond and against appearances: and this trust, when habitual and strong, bears the name of assurance … . But this assurance, though desirable, is not absolutely necessary to our safety, or even to our comfort; for we are not saved by the degree of our assurance, but by the reality of our faith in the Son of God; and He that has begun the good work, will carry it on, in defiance of all opposition, and will perfect it in His own time and way.[7]

---

7 John Newton, *Cardiphonia; or, The Utterance of the Heart* (London: Morgan & Scott, 1911), 336–337.

Newton's pastoral wisdom echoes that of other wise, godly leaders in history and is well worth pondering and taking to heart as we seek assurance of our salvation.

Suggestions to Consider

1. As you seek assurance, pour out your heart to God in prayer, asking Him to grant you the witness of the Spirit, which brings assurance of sonship (Rom. 8:15–16). Pray through the many verses of Scripture discussed in this chapter, focusing on what God has said to us about our adoption in Christ.
2. Don't be overcome by your past but abide in the present; cling to the cross of Jesus and hold tightly to Him. It can be difficult to go back and analyze your conversion to see if you had "enough" faith and repentance, especially if you were converted a long time ago or as a child. Consider instead: Do you currently see evidence that you have turned from your sins and are trusting in Jesus' sacrifice to pay for your sins?
3. Ask God to show you if any sin or resistance to His will is blocking your sense of assurance. If needed, seek counsel and prayer from a wise, godly pastor or elder.

Acknowledgements

Writing this book has made me very aware that I am standing on the shoulders of others. I owe a deep debt of gratitude to the godly teachers and mentors who have invested in me, helped me grow in grace and truth, and encouraged me in this project over the years. Chief among them are Tom Schwanda, who supervised my doctoral work many years ago and has remained a good friend; Bill Kynes, another good friend and unfailing source of biblical and theological wisdom for each chapter; and Michael Wilkins, whose friendship and prodigious scholarship on discipleship have inspired and guided me for many years. Art Lindsley also gave valuable assistance and encouragement in an early theological review and assessment. Not least, I wish to thank my friend and colleague Bill Smith, who advised me and developed the "Questions to Ponder" for each chapter.

In addition, I am very grateful for the close brothers in ministry who have prayed for and supported me in this project. Their biblical and theological learning combined with decades in the trenches of pastoral ministry have been a rich resource upon which to draw. They include Tom Holliday, Stuart McAlpine, and Bill Campbell. I am also grateful to those I have taught in discipleship groups and adult education classes who have given helpful input on the curriculum. A special thank you is due to Matt Miller, who wisely advised me to forego the traditional publishing route and instead to retain the rights to the book so that in addition to providing a hard copy version for ordinary readers, I could also offer the book free on the worldwide web in both English and other languages in order to "make disciples of all nations."

I am also most grateful to my remarkably gifted editors, Steve Halliday and Rebecca Rine, who applied their extraordinary editing skills, biblical wisdom, and theological training to making this book a clear and engaging work to read. They validate the observation that good editors are worth their weight in gold and that the key to good writing is: revise, revise, revise! Additional review, proofreading, editing, and project management were generously provided by Ed Glancy, Steven Keil, Bill Soderberg, Aimee Reigert, and Crystal Sarno, to whom I am grateful. And many thanks are due to Chris Tobias (cover) and Brian Zuckerman (interior) for their excellent design work!

Those dear friends who quietly prayed for and financially supported the writing of this book have played a major role in its development and deserve special recognition. Without them it would not have come to fruition. They are well-known to God but would not wish to be named before man. Their reward awaits them in the world to come.

Finally, I wish to thank the Board of Directors and my colleagues at the C. S. Lewis Institute who have provided good advice, constant encouragement, and every accommodation along the way and allowed me to go to halftime status for an extended period in order to complete this project.

Don't quit now. Press on to maturity!

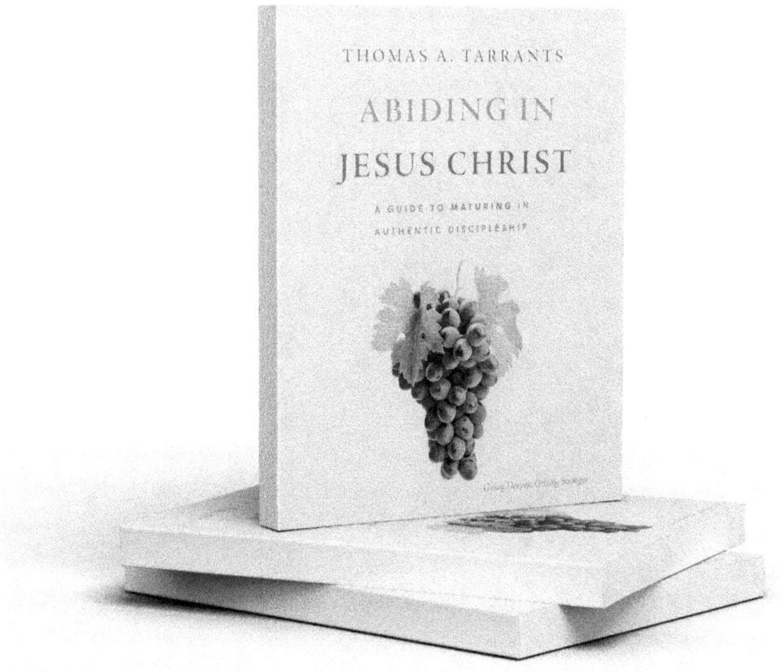

Basic foundations are essential, but there is much more to discipleship and the Christian life. ***Abiding** in Jesus Christ: A Guide to **Maturing** in Authentic Discipleship* provides resources to continue the journey.

Part 1:

Getting Stronger as a Disciple of Jesus

1. Abiding in Christ
2. Resisting the Devil and His Schemes
3. Renouncing the World and Its Snares
4. Understanding the Flesh
5. Battling the Flesh and Its Lusts
6. Forsaking Fleshly Christianity
7. Living in Truth
8. Dying to Pride and Cultivating Humility
9. Resisting Temptation and Sin
10. Prevailing in Testing and Trials
11. Reordering Your Heart's Desires
12. Being Transformed by Word and Spirit

Part 2:

Going Deeper as a Disciple of Jesus

1. Growing in Faith
2. Growing in Hope
3. Growing in Love
4. Growing in Servanthood
5. Preparing for Persecution and Suffering
6. Running the Marathon of Faith
7. Becoming Ready
8. Awaiting Jesus' Return

www.ingramcontent.com/pod-product-compliance
Lightning Source LLC
LaVergne TN
LVHW010601100826
845148LV00014B/2802